POETS
IN
THEIR
YOUTH

POETS
IN
THEIR
YOUTH

A Memoir

EILEEN
SIMPSON

faber and faber

First published in the United States of America 1982
First published in Great Britain 1982
by Faber and Faber Limited
3 Queen Square London WC1N 3AU
Printed in Great Britain by
Redwood Burn Limited
Trowbridge, Wiltshire

© 1982 by Eileen Simpson

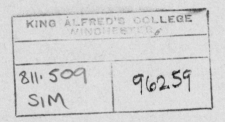
British Library Cataloguing in Publication Data

Simpson, Eileen
Poets in their youth.
1. Simpson, Eileen—Friends and associates
2. Poets, American—20th century—Biography
3. Authors, American—20th century—Biography
I. Title
811′.54   PS3569.I489

ISBN 0–571–11925–5

Grateful acknowledgment is made to the following for permission to reprint previously published material:

Curtis Brown, Ltd.: Except from "Louis MacNeice, 1907–1963" by W. H. Auden from *The Listener,* October 24, 1963. Copyright © 1963 by W. H. Auden. Reprinted by permission of Curtis Brown, Ltd.

Kathleen Donahue: Excerpt from "His Marriage" by John Berryman. Reprinted by permission.

Doubleday & Company, Inc.: Excerpts from "The Would-be Hungarian," copyright 1955 by Delmore Schwartz, from the book *Summer Knowledge* by Delmore Schwartz. Reprinted by permission of Doubleday & Company, Inc.

Doubleday & Company, Inc. and Faber & Faber Ltd.: "Heard in a Violent Ward," Copyright © 1964 by Beatrice Roethke as Administratrix of the Estate of Theodore Roethke. Reprinted by permission of Doubleday & Company, Inc. and Faber & Faber, Ltd.

Farrar, Straus & Giroux, Inc. and Faber & Faber Ltd.: Excerpts from *The Dream Songs* by John Berryman, Copyright © 1959, 1962, 1963, 1964, 1965, 1966, 1967, 1968, 1969 by John Berryman; from *Love & Fame* by John Berryman, Copyright © 1970 by John Berryman; from *Short Poems* by John Berryman, Copyright © 1948, 1958, 1964 by John Berryman; from *Delusions, Etc.* by John Berryman, Copyright © 1969, 1971 by John Berryman, Copyright © 1972 by the Estate of John Berryman; from *Stephen Crane* by John Berryman, Copyright 1950 by John Berryman, Copyright renewed © 1977 by Kate Berryman; from *Berryman's Sonnets* by John Berryman, Copyright © 1952, 1967 by John Berryman; from *Homage to Mistress Bradstreet* by John Berryman, Copyright © 1956 by John Berryman; from *The Third Book of Criticism* by Randall Jarrell, Copyright © 1941, 1945, 1955, 1956, 1962, 1963, 1965 by Mrs. Randall Jarrell, Copyright © 1963, 1965 by Randall Jarrell; from *Life Studies* by Robert Lowell, Copyright © 1956, 1959 by Robert Lowell; from *History* by Robert Lowell, Copyright © 1967, 1968, 1969, 1970, 1973 by Robert Lowell; from *Day by Day* by Robert Lowell, Copyright © 1975, 1976, 1977 by Robert Lowell. Reprinted by permission of Farrar, Straus & Giroux, Inc. British rights are administered by Faber & Faber Ltd.

Dwight Macdonald: Several lines from an unpublished poem by Delmore Schwartz. Reprinted courtesy of Dwight Macdonald.

Macmillan Publishing Company, Inc. and Eyre Methuen Ltd.: Excerpt from "A Night with Lions" ("The Lost World," Part 2) from *The Lost World* by Randall Jarrell. Copyright © Randall Jarrell 1963, 1965. Originally appeared in *Poetry.* Reprinted by permission of Macmillan Publishing Company, Inc. and Eyre Methuen Ltd.

Macmillan Publishing Company, Inc. and A. P. Watt, Ltd.: Excerpt from "The Wild Swans at Coole" from *Collected Poems* by William Butler Yeats. Copyright 1919 by Macmillan Publishing Co., Inc., renewed 1947 by Bertha Georgie Yeats. Excerpt from "John Kinsella's Lament for Mrs. Mary Moore" from *Collected Poems* by William Butler Yeats. Copyright 1940 by Georgie Yeats, renewed 1968 by Bertha Georgie Yeats, Michael Butler Yeats and Anne Yeats. Reprinted with permission from Macmillan Publishing Company, Inc. and A. P. Watt, Ltd.

New Directions Publishing Corp. and David Higham Associates Ltd.: Excerpt

In loving memory of
ROBERT SIMPSON

We poets in our youth begin in gladness;
But thereof comes in the end despondency and madness.

—WORDSWORTH

CONTENTS

POETS
IN
THEIR
YOUTH

I

JOHN
AND
DELMORE

The links between the poets in the generation born around World War I were beginning to be forged by the time I met them in the early forties. On a Friday afternoon in February 1942, I was in Pennsylvania Station waiting for a train from Boston. John Berryman, with whom I had fallen in love the previous summer, was arriving with Delmore Schwartz for the weekend. During the nine months I had known John he had talked so much about his fellow poet and colleague at Harvard that I felt I knew him, too. With dazzling precocity Delmore had made his name following the publication in 1938 of *In Dreams Begin Responsibilities,* a collection of poems and stories. The critics who mattered most to both of them—Allen Tate, R. P. Blackmur, John Crowe Ransom, Mark Van Doren—had concurred in the opinion expressed by Tate that Delmore's poetic style was "the first real innovation we've had since Eliot and Pound." The title story, which had previously been published in *Partisan Review,* had been hailed as a masterpiece. At the age of twenty-six, Delmore was famous in the literary world.

John's career, by contrast, had barely begun. His first publication in book form had been in *Five Young American Poets* (1940), to which

John Berryman in 1941—the irresistible grin

he had contributed twenty poems and, very reluctantly, a photograph. The man in the photograph looked absurdly unlike the one who had been brought to my New Year's Day party in 1941, the man who had kissed me under the mistletoe, saying with an impish grin, "One should respect custom, don't you agree?" Long and hard study of the face made me suspect that if I hoped to understand a character more complex than any I had previously known, I would have to make a composite of the man with the irresistible grin and the proud and introverted poet in the photograph.

The clock at the information booth in the station's great concourse seemed to have stopped. I tried to temper my eagerness and impatience by mingling with the throng of students arriving from Eastern colleges. Anticipation and excitement over the long weekend filled the wintry dusk that filtered down through the clerestory windows. From time to time I took out a pocket mirror and critically examined my new hat. Small, made of black velvet, it perched over one eye, and had a chin veil sprinkled with little dots. It was the height of fashion. Studying it critically, I decided that, yes, it had been worth a week of lean lunches. But would John find it becoming? If I understood his feelings correctly, there was no limit to how attractive I could be for him, although I must somehow arrange it so that I would not be

attractive to other men. The veil was proving troublesome. My
eyelashes kept catching in the little dots.

From January to June of the previous year I had heard from John only
once, at the time he sent me a copy of his book. It wasn't until he came
to New York at the end of the academic year on a brief visit to his
mother that we met again. From then on we were inseparable until
he returned to Harvard in the fall. After it became clear that he was
going to stay on in the city that summer, he rented a "low dark long
damp room" below ground on Lexington Avenue at Thirty-sixth
Street, where he wrote, listened to music and, as he said afterward,
plotted how to seduce me. At five o'clock, when I left the office where
I was working on lower Broadway, we met in the Jumble Shop on
Eighth Street for a drink. Or went to rundown, airless, steaming movie
houses on the Lower East Side to see films like *Potemkin* and *Alexander
Nevsky.* Or to the Apollo on Forty-second Street for any picture with
Louis Jouvet or Jean-Louis Barrault.

Also we walked, walked miles of city streets from river to river,
from the Battery to Inwood, during which John talked about poetry,
the writing of which, he said, quoting Delmore, was "a vocation." It
demanded, and should have, a poet's whole attention. ("Poem" and
"poet" he pronounced with a caress, as if an umlaut hovered vaguely
over the *oe*). He must be engaged in it with his whole being. But how
could he, John, be so engaged when he had to earn a living? Delmore
and he had been born at the wrong time and in the wrong country.
"Pushkin could count on railway workers to know his poems. *Think
of it!* Who reads poetry in America?"

Not I. I had bought the Faber editions of both Eliot's and Pound's
Selected Poems, but I was ashamed to admit that I would not have been
able to quote more than one or two of them had John asked me to.
He never asked. He took it for granted that everyone he met, fellow
poets excepted, needed to be educated to read verse. Crucial to our
relationship was his discovery early on that while reading Keats and
Byron and Shelley (though not Spenser, Milton or Wordsworth) in
college, I had, in some woolly way, come to believe that poetry was
the most powerful and mysterious form of writing. To be the "help-
mate" (wasn't that the word we undergraduates used in the student

cafeteria, talking of such things?) to a poet would be the most interesting and useful way for a woman to spend her life.

Perfect! The combination of near ignorance (no wrong-headed notions to be dislodged), eagerness to learn (from what better teacher?), an exalted view of his craft and the promise of devotion, suited John admirably in a companion. "Take a typical Harvard undergraduate from a good Eastern school," he'd say. "He hates Milton, is pious about Shakespeare, who actually *bores* him. Incredible! The fault of schoolmasters, of course. In Delmore's essay, 'The Isolation of Modern Poetry'—have I given you that issue of *Kenyon*? . . ."

On nights when it was too hot to stir that torrid summer (my first spent in the city working, instead of at the beach on Long Island) we sat at the Brevoort Café on lower Fifth Avenue, where the waiter permitted us to dawdle over a glass of ale until closing time.

If John had spent the day "obsessed" with thoughts about me, instead of working—if I didn't declare unconditional love for him, and *soon,* he was going to lose his mind—he would talk about how old he was, and how little he had accomplished. Twenty-six and all he had to his name was a *fifth* of a book. Still, he didn't envy Delmore his fame. One didn't want success to come too early, or too generously. Precocity was an enemy of promise. "I must find you a copy of Cyril Connolly's book tomorrow." In *Enemies of Promise,* Connolly says that fame sets up expectations in critics, and in writers, which restrict a writer's freedom to experiment, to fail, to fall silent. The ideal is to keep almost completely but not entirely underground ("No harm in a *little* encouragement," John said wryly) until one is sufficiently formed and strong enough to be unaffected by either success or, since success can't be constant if one is developing, failure. "Yeats's way was the ideal way. A long slow development, the work getting better, the character stronger, until the late great poems and world fame. That's what Delmore would have wished for himself."

"Not, mind you," John added with amusement, "that Delmore hasn't schemed for success, even to the point of stage-managing the prepublication promotion of *In Dreams.*" He had told James Laughlin of New Directions what senior poets to solicit for quotes, and had seen to it that the book got into the hands of the right people for review. After publication he suffered not only from the predictable postpartum depression, but also from terrible apprehension about his liter-

ary future: *Was this the summit of his career?* From now on would it
be a downhill slide? The gnawing anxiety exacerbated his insomnia.
"Insomnia Valley" is what Delmore called Cambridge when he and
John commiserated with each other about their white nights.

John was a night owl. If I had not had to be at work at 8:30 in the
morning, he would have resisted taking me home even at 2:00 or 3:00
A.M. There was so much to talk about, so much we had to learn about
each other. What he had to say about poetry, about books, about films,
about his youth, his family, his years abroad, his hopes, his dreams,
about us—especially about our deepening love for each other—made
it difficult to separate at my doorstep. Only the memory of what it
would feel like, mid-morning, as my head nodded over the typewriter
after three or four hours sleep, helped me to resist yet another walk
and another talk before going in.

After he left me at the brownstone on Twelfth Street where I had
a room, John often sat up until dawn in an all-night cafeteria and
wrote. One night, on his way home to Lexington Avenue, he cut across
Union Square and stopped by a cluster of men to listen to a dispute.
Before he knew what was happening, he was caught up in an argument
about the entrance of the United States into the war. When he tried
to inject reason into the "savage" argument, the ringleader told him
to shut up, and called him a Jew. John's objection that he wasn't a Jew
but a Catholic enraged the leader, who shouted at him, "You look like
a Jew, you talk like a Jew, you are a Jew," and challenged John to
disprove the charges by reciting the Apostles' Creed. Partly because by
now John, too, was angry, partly because he hadn't said the Creed in
years, he could recall from his days as an altar boy only phrases of the
Latin—proof, the leader told the crowd, that John *was* a Jew. The
crowd, which was convinced by the leader's reasoning and thought
there was nothing further to be said, lost interest and drifted off to join
other groups.

John walked the streets until morning and, still overwrought, telephoned and asked me to meet him for breakfast. He hoped that by
recounting the events of the night he would understand what had
happened, what it meant to him. Later that day he began writing a
poem called "Union Square," worked on it for a week or so and then
put it aside. I had become so involved in what he was doing that I was
disappointed when he abandoned it. "Abandoned" was too strong a

word, he said. If I wanted to be helpful to him, I must learn not only
to follow him in his enthusiasms, but also to let go of them when he
did. It was as important as not pressing him to write for money. He
was happy to discover that, unlike his mother, I seemed to have no
temptation to do this. If a subject were worth going on with—many
were not—it would surface again in months or even years. (This lesson
in how to be a "writer's ear" I didn't learn at once. I had all but
forgotten about the night in Union Square when, years later, John
began reworking the material in fictional form. Four years after the
episode took place, his story "The Imaginary Jew" appeared in *Partisan
Review* [Autumn 1945].)

The arrival of the train from Boston was being announced. I hurried
to the gate to meet the real and the imaginary Jew, stationing myself
where I could see the passengers getting off: soldiers and sailors, businessmen with briefcases, Boston matrons, Harvard students with green
book bags over their shoulders. And there they were! Far up the
platform I could see the poets, talking animatedly. Delmore was taller
than John, over six feet, heavier, and looked barrel-chested in his
carelessly belted overcoat. He walked with a little running step, giving
the impression that his legs were shorter and less well-developed than
the rest of his body.

John strode by Delmore's side (that it was not easy to keep up with
these giant steps I well knew). His broad-shouldered, slim, narrow-
waisted build made him look the more athletic of the two, yet I knew
that Delmore had beaten him at tennis. John looked younger, now that
he was no longer wearing his book-photograph mustache. I much
preferred the hollow-cheeked, ascetic appearance of his clean-shaven
face, but I knew better than to tell him so, for I suspected that the
mustache, and an earlier beard he'd once grown in England, had been
attempts to make himself look older.

As John spotted me in the crowd and quickened his pace, I lost my
nerve and took off the veil. Delmore would be looking me over. "He's
madly curious about you, of course," John had said, and I didn't want
Delmore to think I was frivolous. Frivolity wouldn't have troubled
him seriously, it turned out. (Would he even have noticed?) He was
going to look me over with another concern in mind.

A shy-sly-smiling Delmore approached to shake my hand. He
looked amused, and a little embarrassed, that John and I had embraced

Delmore Schwartz in his carelessly belted overcoat. Cambridge, 1941 or 1942

openly. His voice was soft as he said how much he had heard about me, how pleased he was that John was finally permitting us to meet.

"John is very secretive. He keeps your visits to Boston dark until they're over."

Word had got out in the small, gossipy literary world of Cambridge that John had been seen that summer (during the week we had spent there so that he could pick up some books and papers) walking through Harvard Yard with a young woman. He had also been spied having breakfast with her in Fiske's. Breakfast! Was she a Radcliffe undergraduate? The English girl he had become engaged to while he was abroad? Delmore, up in Maine on vacation, received intelligence reports by letter, and on his return had been eager to know more.

During term time I had been up to visit John almost every month, but when I was there we had seen no one. The occasion of the two men taking the train together to New York made for an easy meeting, with a plan for the three of us to have a drink together.

On Seventh Avenue we looked for a taxi. John led the way,

jaywalking, skillfully dodging cars, Delmore shouting at him to be careful. Delmore grabbed my arm in mock-serious need for protection against the onrushing traffic. Once in the taxi he collapsed against the back of the seat and said with relief, "Oh, my castration anxiety!" at which we all laughed.

Without a trace of the shyness I thought I had seen at first, he continued in a bantering manner to play the role with John of a worldly-wise advisor to a naïf who didn't know how to look after himself. Sancho Panza and Don Quixote was the way they characterized this part of their relationship. John jaywalking, John being undiplomatic with his publisher, John being stand-offish with his colleagues, John moving from Cambridge to Boston (as he had done following our summer together in New York). This last had isolated him from the academic community, Delmore said to me, and had been bad for his career.

"It's not good for John to be so much alone. He's a recluse, you know."

For some time I hadn't known. Having heard about John for years from my closest friend in college, Jean Bennett (to whom he had been engaged before going to England), as an undergraduate who, as he later put it, "rowed and danced and cut classes and was political," I continued to think of him in this way for some time, although Jean had also told me that he had returned from his two years abroad greatly changed. He had arrived at Harvard following a year of teaching English at Wayne University in Detroit, where he had left behind another poet and colleague, Bhain Campbell, to whom he was devoted. At this time Bhain was:

> yellow with cancer, paper-thin and bent
> even in the hospital bed
> racked with high hopes . . .

hopes which no one shared, for testicular cancer was killing him. Grieving for the loss he knew he would suffer within months, John had plunged into teaching and the drudgery of correcting papers. As a bachelor he hadn't been automatically included in the social life of the Harvard English department, and was too low-spirited to take the initiative with his colleagues.

That apart from Delmore John "saw no one," as he more than once
told me during the summer, I hadn't taken in until mid-August when
we went up to Cambridge together. Appian Way, where he then lived,
not far from Harvard Square, was little more than a paved lane, with
a Radcliffe building on one side, and three or four white frame houses
on the other. Number 10, large and handsome, had an ell to which had
been added, long after the original structure was built, a dependency
so fragile-looking, so amateurishly put together that it was hard to
guess whether it had been intended as an oversized playhouse for
children or undersized quarters for servants. By the time John went to
live there, it had been rented out for some years, usually to a member
of the academic community, and had a number of its own, 10½.

The address—the juxtaposition of the name of the imperial Roman
road with the fraction—was the best thing about the house, John said,
for it was dark, damp, draughty, cramped and, as the previous winter
had shown, unheatable.

"The living room, as you will see," he said, turning the key in the
lock and butting the ill-fitting door with his shoulder, "is like the
cabinet of Dr. Caligari."

Stepping inside, I felt a moment of vertigo. There was not a steadying right angle in sight. The floor tilted sharply, the walls slanted, and
had there been portholes instead of windows, one would have had the
illusion of being afloat in the cabin of a small craft on a choppy sea.
About the interior decorations, however, there was nothing shippy.
The windows were curtained in dark red monk's cloth. Against one
wall was a daybed covered in brown corduroy. There was a red leather
chair, John's chair (which followed him wherever he went), next to
which stood a small table to hold books, paraphernalia for his pipe,
a corkscrew which he ran through his thumb and index finger as he
sat in the chair and talked, and a set-up chessboard. A drop-leaf table
and two chairs were flattened against the wall that led to the galley
of a kitchen. Books, in piles, claimed most of the remaining floor space.

Ten and a half was so outrageously uncomfortable it was a source
of amusement to John. He rented it from a professor emeritus of
classics, the owner of number 10, who also provided amusement. A
chat with him in passing on the Way was often the highlight of an
otherwise gloomy morning. The lease, which the professor had typed
with unlegalistic italics, exclamation points and the erratic use of

capitals, John said was the only one he had ever read to the end. He planned never to throw it out. He fetched it from his file and began reading aloud: "OIL IS KING THIS DAY: OCEAN STEAMERS USE IT."

This oracular pronouncement was followed by a paragraph about the insoluble problem of heating the "half," directions for disposal of garbage, warnings about fire hazards and the like, the whole interlarded with quotations from Horace and Virgil. By now I was laughing so hard at John's laughter, which bubbled up and up until it cut his voice to a high *"eeeeeeeeee,"* befogged his glasses with tears and twisted his trunk into spasms, that I couldn't hear what he was reading. I held up my hand, begging him to stop.

"Wait! Wait! There's more," he cried, as soon as he got his breath, and continued on with the classicist's comments on the lamentable state of the world as well as his reminiscences about his undergraduate days at Christ Church, Oxford (some sixty years earlier).

The little house was not so entertaining, however, that John planned to stay in it for another year. As we walked along the Charles River he said he was thinking of taking an apartment in Boston. Appian Way was so convenient to the Yard that his students had taken to dropping in at all hours of the night. In the coming year, he was going to guard against squandering his time on teaching. He liked teaching, was good at it, also liked the boys. But the important thing, the real thing, the *only* thing was to write poetry. All else was wasted time.

Students were much less of a temptation for Delmore. Because he was married, they didn't think of dropping in on him.

"You yourself warned me against them, Delmore," John said, defending the move to Boston.

"That's why you moved?" Delmore's smile was sly. We were seated at a corner table in the candlelit bar of the Jumble Shop. Seen close to, Delmore had a big head, made bigger by abundant, wavy brown hair. He had high wide Tartar cheekbones and the full, beautifully shaped mouth of a classical Greek statue. His face was divided into two parts, as if by a carelessly drawn line, beginning with a diagonal scar on his brow, running along the crest of his broad nose and ending in a cleft in his chin. (Later, marking the division with his hand, he showed me that the division was not superficial. The two sides of his face were different one from the other and reflected, he thought, a split in his personality.) When he smiled, he smiled broadly, exposing a front tooth that looked as if it might have been injured in a child's game.

One had the feeling that the clothes Delmore was wearing, a conventional suit, tie and shirt, had been selected without interest in color or texture, and that he was not completely comfortable in them, as if their conventionality had been imposed: It was the way an instructor at Harvard dressed. In this, and in other ways that John fought, he fit the mold better than Delmore, although his style, less donnish than it would become, was more formal and old-fashioned than academic—another attempt to look older. I suspected he had copied it, even down to the vest, from his stepfather, an elderly Southern gentleman. On the vest was a gold watch chain that held a Phi Beta Kappa key (useful for cleaning the bowl of his pipe) and his real father's watch. It seemed to me that when he took the watch and chain off and put them back on, he handled them tenderly.

Delmore and I, both New Yorkers by birth, were discovering that we had spent part of our youth in uptown Manhattan, he on Washington Heights and I close by in Inwood. (Earlier he had lived in Brooklyn, and I had been in an Italian convent in Dobbs Ferry.) We had both also attended George Washington High School.

"Did you have Miss Wrinn for English?" Miss Wrinn had encouraged him and his wife Gertrude, who had also gone to George Washington, in their early literary efforts.

None of the English teachers they had had were still there in my day, but our having gone to the same school established a bond between us.

"How lucky you were to go to public school," John said. He, who had been born in the Southwest, and spent his youth on Long Island, had been "shipped off" to South Kent in Connecticut. He had hated it and doubted he had learned anything there. Certainly there was no Miss Wrinn to encourage a student to write poetry, or even read it. He had been a misfit in that philistine atmosphere, with its heavy emphasis on sports. Trying to be a jock like the other boys (which accounted for the chip missing from *his* front tooth) had delayed his intellectual development for years. "I don't remember a *single* book I read. Can you believe it?"

No. Neither Delmore nor I could believe it. As Delmore said, John had lost little time catching up.

"And how I dreaded going back there after vacations! Even today the mourning *whooowhoooo* of a train whistle, the signal that we were rounding the curve before the Kent station, overwhelms me with a feeling of desolation."

Though it was difficult for me to imagine, John had not been physically attractive as an adolescent. His face had been dominated by thick-lensed eyeglasses behind which his eyes, afflicted with nystagmus, moved so jerkily that he was given the nickname "Bleers." It was only when his face grew large enough to support the glasses, and the nystagmus became almost unnoticeable (except in times of stress)—this in his last years in college—that he developed what Delmore called his "mad charm."

We had all three gone to college in New York, John to Columbia, I to Hunter, and Delmore, after a brief period at the University of Wisconsin, to New York University, around the corner, as he pointed out, from where we were sitting. The last time he'd been in the city he had gone there, trying to recapture the past for a scene he was writing in his verse play, *Genesis.*

"Sitting in the lunch room, I felt what it would be like to be old." We sat silently imagining what it would be like to be old.

We had had our drink and were reluctant to separate. "What about having dinner together?" Delmore suggested. Now that the meeting John had been nervous about had gone off well (Suppose Delmore and I hadn't liked each other?), he was all for it.

As we wandered around the Village looking for the restaurant Delmore had in mind, I began to suspect he was no better at such practical matters as finding a restaurant, or a taxi, than John. An English instructor's salary at Harvard didn't allow for doing either very often, but when it did John and I were usually together and it seemed to me there were always difficulties. On one of our first dates he had taken me to a place in the East Fifties, Le Divan Parisien, recommended by his mother. No sooner had we been installed on the red-plush banquette and handed the menu than I felt that he was uncomfortable. What *had* his mother meant, sending him to a restaurant he couldn't possibly afford? Pooling our money, we were able to pay for the olives and celery in crushed ice that had been put on the table, and make an awkward exit.

The next time he took me to dinner he was offended by the waiter's manner. The time after that it was the "vulgarity" of the other diners.

"How much easier it would be if we were abroad," he'd say. "Now if we were in Paris, we could go to La Coupole." Or, "If we were in London . . ." John's brother, Bob, seeing my perplexity at this behavior, said it was a family joke. He and his wife Barbara used to say, "Poor Eileen, there isn't a restaurant in New York she can go to with John. He's made a scene in every one of them." This was an exaggeration, and John laughed at it with us, but it was not much of one.

Ostensibly, Delmore was looking for a restaurant, but as I got colder and colder and hungrier and hungrier, I began to wonder. This one had moved, this one was closed, we were passing up this perfectly good one for reasons that were obscure. Finally he remembered the Jai Alai on Bleecker Street. It was good and it was cheap. It was to become our meeting place for years thereafter, but that first night I was afraid we were going to have another scene, this one staged by Delmore.

On the walk there he had kept up an entertaining flow of reminiscences about his life in an attic room off Washington Square that he had shared with his brother, Kenneth. As soon as the waiter seated us, Delmore's mood changed. He fell silent. When I asked him a question, he responded in whispered monosyllables. His attention seemed to be taken by the people seated nearby. He kept looking over his shoulder, first to one side, then the other. That there was no one he recognized didn't seem to reassure him. In a few minutes he was looking around again. A deep frown made the diagonal scar on his forehead more pronounced. What *was* the matter? I looked to John for an explanation. Infected by Delmore's mood, he too had fallen silent. Just as I was deciding that dinner was going to be a disaster, Delmore stood up and, with some embarrassment, asked if I would mind changing places with him. The waiter had seated me where he wanted to sit. He had to have his back to the wall; it made him anxious to have anyone sitting behind him.

> Do they whisper behind my back? Do they speak
> Of my clumsiness? Do they laugh at me,
> Mimicking my gestures, retailing my shame?

was what he was thinking.

In the poem, "Do the Others Speak of Me Mockingly, Mali-

ciously?" he recognizes that if others do speak of him in this way it
is for "wit's sake." The poet admits that for wit's sake he has also been
cruel, even "behind my dear friend's back." Delmore loved to talk
about people, loved to gossip about his enemies, his friends and even
his heroes, as I learned that evening. Once the seating had been rear-
ranged and he became easy and relaxed again, he referred to the
conversation he and John had been having on the train coming down
about T. S. Eliot's recently published "East Coker," which Delmore
found disappointing and referred to as "East Coca-Cola." In the days
when John had been running around in the mud at South Kent trying
to intercept a pass, Delmore was already reading Eliot. If Eliot was
his hero in much the way Yeats was John's, there was the great
difference that Delmore was not reverential the way John was. Rather,
he seemed eager to reduce his hero to life-size by a kind of unrelenting
private-eye investigation of Eliot's personal life. He was on to a new
bit of gossip about the relationship between "Tom and Vivien" (Eliot's
first wife), he said, touching the tip of his tongue to a back tooth in
a gesture that I began to recognize as characteristic when he was about
to impart gossip. He had reason to believe that Eliot had been compro-
mised into marriage.

"Shakespeare probably was, too," John said. "But how do you
know about Eliot?"

The poems. Other sources. What other sources, Delmore wouldn't
say.

John turned to me and said, "As you will learn, Delmore talks about
the Eliots as if they lived around the corner from him in Cambridge,
and as if he had a pipeline to their bedroom." How accurate Delmore's
information was John didn't know. (More accurate, as I learned long
afterward from James Atlas's biography of him, than we imagined.)
"The *PR* boys? I bet you got it from them," John said.

Until this evening the image that had come to my mind whenever
I heard the editors of *Partisan Review* called "the *PR* boys" was of
three clever little faces above Buster Brown collars. But as Delmore
talked about Philip Rahv, William Phillips, the co-founders of the
Review, and Dwight Macdonald, they appeared instead as a cross
between rabbinical scholars and bookies, who argued and shouted at
one another in a smoke-filled office littered with manuscripts from
writers young and old, American and European, who aspired to be

printed in the liveliest literary magazine in the country. Delmore, at this time, had a particular fondness for Macdonald.

While Macdonald's being a gentile furnished Delmore, the kidder, with material for kidding Dwight, the fact that John was also a gentile figured in their relationship very little as far as I could see. (Delmore rarely used Yiddish expressions. When he did it was always a direct quote from his mother. When I used them, having learned them in college, he thought it very funny.)

After dinner John suggested that since his mother was away we all go to her apartment to listen to music. This pleasant, sunny studio on Madison Avenue and Thirtieth Street was where John and I had lived during the summer, after his mother had gone on vacation and I had "finally" admitted (a bare month since the evening at Le Divan Parisien) that I was as much in love with him as he was with me. It was here that, when we felt like seeing other people, John entertained at tea (serving black China tea prepared with great care, and toasted pound cake followed by a glass of sherry). Among the guests were old friends of his who happened to be in town, like Mark Van Doren, Bob Giroux, Jean Bennett, or my sister, who had married while still in college and was living in the city with her husband and children.

"I have an *amazing* Bessie Smith record I want you to hear, Delmore," John said on the way uptown.

John had become seriously interested in music at about the time I met him. With characteristic enthusiasm and zeal, he had trained himself to listen to records with the help of B. H. Haggin's *Music on Records,* which begins: "For my purpose in this book I am assuming that you have just bought a phonograph, are ready to buy your first set of records, and are asking me what I think it should be."

John had just bought a portable phonograph (or, as he called it, "gramophone"), was ready to buy his first set of records and was indeed asking Haggin's advice. Having found a brilliant instructor, John became the kind of pupil teachers dream of. Haggin said one should begin not with Beethoven, Mozart or Bach, but with Schubert. John began with Schubert. Haggin said to buy this or that recording. John scoured the second-hand shops on Sixth Avenue in the West Forties to find it. He set about building a record library with the same care he had taken in building up his library of books.

When he returned to the below-ground room with his treasure, he followed Haggin's directions about the order in which the movements should be played, put the needle down again and again at a theme Haggin had pointed out, listening to a work twenty, thirty, forty or more times until he knew it. Reading Sir Donald Tovey, also recommended by Haggin, he anchored firmly in mind dates, biographical data, opus numbers and, for Mozart, Köchel listings.

During the recent Christmas vacation he had finally succeeded in meeting his musical mentor through his poetical mentor, Mark Van Doren. With Mark, and his wife Dorothy, we had gone up to Isham Street one freezing cold night for an evening of recorded music in Haggin's apartment. By the end of it John had decided to buy the gramophone we had been listening to (which our host had mentioned he was thinking of selling) as a kind of graduation present to himself: He was now ready to follow music on his own.

The sound track for our summer in New York was put together by Haggin. John associated that period with Haydn's *London* Symphony, I with Beethoven's Op. 59, No. 3. Whenever I hear it, I see us wedged together, knee to knee, in the tiny oven of a booth at the Record Collector's Exchange where we first heard it. John's upper lip, shaved of its mustache, is beaded with perspiration. He bends over, his right ear inclined toward the turntable, listening with his whole brain. From time to time, looking as though he might levitate, he grabs hold of my hand and with an ecstatic expression on his face says, "You *hear*?" as the cello pizzicato plucked at our hearts.

It was Haggin who had introduced John to Bessie Smith. He listened to her singing with the same concentration he gave to a Mozart aria. Delmore clearly didn't find Bessie "amazing." He sat quietly through "Empty Bed Blues," then began to wander around the room restlessly, examining books. At the end of the first side he said, "John, I neither understand nor am capable of responding to such music."

John, who always hoped his friends would share his enthusiasms, and propagandized for them so effectively that they usually did, was disappointed by Delmore's unresponsiveness to the singing. But Delmore had spoken so firmly there was clearly no possibility of changing his mind.

What Delmore preferred was to continue talking. He wanted to hear more about my sister's children (John had inquired about Marie and the children on the way uptown). I was perplexed by this show of interest. It certainly wasn't a matter of making polite conversation. On the other hand, I couldn't imagine that children as children would arouse Delmore's curiosity. He had, I suspected, a literary interest in the striking things they occasionally said. I told Delmore that Billy, my seven-year-old nephew, had come home from his first day in a new school in the Yorkville neighborhood to which the family had recently moved, reporting that all the children in his class were Hungarian. He wanted to be Hungarian too. His mother, who was preparing dinner, didn't at first take in the urgency in his voice. Could he please be Hungarian? Why couldn't he be? Why? Why? When she tried to explain why it was impossible, he burst into tears. The rest of the day he was disconsolate.

Years later Delmore published a poem which begins: "Come, let us meditate upon the fate of a little boy who wished to be Hungarian!" In "The Would-Be Hungarian" he took up, once again, the theme, his theme, of the immigrant in America, this time making the native-born child the alien who learns from his experience in school what it feels like to be an immigrant. Billy in Delmore's poem becomes an imaginary Hungarian, as John, in his story, becomes an imaginary Jew.

Delmore made me promise, as he left us late that night, that I would have John let him know when I was next going to be in Boston. He wanted me to meet Gertrude. The four of us must have dinner together. I said that I would do so, but my visits to Boston were always so short they seemed to be over before they had begun. There was the slow train ride up, slowed further by my excitement and anticipation, the taxi from Back Bay to Grove Street, John at the second-floor landing, pausing an instant with the tension he always felt after the long separation: Would I have changed? Would I look "too New York?" (In the little black hat, yes. It was the first thing to come off.) Silhouetted from behind by the hall light—broad, square shoulders, flat torso, narrow hips, arms close to the body, the stance rigid—he was like an Old Kingdom Pharaonic figure. Running down the stairs to take my suitcase, he'd say, "Damn the train. I've been waiting *hours*. I thought you'd never get here."

In minutes it was Sunday afternoon, time to go back to New York on the six o'clock, which would put me into Grand Central at midnight. I never took the six o'clock, nor the seven, nor the eight, nor the nine—"Stay, Stay. Take the next one"—until we raced to catch the last, the midnight train, on which I would sit up all night with drunken soldiers, crying children, argumentative families in a crowded, smoke-filled, lurching car that was either overheated or refrigerated, arriving in New York the next morning with just enough time to shower and change before going to work, hung over from lack of sleep, played-out but still keyed up from the emotional and intellectual excitement of the weekend.

The letter from John after I'd reported this was always a reminder that we wouldn't have these brief visits and terrible separations if I had agreed to move up to Boston with him in the fall as he had pressed me to do. As autumn approached, John had begun urging me to give

Myself at the time of my engagement to John—his favorite photo of me

up my room and my job and go to live with him. The hope that I would be willing to do so was the reason, he confessed, for his wish to move to Boston. Boston would allow us the kind of privacy impossible to find in Cambridge. The atmosphere at Harvard was puritanical; the faculty inquisitive and gossipy. They were *still* talking about another poet and faculty member who had scandalized them by living openly with his mistress. (The mistress, knowing that she was being gossiped about, played the role to the hilt. On one occasion, when students were in the house for a seminar, she sauntered into the room where they were meeting dressed in a negligee, a boa of marabou feathers around her neck, and cut through the discussion with, "For Christ's sake, honey, where's the gin?")

Although by this time I was deeply and irrevocably in love with John, I was unable to make the kind of commitment I knew going to live with him in Boston would require, because it seemed to me that he was not ready. His relationship with B., the English girl, was still unresolved. They had talked of marrying before he had left England, and talked about it again when she had come to this country for a visit a year later (a visit that had not gone well, he admitted). Full of doubts, they had postponed the decision a second time. They were to meet again, although where and when was not decided, and probably would have done so had the war not intervened. Their two years of correspondence, though episodic, had been for John a bulwark against loneliness. Although he admitted that it had become a phantom relationship even before he and I met, he was unwilling, or, as he said (and I later came to see was true), unable to break it off. How could he write about us when he had no idea what B. was suffering—her country at war, London attacked by air raids? What he yearned for was a letter from her which would release him honorably. I saw the difficulty of his situation, but saw also that until it was resolved we would have to live on weekends and letters.

So it did not seem likely that John would let Delmore know when I was going to be in Boston for a visit. As it turned out, Delmore and I didn't meet again until the following November. The hoped-for letter of release came in the summer. John and I became engaged soon thereafter. In October we married and I moved into his Grove Street apartment.

II

BOSTON
AND
CAMBRIDGE

We were married in the Lady Chapel of St. Patrick's Cathedral. John's choice for best man was his old classmate from Columbia, Bob Giroux. It had been at one of John's little teas that I had first met Bob. He had not squandered his undergraduate days cutting classes and rowing, John said; rather he had been thoroughly intellectual, with highly developed interests in literature, films and music. Bob liked Bessie Smith better than Delmore had, but he obviously didn't feel one had to listen to her in hushed silence, as John tended to do. When Bob laughed at the lyrics, I decided he wasn't as formidable as he at first appeared. An editor at Harcourt Brace, he seemed more adult than John's other friends, perhaps because of the dark business suit he wore and the air of authority he already had.

Bob and his friend Charles Reilly, my sister and Jean Webster (née Bennett) formed the nucleus of a group that met for parties during the engagement period, when John was teaching summer school at Harvard, and Bob and Charlie were waiting to be called into the service. We saw one another frequently and informally, so that by the time October came I, too, counted Bob a friend. When we learned at the last minute that he would not be granted "compassionate" leave by the Navy for October 24, the date set for the wedding, John and I were both crushed. Mark Van Doren, with characteristic grace, agreed to take Bob's place.

Mark's influence on John's life was immense. It was as Mark's student that John had developed his lifelong passion for Shakespeare. It was Mark who introduced him to Stephen Crane, Mark who encouraged him to become a poet, Mark who tried to keep him in line during his unruly undergraduate days when he was dismissed from college one semester, for cutting classes and flagrant neglect of his studies. And it was Mark, when John settled down to become a serious student, who recommended him for the Kellett Fellowship to Clare College, Cambridge.

At the wedding Mark, a tall handsome man with a cap of close-cropped graying hair, played his role with the urbanity John so much admired. ("Will I *ever* have a manner like his?" John asked.) But he played it rather as the father of the groom than as best man, the calm, steadying mentor who understood so well the intellect he had helped develop, the father who felt sympathy and compassion for a difficult temperament so foreign to his own. As the two men waited at the altar, Mark made a sotto voce observation about the chapel's architecture to engage John's attention. This brought the trembling in John's body under control. At the reception, which Jean gave us in her new apartment in the River House, Mark led me in the first waltz, proposed a toast to our happiness and held us in a joint embrace. As we were leaving, we saw him, elegant in his cutaway, whirling John's mother around, his last official act as surrogate parent.

Our honeymoon was brief. Because John had to teach on Monday, we had just time enough for an evening at the ballet to see Nora Kaye in *Pillar of Fire,* and a champagne breakfast the following morning at the old Murray Hill Hotel, in honor of John's twenty-eighth birthday. To show how uxorious he intended to be he carried me with great good humor over the threshold—"One must follow custom"—of his, and now our, Beacon Hill apartment.

In those days the Hill was rundown, even seedy-looking. The façades of the handsome nineteenth-century houses on Louisburg Square were in need of painting, the brass needed polishing, the windows washing. There were signs offering furnished rooms for rent, such as one might see outside tenements. Nevertheless, the bare bones of the architecture here and on neighboring Mount Vernon, Pinckney,

Mark Van Doren dancing with my aunt at our wedding reception

Revere and Joy streets, together with the walled gardens, and tree-covered alleyways, made it far and away the most attractive and desirable section of the city in which to live.

As one came out of our house, 49 Grove, an undistinguished but tidy four-story building at the top of the Hill, turned the corner into Revere (a short distance away from number 91, which in a few years another poet would put firmly on the literary map) and started down to Charles Street, one caught a glimpse of the river, a streak of cerulean blue splashed with white sails in summer, slate gray with snow and ice in winter.

That winter snow and ice came early and stayed late. The daily newspaper confirmed what we felt in our bones. Day after day there were record-breaking temperatures. Indoors and out we froze. The sanitation department was so sluggish about removing the snow that the Hill became a treacherous ski slope as layer piled upon layer, the surface glazed at night with a frosting of ice. When we sat up past midnight, talking and listening to the albums of Mozart operas we'd been given as wedding presents, we kept warm by drinking tongue-blistering hot chocolate from china mugs (another wedding gift), while burning rolled-up newspapers in the fireplace and, on one occasion, early poems taken from between the covers of black binders, poems that had once seemed to their author worthy of a place in his first book and now struck him as "contemptible." As John read aloud a stanza before tossing the page in the fire, he'd say, "Good God! Did I write that?"

At 6:30 each morning, when the alarm went off, we pried our eyes open to see through the frosted window of our igloo-like bedroom the milky, arctic light of almost-day. Knowing that the only other spot of warmth in the apartment would be inside the refrigerator, which was more or less permanently out of order, we felt little temptation to move. Although he didn't have to go to Cambridge until later in the day, it was John who got up first.

"*Quel hiver!*" he'd murmur, as he jogged to the bathroom to run a hot tub for me, then to the kitchen to light the oven for warmth and put the water on for coffee. Was I wearing enough clothing? he asked, as I, wearing almost everything I owned, braced to go out the door, down the Hill and across the Public Garden to my tedious but financially necessary job in the law department of a large insurance company.

One memorable night, the night I became a permanent coward about the cold, Gertrude and Delmore asked us to dinner. The air was so raw and sharp as we came out of the Harvard Square MTA station and started toward Ellery Street that we ran all the way, our scarves over our faces so we could breathe through wool. The Schwartzes' apartment, the upstairs of a modest two-story frame house, was cozy and warm.

Gertrude, short and delicate-looking next to her "heavy bear" of a husband, had a light voice, what John called a "champagne laugh" and a dry wit. She was as soft-spoken and reserved as Delmore was convivial and expansive when he was playing the host. He gave us a glass of sherry and introduced me to the other guest, John Malcolm Brinnin, whom John had met when he was teaching at Wayne (and who had

GEORGE PALMER

Gertrude and Delmore in their Ellery Street apartment

been the victor when they had both submitted poems for the Hopwood Award given by the University of Michigan).

As we sat at the dinner table, listening to Gertrude's stories about Yaddo, where she and Delmore had spent the summer of 1939, and also to Brinnin's talk of Dr. Benjamin Sieve, the Commonwealth Avenue "gland man" about whom Delmore questioned him carefully (for reasons which would later become clear), we forgot the night outside. When the heat went off, Gertrude kept us warm with cup after cup of hot tea, the men fueled by a discussion of Edmund Wilson's essay on *The Turn of the Screw* which had recently appeared. (John was less enthusiastic about it than Delmore, afraid that the psychoanalytic interpretation would overpower the ghost story.)

It was late when we left. At the door we separated, Brinnin to go in one direction, John and I in another. Two steps were all that were necessary to tell us that the temperature had dropped still further. It was below zero, how much below we were afraid to guess. We shouted words of encouragement back and forth until Brinnin was out of hearing. From the Charles Street station up the Hill to our apartment was a short but steep walk. That night the wind from the river

forced its glacial embrace upon us so brutally that we felt as though
we were wrapped in wet sheets. A walk that should have taken ten
minutes took fifty. It seemed absurd to panic so close to home, but
waves of panic were what passed between us, we admitted, when we
were safely inside our icy but windless apartment, and could speak
again.

The next morning Delmore called, eager to hear how we'd got
home. He'd learned from a radio report that at about the time we'd
left his house the temperature had dropped to fourteen below. Brinnin
was so affected that he became ill. Sunday was milder. By midday the
mercury rose to zero. It was that kind of a winter.

For an instructor in English at Harvard, the Grove Street apartment
was an extravagance. While not at all posh, it was, by comparison with
the little house on Appian Way, altogether more serious and solid,
despite the trickle of heat and the out-of-order refrigerator. It had a
good-sized living room, a small bedroom, a tiny storeroom, proper
kitchen and bath. The living room was dominated by an immense desk
covered with books and papers that looked chaotic but had an order
—for my husband was an orderly man—that John understood perfectly. There was also a comfortable sofa, upholstered chairs, a rug (all
lent by John's mother) and the large and powerful speaker of Haggin's
Scott gramophone, next to which sat John's red leather chair. The walls
were lined with books arranged with a care a librarian would have
admired. It was a room for thinking, writing, reading and listening to
music, one which could have been, without alteration, a tutor's study
in an English college.

The bedroom, with its single bed—"I suppose when we have some
money we should buy a larger one, but since we're both slim . . ."—
and straight-backed chair, was as bare as a monk's cell. Because it was
on a courtyard and had no lighting fixture, day and night it was as
dark as a cave. Though the living room was generously supplied with
windows, it too was dark. Soon after John moved in, he'd been
walking around the room, muttering to himself in the act of composition, when he'd become aware that the woman who ran the grocery
store across the street was staring up at him as if he were "gaga."
Thereafter he kept the shades drawn. On weekends when I had visited
him I raised them. After I left he lowered them again.

White curtains, which would allow me light and John privacy, were my modest attempt to brighten the room and add a feminine touch to the otherwise donnish décor. In this John humored me, even putting up the curtain rods. It was only when I banished books (which I suspected would always preempt any living space we shared) from the kitchen that he protested, "All that *beautiful* space will go to waste." No it wouldn't, I assured him. Where books had been, there would now be dishes and glasses. "We can't live on peanut butter sandwiches and Hershey bars as you did in your bachelor days."

Soon after I had installed the few possessions I had had sent from New York, Gertrude called to welcome me, to invite us to dinner and discuss the wedding present she and Delmore would give us. Others had given us records, she knew, and Delmore was for following suit. Was there not something more practical I would like for the apartment? If she remembered correctly, from a time she'd left her coat there, the bedroom had no light. How did I manage? Poorly. John, who had learned a good many spartan habits at prep school, dressed in the dark, even tying his bow ties expertly without the use of a mirror. Thanks to Gertrude, in a few days the bedroom had a pretty lamp, and John wondered how he had lived so long without one.

Since Gertrude had said she was going to New York to spend Thanksgiving with her mother, I suggested that we invite Delmore to have dinner with us. We had been married a month and had seen no one, not even the Schwartzes (the night of record cold was still two months in the future). John had refused Gertrude's dinner invitation with a fabricated excuse. When I asked him what the real reason was —for I knew he was very fond of her and ordinarily wouldn't have missed a chance to go to Ellery Street—he said he needed more time to become accustomed to his new state. (He had been unnerved, going into his first class the Monday after we married, when a student hummed the opening bars of the wedding march.) To break out of his reclusiveness at Harvard was difficult, especially since, for the first time in years, he wasn't lonely, while I, though immensely happy, missed having a circle of women friends such as I'd had in New York. Letters, which I exchanged with my sister two or three times a week, and less frequently with Jean Webster and others, seemed a poor substitute for their company.

Delmore telephoned one day in John's absence. He'd been hoping to catch me alone. "Your husband is insane, do you realize that? He's behaving like an Arab, keeping you in hiding. He's refusing invitations right and left." This was news to me. "It offends people and is bad for his academic career. Tell him to bring you out Saturday afternoon. Say Gertrude has to go to New York again and I'll be at loose ends."

Saturday afternoon John was settling himself down in Delmore's living room for a good long talk, when Delmore announced that we had all been invited to the Mark Schorers' for cocktails.

"A plot," John said, turning to me. "Were you in on this?" I said I had not been, but that I would very much like to go to the party. It was time for him to allow me out of purdah.

During the first summer we were together I had asked John what faculty wives were like; he had said they were badly dressed, dreary-looking bluestockings, and told me the story about Thorstein Veblen. When Veblen's appointment at Harvard was being considered, the head of his department, who had heard that the famous economist was a womanizer, said, after much throat-clearing, "Professor Veblen, we can't have any of that at Harvard." Veblen replied suavely that there was no need to be concerned on this score. He had seen the women of Cambridge: They offered no temptation.

Veblen hadn't seen Ruth Schorer in a long black dinner dress, I whispered to John, as Delmore introduced us. Mark Schorer, who looked and sounded like Humphrey Bogart, said, "I won't pretend we haven't been dying to see the girl Berryman married. Is it true you were a model?" Briefly. No, I had not been a dancer, another rumor I was asked about as Mark took me around. The Schorers' living room, which had white leather couches, high-backed Mexican chairs and a rug so thick one's heels sank into it, was like a page out of *House and Garden*. Dry martinis, drier wit, flirtatious laughter, talk of models and dancers (where I had expected the conversation to be about Words-worth and Coleridge): If this was Cambridge society, John had very much misled me.

After John got over his initial stiffness—aided by Delmore's asides about the other guests—John behaved, greatly to the surprise of his colleagues, like the man I had known in New York. He was having such a good time that we stayed on and on, and when we left I heard him inviting the Schorers to come to Grove Street.

On Thanksgiving, which followed the party by a few days, Del-

MRS. FORBES JOHNSON-STOREY

Delmore as the youthful, handsome and brooding poet

more arrived at our apartment with a bulky package under his arm:
the proofs of *Genesis* which John had offered to read for him.

"It's going to be a terrible job, John. A thousand pages! Four others
have been over them . . . but your sharp eye. . . . I'll be eternally
grateful." The villanelle he had also promised to bring (it was to have
accompanied the lamp) was not quite right yet. Instead he presented
us with a photograph of himself that we had both admired. A studio
portrait taken by Mrs. Forbes Johnson-Storey, it showed him looking
into a mirror, a youthful, handsome, brooding poet. With rue, he said
that in this romanticized view one didn't see the split down the middle
of his face which he confronted every morning when he shaved, asking
himself, as did his character Shenandoah, "What will become of me?"

"There's another photograph of you prominently displayed in the
window of the Coop. Did you know?" John asked. "It's right next
to the one of Joyce. Not bad company, old boy."

Delmore, who revered Joyce (while at the same time keeping a
dossier on his private life), agreed the company couldn't be better.

How cheerful the curtains made the room! Delmore said, looking
around. Having just read John's poem "For His Marriage," he quoted:

> comes lover to my side
> the terrifying bride.

"What else has the 'terrifying' bride been up to?"

"She's thrown my books out of the kitchen." John got no sympathy
for this. "You can't eat books, John." To me, Delmore said, "One of
the hazards of being married to a poet, and there are many—'All poets'
wives have rotten lives'—is that there's no telling how one will be
characterized in verse. 'Terrifying,' for example. On the other hand,
when you're old, and your hair has turned gray"—My hair turn gray?
I couldn't imagine that it wouldn't always be red—"its color, recorded
in the poem, will remain forever 'the conflagration' it is today."

While I was struggling in the kitchen with my first elaborate dinner
(how, I asked my sister in a letter the next day, did one learn to time
the dishes so that they were all ready to serve at once?), Delmore asked
John what news he had about *Poems,* my copy of which he picked up
from the table next to my chair. John's second publication, a slim
volume in the New Directions "Poet of the Month Series" had come

out shortly before we married. If, indeed, it had come out, John said. Apart from the free copies he had received from Laughlin, there had been no sign that it had. No reviews, not a single notice of its existence. Even *The Nation,* where John had been poetry editor, had not listed it among the books of verse that had appeared during the year. "What's the point of publishing?" he asked gloomily.

"The advance," Delmore said. We all laughed. The advance had been $25.

The jacket copy, which Delmore now read aloud, said that of the contributors to *Five Young American Poets* (Randall Jarrell, George Marion O'Donnell, Mary Barnard and W. R. Moses were the others) John had received the most critical praise. Delmore, imitating Laughlin who had written the copy, read, " 'a cerebral poet whose gifts augur a brilliant future. He is young, he has faults—sometimes his sensibility seems almost too acute' —(You hear that, Eileen . . . about the almost-too-acute sensibility?)— 'but few of his contemporaries make better reading for someone with a cultivated poetical taste.' "

"That, of course, is the trouble," Delmore said. "How many readers have 'a cultivated poetical taste'?" With John, whose discouragement was patent, Delmore turned serious. "You know that in any other country you would have a wide and immediate audience." And he repeated what John had reported his having said before: that no one of their generation was writing poems as rich and complex as John's.

As I was beginning to discover, praise in general meant little to John. Praise from Delmore or Mark, or Allen Tate or R. P. Blackmur was what mattered. At this period, Delmore's encouragement was what kept him afloat. When, on the way out the door, John would say with his crooked grin, "I'm off to Cambridge, to show my new poem to God," what he meant was that Delmore's opinion mattered more to him than anyone else's. If Delmore remained silent, that meant he didn't like the work (the stiffest review John could have). If Delmore offered suggestions, John always thought them over long and hard. So, when, during dinner, Delmore talked about "A Point of Age," quoted a stanza, and singled out the line, "We must travel in the direction of our fear," which he thought particularly good, John feasted on his words. Going even further, again to help John overcome the sense of frustration he felt at having *Poems* ignored, Delmore linked his name with masters like Yeats and Stevens. I began to love Delmore for his thoughtfulness and generosity.

John in turn had been Delmore's critic, although, until his recent anxiety about the publication of *Genesis,* he had needed little encouragement, for he was "blazing" with success. Nevertheless, he counted on John's judgment, which he thoroughly trusted.

"You must get John to put together a book for a commercial publisher, like Frank Morley at Harcourt Brace," Delmore said to me at the table, "because if John has his faults as a poet, Laughlin has *his* as a publisher. Who knows? Maybe Jay was on the ski slopes and forgot to send out review copies of the *Poems.* A book by a commercial publisher like Harcourt could not be ignored. It would have to be reviewed."

Soaking in the balm Delmore offered that evening, John fortunately could not imagine how many years it would be before he found a commercial publisher. As he listened to Delmore stage-manage his future, he could almost see Morley's letter of acceptance.

After we moved away from the table to have coffee, Delmore asked how I had enjoyed my debut in Cambridge society. I told him I thought John had misled me about what to expect: The Schorers' party had been great fun.

"What John was talking about was faculty teas. Nevertheless you must make him go to them. And as soon as you're settled, you should have the Morrisons [Theodore Morrison directed English A, the required freshman composition course] and others in."

"Machiavelli," as John called Delmore whenever he urged John to be politic, was delighted to hear that John had already invited the Schorers.

"For tea? You'd better offer them something stronger if you want things to go well."

"Sherry?" John suggested. "Ale?"

"Gin. And invite some others from the department."

(Gin it was, and the evening, with the help of Gertrude and Delmore, who also came, was a success, though one of the faculty wives was shocked to discover that John and I slept in a single bed and John predicted that by the time this news hit Harvard Yard, Cambridge gossip being what it was, we would probably be said to have a mirror on the ceiling.)

Thanksgiving evening was a good time to go to the Statler Hotel bar, according to Delmore. He had heard it was a homosexual hangout. What about going for a drink, to take in the scene? The couples sitting at little tables looked to me like undergraduates and their dates, carbon copies of those I had seen at the Biltmore bar in New York in the days when I had gone there. If there were any exotics in the room, it was the two men I was with. I had often wondered whether Delmore and John exaggerated how much they were discussed by both faculty and undergraduates. This evening I saw that they hadn't exaggerated. Their appearance was causing a stir. Delmore, who became uncomfortable in the way he had at the restaurant in New York, said that perhaps he had made a mistake. It was the Lincolnshire, not the Statler, that was interesting. The scene at the Lincolnshire was equally heterosexual, although the couples here looked like young married Bostonians.

After a cursory look around Delmore, seeing that there was nothing to interest him, began to question me about my early life. Unlike many brilliant talkers Delmore was also eager to listen, and had a flattering way of quoting what one had said on another occasion as if it had been a brilliant insight or extremely witty. When one was telling a story, or recounting an incident, he turned his head to the side and nodded reflectively, like a confessor. This kind of concentrated attention (which I had never experienced until I met John, who listened with the same intensity), made me uneasy. Surely what I had to say was not weighty enough. Delmore pushed past the timidity I felt with him in the beginning, leading me on with his questions.

What interested him most about my history was that I was an orphan, my mother having died when I was ten months old, my father when I was five. So it was that, was it, that explained my closeness to my sister? He wanted to hear all about the convent school run by Italian nuns that Marie and I had gone to. What did the convent look like? What did the nuns wear? What kind of room had my sister and I slept in? From his questions I felt that what I looked upon as a commonplace childhood seemed to him exotic in a way in which it had not been to John, who had also been in a convent school briefly as a child (and had felt orphaned, though he then still had both parents).

How different his own childhood had been! Delmore said. Like the young man in his story, "America, America," he had sat for hours in his mother's kitchen, listening to her tales about her youth, her courtship and marriage, the Sunday night get-togethers of her friends. Over her "genre studies," as he called them in the story, he painted his own genre studies of the life of middle-class New York Jews of his parents' generation, the composite rich in color and specificity. Ironic though he was about the aspirations of these people and their attitude toward America, he nevertheless envied the sense of community they shared in their cozy, tea-drinking social life and was saddened that he could not re-create it, as he had imagined he would after he married.

"Jews aren't drinkers," he said, in a long aside about the differences between Irish and Jewish immigrants. Wine being part of their religious ritual, Jews learned moderation at home, at the Seder. "The Irish have no built-in control. Take Joyce . . ."

"An alcoholic, wasn't he?" John asked.

"His younger brother Stani had to scour the streets of Trieste looking for him, and more than once found him in the gutter. No bed of roses for Nora . . ."

"Incredible that it didn't affect his writing," John said. The two men, who drank little at that time, talked about alcoholism as if it were a rare disease, like dengue fever.

When I asked what his father had been like, Delmore said he had been a handsome, charming, philandering man and a natty dresser. With an intake of breath coupled with a smile, which usually meant he was going to make a self-deprecatory remark, he said, "I didn't inherit his nattiness. John now: If he had any clothes but the suit he has on, he'd be a clotheshorse."

Harry Schwartz had made a fortune in real estate. Success came to him early. "My father wasn't able to enjoy his success because he was haunted by the fear that what had come to him early and easily would vanish in the same way."

The very anxiety that gnawed at his son, I thought.

Listening to Delmore talk was like reading his long poem "Shenandoah," "America, America," or, as I was to see in the coming days, when I read the proofs as John finished them, like *Genesis*. His life was his subject. He was frankly and unashamedly autobiographical. Long before the word came into fashion, he was "confessional." Having worked through and discarded the styles of his mentors at an early age, after taking from them what he needed, he developed the flat, conversational voice that recorded so well the speech of the milieu in which he had grown up, while the other poets of his generation were using material from their lives, when they used it at all, in an abstract, symbolic way, expressing it in "cerebral" language.

How far John was from using his life in this undisguised way was clear from his conversation. As Delmore talked about his parents, his beloved grandmother and his brother Kenneth on this and other evenings, I was struck by how little John said about his own family. Yet the similarities between their situations were striking. Each was the older of two boys. Each was intellectually precocious, observing, inquisitive. Each overheard his parents' terrible disputes and suffered from divided loyalties. Delmore sometimes said that his mother preferred Kenneth, but I suspect that he, like John, was the favorite—at least until, in order to survive, he tried to escape her domination.

With evident nostalgia, he spoke of Rose Schwartz as she had been when he was a small boy, and said he thought his storytelling talent came from her. He repeated, with amusement, some of the expressions she used. When he misbehaved, she'd say, "You should grow like an onion with your head in the ground." Or, if he complained of having no one to play with, nothing to do, she'd say, "Go knock your head against the wall." Though the words were harsh, they were said in an amused, maternal way. But as she grew older and became embittered, as she was by the time he and Gertrude married—"I told you, John, that she threatened to kill herself when I announced that Gertrude and I were going to get married, didn't I?"—she turned into a virago who poisoned his life with her paranoia.

After one of these long evenings (which sometimes lasted six or seven hours), John often wondered aloud how it was that he, who with other people was so articulate, was so silent with Delmore. There was little mystery about that, it seemed to me: If the four of us were together, or there were guests at the Schwartzes', the talk was literary and John did almost as much talking as Delmore. It was when it was just the three of us, and Delmore's conversation was autobiographical rather than bookish, that John (though keenly interested in what Delmore had to say) was likely to be silent. The natural thing would have been for him to talk about his family too, but it was a subject about which he was reticent in the beginning, even with me. He rarely mentioned his father. His mother, who was so actively involved in his life that he couldn't have left her out of his conversation had he wanted to, he talked about in the present tense. About their clashes of personality, the most he permitted himself to say with anyone outside the family was a comically exasperated, "My mother!" when she had done something outrageous.

So Delmore's candor about the flaws in Harry Schwartz's character, his efforts to distance himself from Rose's hysteria, and his bluntness in describing the defects of her personality, astonished John. Once, pushed beyond endurance by something his mother had done, Delmore said he hated her. John, who had learned his catechism well, was shocked. One must honor one's father and mother. He was struggling to honor his.

At closing time at the Lincolnshire, Delmore was reluctant to go home. He held us on the sidewalk with another and still another recollection. His mood, which had been sprightly early in the evening, had grown somber. When we parted at Revere Street, and looked after him as he walked heavily toward the Charles Street station, John said, "He knows he won't sleep at all tonight." Though he didn't tell me at the time, because he had been sworn to secrecy, John suspected that Delmore's preoccupation with family on this holiday night, his change of mood toward the end and his reluctance to go home to an empty house, were caused by a grave concern that I wouldn't know about until April.

What I did know, however, was that some months before we were married Delmore had asked to see John, and had talked about his private life in a way he never had before (the conversation marked an increased intimacy in their relationship). And John, reciprocating, had told him that he was thinking of asking me to marry him. At first Delmore was delighted, but on reflection his deep pessimism about poets as husbands, poets in marriage, made him urge John to find out first if I was neurotic.

"How do you suggest I go about it?" John asked, not taking him seriously. "Have a psychiatrist look her over?'

There was nothing funny about this subject. "Think of the hell Vivien made Eliot's life, John. We're enough trouble to ourselves without having to worry about whether our wives are unstable."

John, who was in a state of (comparative) pre-Freudian innocence in those days, reported this part of the conversation to me with amusement. Certainly he cared more that I should be psychologically rather than physically strong. While he claimed that what had attracted him to me were my ankles, what he had looked for in a wife were deep wells of sympathy for his work, and a conviction that the work was sufficiently important to make sacrifices for. Beyond that he hoped for an equable temperament (as unlike his as possible), and a gift for fidelity.

During the brief Thanksgiving holiday John began reading the proofs of *Genesis*. It was indeed a labor of love. He worked on them four and five hours at a stretch, the only interruptions being telephone calls from a very jittery Delmore, who was going over another set at home. When John finished the section he had, he'd take it out to Cambridge to go over his corrections with Delmore. Delmore's nervousness before the publication of a large and ambitious work, for which he had the highest hopes, was compounded by a fear that reviewers would pounce on this book as they had on his translation of *Une Saison en enfer.* The attacks on the Rimbaud, the first he had suffered, were provoked by errors due, he admitted (at least to John), to haste, carelessness and a slippery grip on the French language. He had needed money and had rushed the job into print. The criticisms had made him feel as humiliated as a schoolboy. Worse than ridicule, however, was the terrible anxiety that the attacks were a sign that he was falling out of favor: *Was this the first step in the downward slide?*

"Delmore's in a terrible state," John reported over dinner. As John went over the corrections, most of them errors of spelling and meaning in the foreign quotations that studded the book, Delmore paced the floor, pulled his hair and groaned, *"Je rêvais, je rêvais,"* which made both of them howl with laughter. (Rimbaud's phrase *"Je rêvais"* he had translated as "I review." Mary Colum, whom he ever after called "Mary Whatchamacolum," rapped him on the knuckles for it in *Book Forum* [March 4, 1940].)

To cheer him up, John said, "You may not be the most reliable translator of French around, but you're the greatest writer on sex in modern times."

To which Delmore replied, "It's the strength of nonparticipation, John."

During the early months of our marriage I had thought of Delmore as the one person who could make John optimistic about his literary future. On the days when the two men

> meeting on the walk down to Warren
>   House
> so long ago we were almost anonymous
> waiting for fame to descend
> with a scarlet mantle & tell us
>   who we were,

would have coffee together and talk, John usually came home so cheerful I knew that Delmore had praised a poem he'd shown him or in a more general way had encouraged him about his future. On one occasion, however, shortly before Christmas, John returned in the blackest mood I'd seen him in since before we'd married. Delmore, who had the latest issue of *The New Republic* in hand, pointed out that *Poems* was not listed there either. When John said it hardly mattered, he'd already accepted that his book would be ignored, Delmore gave him more bad news. Another poet in their department had been invited to give the Morris Gray Poetry Reading. This was no news to John because he had helped the man prepare for his performance. "But don't you see, John? This is a slap at you. If a member of the department was going to be invited (and not an outsider), you were the obvious choice." John said defensively that even if he'd been invited he would have refused. Delmore, who sometimes admired John's unwillingness to be political, came down on him hard that day, accusing him of "demonic pride." If John's memory tricked him years later when, in *Love & Fame,* he replaced "demonic" with "satanic," he never forgot the substance of Delmore's lecture: The danger of being ignored as a writer for a long time is that it deforms the personality. To protect his talent John would have to be on guard against bitterness, Delmore said.

Reporting Delmore's warning, John said, "I don't feel bitter—*yet,* but Delmore is, as so often about me, right. It's a danger I will have to fight."

In the spring the question of the Morris Gray came up again when Theodore Spencer, a powerful professor in the English department, startled John after a staff meeting by inviting him to give the reading. John's stiff-necked reply was, "Surely you can't be serious." I arrived at the cafeteria where I was to meet Delmore and John minutes after this scene had taken place. Delmore was red, John white in the face. "You won't believe what happened," Delmore burst out, reporting John's response and imitating his hauteur. "Spencer concealed his astonishment and said that, on the contrary, he was quite serious. You know what John has done, don't you, Eileen? He's committed *academic suicide.*"

I was as distressed as Delmore, but suspecting that there was more than wounded pride involved, put off a discussion about it until John and I were alone. Then I discovered what was at first difficult for me to credit: The thought of having to read in public made him "madly nervous." He wasn't sure he could do it. That he was a superb reader in private and in class was no guarantee that he could perform before an audience. Delmore would have found this concern incomprehensible because he admired enormously the way John read, and deprecated his own performance. (After hearing a record he made for the Poetry Room collection, he said to John, "I see now why they consider me simple-minded. That lisp!"—though was there anyone who considered Delmore simple-minded?)

John's fear was easier for me to deal with than his pride. Once I understood that fear was in part responsible for his answer to Spencer, I was able to convince him to accept—which, in his typically ambivalent fashion, he was dying to do. Having observed that he reacted in the same way when anyone attempted to talk to him about a poem he'd published, or asked for his autograph (both rare occurrences in those days, but they did happen), I realized that the nervousness had a complex source. It was as dangerous to have one's work recognized as it was to have it ignored.

The Morris Gray was a success. During John's opening remarks his voice was tremulous, but as he began to recite, the poetry took hold of him. His voice steadied, his confidence grew and he gave his lines the shading and drama they had when he said them to himself. By the end he felt he had interested and moved his audience. The following morning he got up at dawn, took the train to Cambridge while I was still asleep and, climbing a wall in Harvard Square, stole the poster announcing the reading. With a note of thanks "for helping me through," he presented this "literary edelweiss" to me at breakfast.

Though he read hundreds of times thereafter, in the years I knew

him the "mad nervousness," though concealed more and more skillfully, never left him.

Shortly after Delmore's "demonic pride" speech, John, who knew
what a trap self-pity was for him, found a way to combat his disappointment over *Poems* that delighted me. Since there was no pleasure
to be had in publishing, what if we were to engage in a little private
venture, one we could control down to the last detail? His idea was
to select two recent poems, find a printer who would run them off,
using a typeface and paper we had selected, and send them out in lieu
of Christmas gifts which, this year, we couldn't afford. Harvard University Press, it turned out, would do the printing as cheaply as, and
better than, anyone else. We chose the typeface, the paper (vanilla in
color, a heavy, agreeable stock) and John selected "For His Marriage"
and "The Ball Poem." I drew up a list of friends, we signed our names
and sent out sixty copies of *Two Poems*. Until *Homage to Mistress
Bradstreet* appeared fourteen years later, it was the only publication that
pleased John in every way.

On December 31st, at the end of the day, I found John standing outside
the office building where I worked, his face closely shaven, his hair
newly cut, two long-stemmed roses clutched in his hand. As I told him,
he looked as though he were about to propose. While he was reluctant,
for superstitious reasons, to celebrate New Year's Eve, he suggested
that we go to a movie and then have dinner: a rare treat. In the
restaurant, he told me he had made up a list of resolutions for the New
Year. I knew from early journals he'd given me to read that his
resolutions usually fell into three categories: reforms he hoped to make
in his character, outlines of writing projects, a list of books to be read.
At midnight, as we toasted each other, he said that the list of writing
projects was long. A series of dream songs headed it. Now that he had
sent off his book to Morley at Harcourt Brace, he was eager to begin
something new. Rubbing his hands together in a gesture of anticipation he said, "Ha! You'll see. I'll make my name yet."
     The dream songs, which appeared years later in *The Dispossessed* as
"The Nervous Songs," were begun early in the New Year. Determined
to put *Partisan Review*'s rejection of "Boston Common" and the silence

from Morley out of his mind, he worked with greater concentration than he had since we married. That Delmore liked "Young Woman's Song," and remarked that it showed no strong influence, pleased and encouraged him. The rush of ideas for other songs—"The Demented Priest," "The Young Hawaiian"—led him to set himself the impossible goal of writing one a week. Unable to satisfy this unrealistic ambition, he became discouraged and began to wonder whether he might not get more work done if he were to go off alone somewhere.

Responsibility toward marriage vs. responsibility toward art became a serious conflict for one who was almost as ambitious to be a good husband as a good poet. With a nervous system such as John's, lapses in the former were inevitable. When I telephoned him one day from the office and interrupted him in the act of composition, he exploded. Often after he had lost his temper he could recover and say, with a rueful smile, quoting George Gibbs in *Our Town,* "I'm afraid I have a fault in my character." Or, "I told you you were marrying the most difficult man in the Western Hemisphere." On this occasion, however, remorse over his lack of control killed the afternoon for work. Maybe he should go away while he was writing. But where? And with what money?

The uncertainty about his academic future, which was becoming more difficult to ignore, proved a more serious impediment to writing than domestic life. It looked as though he would be asked to stay on . . . It looked as though he would not be asked to stay on . . . His head of department couldn't say . . . It depended . . . The only thing that was clear was that the war was turning Harvard upside down. In the early months of 1943 the students seemed feverishly eager to learn, to squeeze as much as they could out of their last days as undergraduates for no one knew how long. The bright boys became brilliant. In months they matured years. Greedy for more than they could learn in class, they began appearing at Grove Street.

Apart from our evenings with the Schwartzes and another instructor in English A, Eddie Weismiller, and his wife (who dandled their baby to sleep with A. A. Milne, substituting for "James, James, Morrison, Morrison," "John, John, Berryman, Berryman"), apart from an occasional movie or concert, what diversion John and I had we made for each other with conversation, music and reading. More and more frequently students shared these evenings at home. There was Stephen

Elliston, articulate and self-assured, Claude Fredericks, introverted and intense (who years later printed John's *His Thought Made Pockets & The Plane Buckt* in an elegant edition at his Pawlet Press), Tony Clark, as knowledgeable about painting as about poetry, and the *spirituel* Roberts Blossom, who was adored by a group that had come from prep school with him and called him, appropriately, "The Spirit." All the prickliness John displayed with his colleagues vanished when he was with undergraduates. In speaking of his students to me or to others, he called them affectionately, "my boy Elliston," or "my boy Clark" (as if he were fifty rather than ten years older than they!). He was witty, open, relaxed with them, advised and cosseted them, and was as hopeful of their futures as a father might have been. In return for our hospitality, the students invited us to Eliot and Dunster House for their cocktail parties, where the animation was in marked contrast to the stuffiness of the faculty teas to which we went out of duty.

It was through "The Spirit" that we were invited to the most brilliant cocktail party of the season. The boys led us to a high gray fence, from which an electrically operated door opened onto a small, snow-covered courtyard and a façade of glass so highly polished there appeared to be no break between indoors and out. It was difficult to believe one was a few steps from the Yard and the lean-to at 10½ Appian Way. This "modern" house had been built by our host, the architect Philip Johnson. Greeting us, he asked what John was studying, which caused John to square his shoulders and made the students, who always called him "Sir" and behaved toward him despite their liveliness and candor with the deference they felt due a poet, if not an instructor, try to hide their amusement. (I was less amused, because I knew that when we got home John would once again threaten to grow a beard.)

A hundred or so guests, graduate students from the School of Architecture and their wives, the staff of the *Advocate* and other college stars, and a few decorative Orientals, draped themselves over the low-slung couches in the sumptuous living room, clustered together on pillows on the floor or, with chilled glass in hand, studied the dazzling Miró wall hanging and made knowledgeable comments about the paintings. MacPearson Clark (no relation to Tony), a modest young man who spent most of his time talking up the talents of the others, told me that when the news came out that Mr. Berryman was marrying a girl who lived in Greenwich Village, the students decided she probably wore bangs, harlequin glasses and was "different." (Only about the bangs had they guessed right.) MacPearson also reported some of John's antics in class, a favorite being to walk around holding a chair in the air by one leg, a device for shaking up the students who had been out all night and were less attentive than they might be. (In the previous year, when his students had been altogether less lively than the current group, he had been teaching *The Sun Also Rises* and, feeling that the discussion was sluggish, said, "Tell me, what do you think was *wrong* with Jake? Anyone?" "Well, sir," one of them said, "He had this accident to his leg." "Anyone else?" John asked. General puzzlement in the room. "Gentlemen, I will have to tell you the facts of life. Jake was impotent." When John reported this lesson to me he said, "My God! Was I ever as young as they are?")

Soon after the Philip Johnson party, the boys began to leave Cambridge for military training, first Tony Clark, then the others. The Harvard we knew was slowly shutting down. By fall, instead of undergraduates there would be officers in training with a curriculum dictated from Washington. Delmore, who was being considered for a five-year appointment, was not at all sure he wanted to stay on. There was something intimidating about teaching men in uniform, he felt, especially if one had to teach them speech. "*Speech*! With my lisp?" With restless apathy, he considered leaving Cambridge and going to New York to devote himself full-time to writing a novel. He was fed up with teaching, he complained.

More than once, in a panic, he called John, begging for assistance in preparing for a class on Shakespeare. John would return from these sessions with Delmore saying he was seriously concerned about him. This was more than fed-upness. Delmore was not in good shape. Apathy and mutism before a room full of students were what he feared. What if one day he stood there and could think of *nothing to say*? Was it prepublication panic over *Genesis*? Or ambivalence about committing himself to another five years at Harvard? Or the strains of his marriage? None of these was a sufficient explanation, Delmore said. He was afraid he suffered from "manic-depressiveness." The high he had been on since September had been followed by a February low. What brought on these swings, how long they'd last, he didn't know. He knew only that he was at their mercy:

> We poets in our youth begin in sadness
> Thereof in the end come despondency and madness

he'd say, revising Wordsworth. Dr. Sieve, whom he consulted in
desperation, diagnosed a glandular disorder and prescribed injections
and nine kinds of pills.

What I had observed during the months I'd been seeing Delmore
had not looked to me like a high. But then I had barely heard the term
"manic-depressive" in an undergraduate course in psychology, and
would have recognized the symptoms only if they had been dramatic.
The low he was in now was more obviously a low, so obviously that
at one moment John became alarmed. He and Delmore had been
talking, as so often happened, about *Genesis*. John had been thinking
more and more that Delmore should not go on with the projected
second volume. Rather he should put aside autobiographical writing
for a time and work on lyrics again. When he suggested this, Delmore,
looking bleak and speaking in an uninflected voice, said he'd never
write verse, any verse, again. John had a moment of acute apprehension
during which it flashed through his mind that Delmore was contemplating suicide, at the same instant remembering that Delmore had
asked to borrow a book on the subject and had not returned it.

The next time the two men met, waiting to go into a staff meeting
—would they learn about their futures today?—John complained that
he never received any mail (by which he meant that he still hadn't
heard from Harcourt Brace), and Delmore told him how lucky he was.
"My morning delivery brought me three letters: One from Laughlin
threatening not to publish *Genesis* at all. Another from Dwight Macdonald addressing me as 'You rat,' and a third from Will Barrett
ending, 'You go to hell.' " Delmore's smile was wan as he said, "It's
the literary life, John." But it was a smile, and John decided that he
had been worrying needlessly.

As could be surmised from the third letter, Delmore and his old
friend from New York student days, and the man to whom he felt
closest, the philosopher William Barrett, who later became "the principle historian of 'the Marxist Decade,' " were not on speaking terms.
A troublemaker had reported to Delmore that when the Rimbaud
attacks began to appear, Barrett, instead of coming to his defense, had
mocked him. Delmore believed what he had been told instead of

asking Will himself if it was true. During this low period he seemed hypersensitive to treachery. He returned from a trip to New York with a suitcase full of plots and counterplots: Allen Tate was behind the Robert Penn Warren attack on Mark's new book. Laughlin, who was more interested in skiing than in literature, was seriously trying to wiggle out of his commitment to *Genesis*. And if he ever did get around to bringing it out, Louise Bogan at *The New Yorker* was ready to do a hatchet job on it.

Nor was it just the literary life. At Harvard the big guns were trying to get rid of him. "They're threatening to send an observer to one of my sections to judge my teaching . . . *at a time when I can barely talk.*" To assuage Delmore's anxiety about this last threat, John suggested they plan a lesson together, so that when the observer came Delmore would be prepared.

Delmore, the brilliant storyteller (when not in class), would spin out these New York literary plots in a richly detailed and persuasive way. John was easily persuaded. I was often skeptical, but since I didn't know the people involved it was difficult for me to judge. John's files of correspondence with the cast of characters, which he gave me to read, were engrossing, but not very helpful. Laughlin was hilariously funny and offhand. Was that the same as being irresponsible, as Delmore claimed? Tate was suave and convoluted. But was he an intriguer? As for Barrett, whom I had met and liked, had he really been disloyal? About all of these accusations I had doubts, but small ones, just as I had doubts about the mysterious Dr. Sieve.

With the egocentricity of the newly married, neither John nor I paid sufficient attention to what Sieve was up to. So, in April, when Delmore's mood suddenly lifted, and he talked about feeling like "Superman," and said that his sluggish brain was beginning to spin:

> You said, "My head's on fire"
> meaning inspired O

we rejoiced with him and didn't wonder, as we should have done, what price he was paying for this magic cure. Evenings at Ellery Street were displays of verbal fireworks. Delmore fabulated about baseball players, Mae West, gangsters, literary personalities: He had the goods on all of them. Frost was irresponsible about earning a living and neglected his

family. Edwin Arlington Robinson was an alcoholic. Eliot's wife was
in a mental institution. "Tom" had a secret apartment in London.

What slowly penetrated our self-absorption was that Gertrude was
away more and more, and when she was home there was tension
between her and Delmore. I allowed myself to think that such disagreements as they permitted us to see (and they permitted them rarely)
were to be expected in a marriage between two complex personalities.
So I was distressed when I called Gertrude at the end of April to invite
them to dinner and learned that she was leaving in an hour. Making
an effort to control her voice, she said she might not be back for
months. So quietly did she and Delmore arrange their separation that
no one in Cambridge was aware of what was happening. She simply
never returned from this visit to New York. With Delmore's reap-
pointment being considered, it seemed the most prudent way.

Restless, lonely, hating the empty apartment, Delmore at one moment wished Gertrude would come back, and the next he'd say it was
no good—they made each other far more unhappy than anyone could
have guessed, more unhappy even than he'd confessed to John. What
Gertrude wanted out of life he didn't know. Certainly it was not what
he wanted. He was gregarious. She was not. He was hospitable. She
was not. He wanted children. She did not. Or at least he thought he
wanted children. About this, I never found him very convincing. It
seemed to me his desire was as vague and abstract as his interest in his
friends' children was literary. (Years later, with greater self-knowledge, he said: "It's not a wife and children I want, but grandchildren.")
At least on the surface he did not share the concern of John and other
writers that children might be enemies of promise.

During his boyhood Delmore had been obsessed with the fear that
he would make an unhappy marriage in the way his father had. Then,
just like his father, he had rushed into it, badgering Gertrude to accept
him, aware of what he was doing yet unable to stop. What alarmed
John were signs that Delmore was going to rush into another relationship with a woman who, Delmore admitted gloomily and fatalisti-
cally, was totally unsuitable for him.

He claimed that he wanted, needed affection. Would he have been
able to accept it from a wife, I wondered? Any sign of it in others made
him avert his eyes. John, who was both affectionate and demonstrative,
always felt constraint in Delmore's presence, as I had sensed the day

I met the two of them in Pennsylvania Station. There was also what Delmore referred to as his "squeamishness about sex" and his recoil at the sound of four-letter Anglo-Saxon words. "Sometimes he's positively *virginal* and talks about the strength of nonparticipation. At other times he hints that he has love affairs. I can't make him out," John said. In the end we decided that it would take a shrewd psychoanalyst to sort out Delmore's true feelings, and to know how much they were governed by his childhood, by his mood swings, and by Dr. Sieve's treatments.

The day after Gertrude left, Delmore's mother appeared, as if in response to a stage direction. She called him from South Station to say she had come on a "surprise" visit. Things went very badly between them. Rose criticized the way the apartment was furnished, made derogatory remarks about the pictures he and Gertrude had hung— "*That's* a painting? You paid money for it?"—complained of Delmore's housekeeping and ridiculed the suit he was wearing, a new suit, which she said was too big. A weekend of this was all Delmore could take. He packed her off to New York with the excuse that he was going away and had to close the apartment. When he and I had dinner that night, he asked me what I thought of his suit. Standing, he turned around self-consciously for me to inspect it. His mother was right. It was too large. Unwilling to reinforce anything she had said, I hedged: The tailor might shorten the sleeves and the trouser cuffs a little. (I turned up one sleeve to show him what I meant.) That evening, wearing his oversized suit and mismatched socks, with his hair looking as if he'd been pulling it in all directions, his eyes red from lack of sleep, and his face pale and haggard, he was hardly recognizable as the young poet of the Johnson-Storey photograph.

John had not been with us at dinner. The final word having come through that he would not be reappointed, he had gone to New York for a series of interviews with other colleges. Delmore was unhappy that Harvard was keeping him on, John that Harvard was letting him go. Though they had both complained chronically about the drudgery of reading papers, and the time teaching took from writing, they were beginning to realize that any job they had for the duration of the war would require three or four times as many hours of work. An even less attractive alternative to teaching was the draft. Delmore was unwilling to go into the Army because he opposed the war on moral grounds, but John had been hoping to follow other members of the English staff who were going into intelligence work in the OSS. After a series of interviews in Washington, however, he was disqualified because of poor vision. So it had to be teaching. We decided to close the apartment and go to New York. From there John would be able to look around more efficiently, I could easily find a job and my sister would put us up. Full of optimism, we told ourselves it was only for a few weeks. A Princeton opening, which John had heard of through R. P. Blackmur, might come through at any moment.

The late spring had finally driven the ice and snow away. The trees in the Yard were in leaf, the air balmy as John cleaned out his office in Warren House and returned armloads of books to Widener. At the moment when he would have been most willing to stay, it was time to go. In the past six months he had begun to enjoy being at Harvard. His students were the most rewarding he had ever had. The success of his Morris Gray reading had subtly changed his relationship with his colleagues. Delmore and he had grown closer. Despite the brutal winter, the failure to find a publisher and the lack of money, John admitted, as we walked by the river, that he had never had a better year. He was touched to hear me say what he already knew, that I too

By the Charles River in Boston

had never been happier. "What the hell is happiness?" he asked with a happy laugh. And, more uneasily, "Should a poet seek it?"

In the months to come, I often thought of this conversation. It seemed to me that it had taken place in another world, in another life.

III

JOBLESS
IN
NEW YORK

Despair, rather than happiness, was the subject of our conversations as we walked by the East River during the months we lived in New York and John looked for a job. The optimism he had felt as he'd drawn up a list of government agencies and colleges gave way to uneasiness as one possibility after another came to nothing. Washington did not need a man of his talents. Ivy League colleges couldn't make new appointments, chairmen of English departments wrote, until they knew how many students the Army and Navy would send them. Princeton, the strongest possibility, was reluctant to ask him to hold out until fall, when they would know their needs, because the chances were so slim. That left smaller colleges and preparatory schools. John sent out fifty letters of application and waited. New York publishing houses might need an editor, magazines a writer. He sent out more letters and waited. Twice a day he waited for the mail. All day he waited for the phone to ring. James Agee, whom Delmore knew and thought would be helpful at *Time,* would return John's call at any moment, so the secretary said. John waited. While waiting, he read the want ads and typed more letters of application to tutoring schools, night schools, teachers' agencies, libraries—any place where he thought he could do the job. Through June, July and August he waited.

Often as I was leaving the office at Rockefeller Plaza where I had taken a temporary job as a typist, I found John at the door. His expression told me there was nothing but bad news. Agee hadn't called. Or the mail had contained news of near misses: The college had just hired an English instructor, the magazine a writer, the night school a teacher. As he pointed out, the wartime economy was thriving, people were earning more money than they had in years and he couldn't find work no matter how much he lowered his sights. He forced himself to tolerate the painful intrusion on his privacy that applications and interviews demanded. "Every day I'm made to peel off my skin—to no purpose." He wasn't sleeping, he wasn't eating, he was plagued by a host of physical ailments.

In little better shape myself, I tried to fight off panic. Agee was probably working toward a deadline on the Ingrid Bergman article and would call as soon as he'd handed it in. Tomorrow's mail was bound to bring an offer. What about going to a movie?

Movies were now less an entertainment than a drug. Four or five hours at a double feature brought the next day, with its possible phone calls, its possible offers, that much closer. At the Apollo on Forty-second Street, our opium den, we saw *La Kermesse Héroique, Un Carnet de Bal, Hôtel du Nord, Doctor Knock, Topaze, Drôle de Drame, Bizarre Bizarre.* Or we went to another cheap movie house nearby and saw *Mr. Lucky, Top Hat, Mission to Moscow.* We saw all these and more, some for the second and third time, while we waited. Movie houses were cheaper than the book and record shops we had haunted our first summer together. In any case we were too restless to listen to music, or even to read very much, and besides we were camping out in my sister's apartment, or my aunt's, without a phonograph or a library.

Once, on the palest promise of good news, we forsook Forty-second Street and crossed the Hudson to the Palisades Amusement Park. The rides, which hurled us up, threw us down, jerked us around in a trope of our daily existence, were hardly amusing but worth the price of admission. Briefly and violently they wrenched us out of an intolerable reality.

It was just before my semimonthly pay envelope arrived, when we didn't have the price of admission to a movie house no matter how cheap, that we walked by the East River. Although I thought that day-to-day I was hearing all the indignities John was exposed to, it was on these drugless walks that those he had tried to conceal came out, often in response to an unguarded question of mine. Was the pain he had complained of any better? It was so bad, and so like the pain Bhain Campbell had suffered before his illness was diagnosed, that John was certain he had cancer. The image of his friend in the agony of his terminal illness, glittering eyes in a skeletal face, haunted John's dreams.

Or I'd ask about developments at *Time.* Agee, who had finally returned his call, had arranged for an interview with Whittaker Chambers, a senior editor. Chambers asked John to write a book review, shredded it, asked him to write another, shredded that, then dismissed him with the question, "Have you ever blown up a bridge?" "The pretentious bastard!" John shook with rage reporting it. "As if one had to have the daring of a revolutionary to write Timese, for Christ's sake." To be in a position where he could be patronized by "a hack writer" like Chambers *and,* instead of being able to tell him what to do with his "back of the book," go away with a hook in the throat that there were "frequently" openings, and that Chambers would keep him in mind, was degrading. What did Chambers care that John was desperate enough to read meaning into his thoughtlessly used "frequently"?

On one of our walks, John showed me a letter from the headmaster of a prep school where he had been considered and where, we both thought, an appointment was certain. Early one Saturday we had taken the train from Grand Central to northern Connecticut, a ride that carried John back to his adolescence, as we traveled the route and heard the mournful whistle so familiar from his return trips to South Kent. The stirring up of old memories, and the recognition of the passage of time (what had he to show for the years since his schooldays?) absorbed him so thoroughly that he seemed not to be taking in what the headmaster was saying about the duties that would be expected of him: teacher of English, supervisor of a dormitory, hockey coach. John was the very model of a good applicant, making all the right responses, displaying interest in the hockey field, the kitchen, the assembly hall, even engaging in small talk with the headmaster's wife.

The jaunty headmaster looked positively boyish in a tweed jacket and brown-and-white saddle shoes. An expression of low-grade anxiety never left his wife's face, making her look old enough to be his mother. This is what happens to women at a boys' school, I thought as she showed me around. Our spacious quarters had a kitchen, but we'd find we didn't need it, she said, for we'd take all our meals with the boys, John at the head of one table, I at the head of another. The school was so isolated, and there was "so much doing," that I'd find I was kept very busy. For diversion, once a week a group of faculty members "piled into a car and drove to the nearest town to the pictures." I'd find it was like being part of a large family.

John living in a large family? Taking all his meals with the boys? Coaching hockey? So great was his eagerness to be employed again that he told himself, and tried to convince me, that he could manage it. Just think: with room and board provided, we could save most of his salary, on which we could live abroad after a couple of years. Until then there would be the long summer vacation, during which he could write. And as for the isolation, with New York only four hours away by train, it wouldn't be as though we were in the Maine woods.

Yes, it would, I thought, remembering John's stories of the interminable snowbound winters at South Kent. John wouldn't last more than a month in such a place, and while I could, I'd hate it. I needn't have worried. The headmaster's letter said they had decided that what they needed was a coach who could teach English rather than an English master who could coach hockey.

How much John had counted on the appointment I realized when he admitted (I had noticed the date on the letter and asked about it) that he had had this bit of bad news for more than a week. The day he received it, he had answered a want ad and had been hired as an encyclopedia salesman because he couldn't bear going another day without earning some money. Without my knowing it, he had been ringing doorbells in Harlem, the district to which he had been assigned, trying to sell to occupants of tenements who couldn't afford the daily paper a set of reference books they'd have to go into debt to buy and would never read. When he saw their circumstances, he went through the prepared sales pitch he'd been taught with so little conviction that he left relieved in conscience at not having made a sale, while at the same time being crushed that he had walked the burning pavement for nothing.

The cycle of supplication and rejection which had been his daily round for three months was so speeded up in his attempts to make himself into a salesman that he felt like an animal. "I am no longer a man, but a dog, *a begging dog.*" He, whose ruling passion was the love of poetry and the desire to make it, had not written a word in months. His mind had been so little free that images didn't occur to him. Was it possible that only a few months ago he had lived the life so natural to him, spending his days reading, thinking and writing? Was it possible that he had put together a book of poems and had even hoped to find a publisher? How, in so short a time, had be been reduced to the person he was now—a man on the run, pleading for one job after another for which he was unsuited by training and temperament. In his wildest nightmares he had never imagined himself trying to sell encyclopedias to keep afloat financially—and *not* selling them, so that he had to continue imposing on my family's hospitality as we limped along on my salary.

What kind of man was it who, with his intelligence and education —honors from Columbia, the Kellett Fellowship to Cambridge, the Charles Oldham Shakespeare Scholarship while at Clare, poetry editorship of *The Nation,* four years of teaching experience at Wayne and Harvard—couldn't support a wife? The fault must be his. He was in some way responsible. The burden of guilt, never light, that he carried around, had become so crushing that he could hardly drag himself out of bed in the morning. He honestly believed he was making every effort to find work. But *was* he? He tortured himself with uncertainty. Once before I had not believed him. Why should I now? How could I believe in him when he no longer believed in himself?

All this he shouted into the night, walking by the river at such a furious pace that I had to run to keep up with him. Rushing to the railing that bordered the esplanade, he cried in anguish that there was no way out but suicide. That he was capable of leaping onto the railing, I knew. That he was unhinged enough to jump was terrifyingly possible.

John balancing on a ledge. Below, danger. I had seen it once before. At the time it had been as exotic as a bit of pantomime from a Nō play, and had been followed by so much real drama that the scene had remained in my mind as a one-of-a-kind still that couldn't be fitted into a context.

A prenuptial party had been given for us by a group of Russian émigrés my aunt had come to know when I was about fourteen. On our holidays, we entertained them. On theirs, they entertained us. In between they found frequent excuses to have people in for evenings of singing Russian songs, dancing Russian dances, eating Russian dishes, the only respite they allowed themselves from their otherwise ceaseless struggle to become Americans and make their way in their professions as engineers and doctors in a puzzling and highly competitive city. Throughout my high school days their parties had been a counterpoint to dates and dances. The urbanity of the men in the group, their hand-kissing, their "Kreutzer Sonata"-like conversations studded with French expressions, their grace as partners in a mazurka, had made the young men I was going out with seem callow.

The Solkonikoffs, the couple to whom I had been closest, had given the party. John, in excellent spirits, was a success with the Russians, they with him. His mother and my aunt pretended cordiality. Home on leave, Bob Giroux (who still thought he could be John's best man) looked handsome in his Navy uniform. He charmed the women and warmed the hearts of the men in the group, all of whom had been doing their service in the Imperial Navy at the time of the revolution. We danced the dances and sang the songs I loved. It being an especially festive occasion, Vladimir, the host, poured more than the usual

LESTER GIROUX, COURTESY OF ROBERT GIROUX

Robert Giroux, in his Navy uniform, at the time of our engagement party

amount of vodka for the men and wine for the women, as I realized
when someone proposed that a toast be drunk out of Bob's officer's
cap (which my aunt rescued in the nick of time).

The dashing Vladimir—black hair parted in the middle and slicked
down, lynx-eyed, dressed in a chalk-striped suit nipped in at the waist
—had taken a great interest in what he called my *formation* during my
high school and college days, inviting me to the ballet, to the opera,
to hear the Don Cossacks and to supper afterward at the Russian Tea
Room. When not looking after his guests, he leaned against the wall
one hand in his trouser pocket, the other holding a cigarette, and
trained his gaze on my fiancé. He could not claim, as he had done about
the college boys I'd brought to their parties, that John was too young
for me. Or that he was insufficiently worldly. But was he a . . .?

The climax of the evening was a series of toasts to our future, during
which a drinking song was sung. Then came John's turn to propose
a toast. Vladimir passed him a tumbler of vodka. After John had had
a swallow, he made as if to pass the tumbler back. No, to prove he
was "a real man," John must drink *"Piei do dna*—to the bottom." It
was John's first taste of vodka. He didn't like it. Even less did he like
having his manliness questioned. While the others sang the refrain,
"Piei do dna, piei do dna" faster and faster, John drained the glass.

Soon afterward the party broke up. John and I were staying with
his mother so that we could all get an early start the next morning to
drive to Westchester for lunch with my great-uncle and aunt, who had
not yet met the groom-to-be. On the way back to the apartment John
sang *"Piei do dna"* in full voice and slightly off key. He was, as he said,
high as a kite. Never having seen him either high or boisterous before,
I was amused. The singing was less amusing when it continued in his
mother's kitchen. The vodka had done its work; he was not merely
high, he was drunk. I had just taken this in when there was an exchange
between mother and son to which John reacted with a flare-up of anger
such as I'd come to expect whenever they were together for too long.
I entered the kitchen at the moment when he turned from her, threw
open the door to the terrace and with the skill of a gymnast leaped
onto the ledge of the shoulder-high wall that enclosed it. The ledge
was wider than his foot, but not much. Below was the cement sidewalk. As Mrs. Berryman shrieked, John started walking, slowly putting one foot in front of the other: the drunk giving himself the test

he always fails. It was this scene, and the moment of paralysis I felt before going to him, that remained framed in my memory.

At my great-uncle's luncheon table the next day, a very subdued John toyed with his food, had an obligatory sip of champagne and impressed my relatives with his seriousness. On the way back to the city, he wondered aloud why drinkers drank if the following day they felt the way he had been feeling. About the incident on the terrace, he and his mother said not a word. They behaved as if it hadn't occurred (was it possible that John didn't remember it?). I so wished it hadn't occurred that, after a sleepless night, I told myself I was exaggerating its seriousness. John, who drank very little—a bottle of ale, a glass or two of sherry, "a little Scotch with a lot of water"— had been made drunk by *my* friend, and in an explosion of anger that had been building up toward his mother since he had been down from Boston, had tried to frighten her.

Terrorize her, was the way Mrs. Berryman put it to me later. It had been his way as a boy, and it always worked. As a child he had had an "angelic" disposition, was all a mother could want in a son— intellectually precocious, affectionate, obedient, and when not obedi-ent, which was rare, *so* winning. (Once when she'd sat him down on his little chair to reprimand him for a minor infraction of the rules— for not putting his toys in their box?—he had looked up at her as she talked with what she thought was touching earnestness. When she had finished and asked, "Do you understand?" he had said, so pleased with his observation he couldn't bear not to share it with her, "I can see myself in your eyeglasses.")

He had been wonderful company during those years when Allyn (John's father), had often been away from home on his job as a bank examiner. In the small Southwestern towns in Oklahoma where they lived, first McAlester, then Anadarko, where Mrs. Berryman had imag-ined herself as Carol Kennicott in *Main Street,* her son had been more rewarding company than her contemporaries. They shared the same magazines, through which she had introduced him to Faulkner and Hemingway, the same library books. It was later, when he was ten and eleven and was allowed to go about independently, that he and the other boys began to climb oil derricks. As her perceptive son quickly discovered, his mother had a horror of two things, snakes and heights. He was sure-footed and agile. The derricks were an attractive jungle gym for boys to climb. Only after he saw her reaction did his play become a weapon.

It was a weapon he used infrequently in those days. If his conscience, which told him that disobedience was a sin, hadn't been sufficient reason for renouncing an activity other boys were permitted to engage in, his lack of tolerance for his mother's show of displeasure would have been. Despite the birth of his younger brother Bob, five years his junior, he was still her favorite. Nevertheless, he had become vaguely aware that he was no longer the sole object of her love at the moment when tension developed between his parents that he was almost old enough to understand.

His mother had fallen "madly and irrevocably" in love with another man, as she told me when she talked about this period in her life. In refusing to leave her husband and sons for Bob Kerr, she had thrown away her only chance for happiness. Kerr, who was on his way to becoming a senator when she knew him, later served as governor of Oklahoma. How different a life with him would have been! For as Bob Kerr's star was rising, Allyn's was sinking. As the result of a disagreement with a colleague at the bank, Allyn felt he had to resign. Although he found another job quickly enough, he decided to move his family to Florida. It was the mid-twenties. The land boom was on. The family, including John's grandmother, who owned property in Tampa, half of which she had given her daughter and son-in-law as a wedding present, moved to what was thought to be the land of opportunity. They arrived in 1925. By the following year the boom was over. So, too, it turned out, was Allyn's life.

The circumstances of his death I heard recounted so often, and so variously, that to this day they remain a puzzle. John tried to tell me what he thought happened shortly before he returned to Harvard at the end of our first summer together. Previously he had said only that his father was a Minnesotan, from a Roman Catholic family, who had become a small-town banker in Oklahoma. There he met Martha Little, a local schoolteacher, and when she was eighteen and he twenty-seven they married. For unexplained reasons, the family moved to Florida where Allyn died when John was twelve. There were no photographs of Allyn around, nor were there any of his artifacts, except the gold watch John wore. There was also John's habit of arranging dollar bills so that they faced the same way before he put them in his wallet, which I suspected mimicked a mannerism of his father's. (It was the only way in which John's handling of money resembled a banker's.)

On the occasion when he said there was something he had been trying to tell me about his father, must tell me before he returned to Boston, the cigarette in his hand trembled. I wished I could admit that I already knew what he had been nerving himself up to say, but couldn't do so without betraying that what he thought was a dark family secret his mother had revealed to many people, among them Jean Webster, from whom I had heard it. So as we sat opposite each other at a table in a coffee shop I watched the color drain from his face as he struggled to begin.

"The move to Tampa had been a disastrous mistake. How my sensible grandmother—or I *think* she was sensible—could have been so misguided as to join the speculators rushing to Florida is difficult for me to understand. They put my brother and me in a convent school (for how long I'm not sure; long enough to teach me what it must feel like to be an orphan), and went off on a reconnaissance trip. Sounds sensible, doesn't it? They returned from the trip convinced that it would be a good move. They collected us from the convent and back we went. Daddy opened a real estate office in Tampa, and with their pooled capital they bought land, which he then tried to resell. There were no buyers. How soon he began to panic I don't know. The newspapers reported that other speculators were committing suicide every day . . ." John broke off. Gripping his head in his hands, he sat, trembling. After a while he said, "This will have to wait. I'll try to tell you another time."

Since I knew it would never get any easier, I urged him to continue, reassuring him that no matter what it was, it would make no difference to our relationship.

"They began to quarrel. At night I'd hear them in the next room. Or, braced for the angry voices to begin, I couldn't fall asleep."

Was this the beginning of his insomnia? I wondered.

"One day, Daddy, agitated and depressed, took me on his back and swam far out in the Gulf at Clearwater, threatening to drown us both. Or so Mother claimed. Another time he took Bob. Early one morning he got out his gun and put a bullet through his head."

John sank back in the booth, exhausted by the effort he had made.

Throughout the narration he had behaved, as I told him, as if he were confessing a crime *he* had committed, as if he had been responsible for his father's death. Shame and culpability were what he clearly felt. Why? At first he was startled by my reaction and said he wasn't sure why he felt this way. Perhaps it was the sense of having somehow been responsible that everyone close to a suicide feels. As for shame—yes, there was that. Soon after the tragedy, his mother remarried. His stepfather wanted to adopt him and Bob. With his mother's consent that, too, was quickly arranged. Should he not, young as he was, have protested out of loyalty to his dead father? He did not, and his name became John Berryman. "A good name for a poet, isn't it? Well it's a damn lie. My real name is ludicrously unpoetic. It is Smith. John Smith."*

The reaction I had been unable to simulate about his father's suicide I showed at the revelation about his name. I had not heard it before. Nor, I suspect, had Jean, Mark Van Doren or any of the other friends of John's his mother had talked to. (I say "I suspect" because John asked me never to talk about this outside the family, so I wasn't able to check.)

John Allyn McAlpin Berryman was the way he had signed his earliest published poems, John went on to say. Discarding one of his father's names, and one of his stepfather's, he adopted the shortened form when the long form began to strike him as pretentious. "What I should have done, what I cannot forgive myself for not having done, was to take the name John Smith. This act of disloyalty I will never, never be able to repair. To 'make a name' for myself . . . Can you see how ambivalent my feelings are about this ambition?"

John's mother's version of the events of June 1926 I heard after John had returned to Boston at the end of our first summer together. She invited me to dinner so we could get to know each other better.

---

*There was an instability about the names in this family that was often confusing to outsiders. Martha Little took the nickname Peggy after her marriage to John Allyn Smith. He was known as Allyn or John Allyn. Their first son was named for him at baptism, but was called Billy as a baby, then John when he reached school age. Robert Jefferson, his brother, was Bob in the family, but he called himself Jeff, and was Jeff to his wife and friends.

When John's mother remarried she changed her first name from Martha to Jill, or Jill Angel. Her second husband, John Angus McAlpin Berryman, was called John Angus by everyone except his stepsons. To them he was Uncle Jack. Bob's wives and I called our mother-in-law Mir, a name which, like Jill Angel, she had invented.

Striding into the restaurant dressed in the bright colors and bold jewelry she favored, she commanded a different table from the one the headwaiter had seated me at and issued a series of commands in a voice that echoed of the Southwest, the twang only partly hidden by acquired Northern inflections. She was not beautiful (as John thought she was), but she was attractive and, to my eyes, glamorous because of her youthful appearance, her élan and vitality. Mother and son looked alike and they didn't. What resemblance there was was heightened because each wore eyeglasses. Although Mrs. Berryman frequently pointed to one physical characteristic they shared, the shape of the thumb, I suspected that the rest of John's hand, as well as a good deal of his angularity, his hollow cheeks and broad shoulders, he had inherited from his father's people, whom she described, with amusement at her exaggeration, as "Grant Wood types."

My future mother-in-law was as eager to talk about Allyn as her son had been reluctant to do so. During the first dinner together, and others we had that fall and winter, John Allyn Smith's biography was often her subject. The defects in his personality undoubtedly were caused by his mother, she said. Mrs. Smith was a formidable, even a cold woman, which explained why Allyn, though not intentionally cruel, was unfeeling and egocentric, never aware of any desires but his own.

The only child of a domineering widowed mother, Martha, as she was then called, had been living away from home only a short time when she had met Allyn. Encouraged by her mother, she married this man nine years her senior. "What does a girl of eighteen know about life? Especially a girl raised as I was. In those days it was Mother and Allyn who made the decisions. The move to Florida was their idea. Allyn didn't have the temperament to be a speculator. When things began to go badly, he became frantic, depressed; he couldn't sleep, and walked the beach at night. At dawn one day he was cleaning his gun; it went off and killed him."

After a moment of astonishment, I took it that Mrs. Berryman, not realizing that John had already told me about the suicide, was giving me the version she had invented to tell outsiders. Or, rather, some outsiders, some of the time, for Jean, Mark and undoubtedly others had heard about the suicide. At another dinner she approached the truth more closely. During that terrible period before the end, "Allyn threatened suicide more than once. But when I saw the gun, I knew he had been cleaning it. You see, Allyn was a weak man. He wouldn't have had the courage to kill himself."

In the years to come, I realized that the circumstances of her first husband's death were part of an ever-changing myth she periodically reworked, usually in response to her older son's longing to be convinced that she was not responsible for driving his father to suicide. For extended periods the subject did not come up between them (though it was never far from their minds). At a time of crisis, either following a violent quarrel or when John was re-examining his life, he would turn to her and ask her to go over the ground anew. She would oblige, sometimes in person, sometimes in three- and four-page single-spaced typewritten letters, with fresh inventions and interpretations, which he accepted or (privately) ridiculed, depending on his need at the moment.

The first summer we knew each other, John had given me an expurgated version of what he believed had happened. After we married, when he began to talk somewhat more candidly about his mother, he said that the quarrels between his parents had not only been over money. They had been over another man. His mother wanted a divorce. The simultaneous failure of his father's business and his marriage, which brought with it the possibility of losing his sons, drove

John and his mother in the difficult months following his return from England

him to despair and to suicide. With "unseemly haste" his mother married the much older and more successful Berryman. She accepted his wish to adopt her sons and change their name (if, indeed, she hadn't herself suggested it, in part to protect them from scandal that might grow out of the newspaper reports and legal proceedings that followed Allyn's death). She also made a rapid shift from Catholicism, to which she had been converted on her marriage to Allyn, to the Episcopal church, changing her children's religion at the same time.

The accidental-death ending John never for a moment accepted, at least not as an adult. What he did waver over was the degree to which he believed in his mother's responsibility. The Smiths and John Angus Berryman lived in the same building. Did his mother drive his father to despair by flirting under his nose with the courtly older man? By insisting on a divorce when her husband was frantic with worry, had she not pushed him to that last, desperate act?

If, in one of the confrontations between mother and son, Mrs. Berryman was able to convince John that his father had been a failure not only as a breadwinner but also as a lover and that, having given up her chance of happiness with Bob Kerr she had a right to insist on it with Berryman, John was won over and became sympathetic with her point of view. The price he paid for this sympathy was a damaging view of his father's manliness and, by extension, his own. If, however, her behavior convinced him that her flirtatiousness with Berryman and her insensitivity to what his father was suffering drove him to suicide, he believed her responsible.*

---

*The evolving myth, which not only I but my sisters-in-law and my sister heard throughout the years, was the subject of countless hours of speculation among us. What had really happened? We had always to remain tentative about our conclusions because all our information came from one eyewitness reporter. John's maternal grandmother, who might have given another view, was seldom in New York, and when she was I never saw her alone.

Was Allyn less intelligent than his wife? Was he "weak?" Certainly he had been successful in his career up to the moment when he resigned from the bank, a gesture motivated by a scruple which made it impossible for him to continue working alongside of a colleague with whom he had had a serious disagreement. If John's strong conscience, even scrupulosity, in his youth and the early years of our marriage came from either parent, it was from his father.

While the Bob Kerr "affair" did not have the ring of authenticity, and may have been little more than the crush of a restless young wife, Allyn was probably unable to ignore Martha's flirtations with other men in their bridge-playing circle. Whether this influenced his decision to move to Florida is not clear.

It was in Tampa that Allyn's instability seems to have shown up for the first time. His profound depression was probably caused in equal part by financial failure and the breakup of his marriage. (That he was unfaithful, and had previously asked for a divorce, a variant

In the difficult months following John's return from England he blamed his mother for his father's suicide. Throughout his two years abroad he had been writing long and intimate letters ("nauseatingly intimate" was the way he characterized them when he reread them years later) to the mother who, once again, had made him the center of her life. As her second husband became elderly, it was to her older son she had turned for interest and excitement, closely following his intellectual development in college, reading the books he read, encouraging him in his ambition to become a writer, entertaining his friends. His letters from Cambridge told her in detail about his study of Shakespeare, about B., about the London theater, about travel to Heidelberg and Paris and, most importantly, about his writing plans.

Reading the letters from New York she sent him in return, John had not taken in how greatly her life was changing in his absence. After the failure of Mr. Berryman's business she had taken a job in advertis-

---

which entered the myth late, none of us credited, except perhaps John, upon occasion.)

If the incident of swimming out in the Gulf at Clearwater occurred early in the family's stay in Florida, as is possible, it may have been no more of a suicide attempt than John's first effort to climb a derrick had been. Allyn, a strong swimmer, took Bob for the kind of ride in the water a small boy would have loved. His mother, who was more timid in the water, would have been frightened, not the small boy. I say Bob rather than John because that's the way we all heard it. I think that when John was told the story his mother said he was the one who was on his father's back. Later, this hardened into the official version. John was permanently substituted for Bob at the time when John questioned his mother as to whether Allyn had favored either son, suspecting, with reason, that Allyn might have felt a closer kinship with Bob. Both were excluded from the "passionate devotion" Martha felt for her firstborn.

After weeks of begging Martha not to leave him, of threatening to commit suicide, Allyn chose:

> A bullet on a concrete stoop
> close by a smothering southern sea
> spreadeagled on an island, by my knee.

There is little likelihood that John saw his father dead. Martha found Allyn. While she and Berryman were making arrangements, John's grandmother, who also lived in the house, looked after the boys.

Soon after the "departure," Martha and Berryman married, the family moved north, the boys were adopted and their names changed. Mr. Berryman, a kindly and sensible man from all reports, adopted an avuncular attitude toward the boys. John's style of dress when I first met him derived from his stepfather, as did many of his notions about how things should be done in the house. (No matter what the temperature, John never appeared at the table without a jacket and tie. Nor would he permit any deviation from Uncle Jack's recipes—he was something of a gourmet—for preparing certain dishes.) How much this man had displaced him in his mother's affections John seemed not to have taken in until he was sent away to school.

ing, where, with her intelligence, energy and gift for language, she made a success. The account executive she became had adopted speech mannerisms and a style of dressing that reflected her new milieu, and that John felt had coarsened her. The most shocking concession she had made to the business world, one she felt necessary for a woman entering it over the age of forty, was to present an appearance so youthful as to rule out having grown sons, especially one who, in his efforts to look older than he was, had raised a beard. John and Bob were her younger brothers, she told her colleagues. It was as a brother that, on his return from England, she introduced John to her new friends.

The deception about her sons being her brothers she was sorry for, Mrs. Berryman said. But why had John taken it so hard? "Poor lamb! When he came home from England, did he expect to find me sitting by the fire in a rocker, like Whistler's mother?" Her laughter filled the restaurant.

John had taken it so hard because he needed to believe in her as a reliable reporter. If she was capable of saying he was her brother, what was she not capable of saying about other relationships? About his father above all, but also about Uncle Jack. Had he really retired to Maryland, as she'd written in one of her letters to England? Or had he been rusticated there after his mother fell in love with a colleague and found it inconvenient to have an elderly husband in the house? Had his mother been unfaithful with the new man under Uncle Jack's eyes, driving him away?

As for his mother's insensitivity, wasn't her complete lack of understanding of what he, John, was going through during the painful transition after he returned from England, when he felt estranged from America, couldn't find a job and was ill, indicative of how she must have behaved with his father during the weeks when he was contemplating suicide?

In their outbursts, which occurred whenever they were together for too long, each feared to say unforgettable and unforgivable things that would cause an irreparable break. Mrs. Berryman, denying this in the beginning, said, "You mustn't make too much of our scenes (I see you're very sensitive to them). John and I love each other dearly. But in a close relationship between two people with strong personalities there are bound to be occasions when the strong bully the strong."

From her laugh as she said this, one got the feeling that she recuperated quickly.

Not so John. He so little felt that the contest was between equals that he resorted to the use of two weapons, each more damaging to himself than to her: the threat of suicide, and episodes of fainting. She was not so convinced Allyn's death was accidental that she didn't tremble when John said, in effect: I will do what my father did. The fainting spells frightened her almost as much. They turned her from an adversary into the mother John had known as a small boy.

To determine the cause of these episodes John underwent a neurological examination while he was teaching at Wayne. During part of the time when he was living with Bhain Campbell and his wife (before Bhain's illness), John's behavior had been so bizarre, withdrawn, suspicious, irritable, explosive and depressed, that Bhain had called in a psychiatrist. Schizophrenia and a brain tumor, both of which had been considered, were ruled out. The electroencephalogram showed a pattern of irregular brain waves. On the basis of the readings (which in those days were often crude), a diagnosis of petit mal epilepsy was made and Dilantin, a specific for epilepsy, prescribed.

The first of these episodes I witnessed was brought on, as the initial one had been, by a quarrel with his mother. At a moment when I was afraid he might strike out at her in rage and frustration, a gesture which would have been shockingly foreign to him, he fell to the ground instead. As if by the throw of a switch, Mrs. Berryman's hysteria dropped away and she became a ministering angel. She removed John's tie, opened his collar, asked me to help her lift his seemingly lifeless body to the couch, put a cold compress on his brow, covered him with a blanket and, tiptoeing out of the room, closed the door, saying we must let him rest. From past experience she knew he would remain in a semicomatose state for hours.

Had John been taking care of himself? she asked. Her son had no idea of the most elementary rules of health, as I would discover. He didn't know what it was to live by a routine, with regular meals, daily exercise and sufficient sleep. He behaved as if these rules didn't apply to him, when he actually needed them more than most people. Had he been up all night working?

He had. So, too, had she. One reason for the ferocity of the quarrel was that they were both irritable from lack of sleep. Mother, like son, often worked through the night and went for long periods without eating. Mother, like son, seemed incapable of predicting that action *a* (staying up all night) frequently resulted in consequence *b* (fatigue and irritability the following day). In John's style of living, as in much else, he followed his mother's example rather than her sage counsel. A stronger nervous system and better recuperative powers permitted her to get away with what for him was dangerous.

During this, the first of countless scenes that I was to witness between them, I had been a helpless observer; exasperated with both at first for not seeing that it was obviously fatigue that was making them hypersensitive to the slights of which each accused the other, becoming sympathetic with John as his mother goaded him, then fearful for both as, at the climax, the very air became electrified. The so-called seizure that followed I watched not with horror—as I had supposed I would when John confessed his medical history and I, in ignorance of the disease, imagined a grand mal episode with thrashing arms and legs and foaming at the mouth—but with disbelief. It looked to me as though an impulse John had had to attack his mother physically when he could no longer reach her with words had been subverted, striking him down instead. He had prevented himself from doing the unforgivable and simultaneously transformed his enemy into a devoted nurse.

I knew nothing of neurology, but I felt certain that a misdiagnosis had been made. Nor did anything I read in the public library change my view. Perhaps he had had a real seizure while living with the Campbells in Detroit. What I had seen was not one. At the time John and I had our first serious disagreement (over my unwillingness to go to live with him in Boston until his relationship with B. was resolved), and he again seemed to be on the verge of fainting, I told him I didn't believe he had epilepsy. The episode was aborted, but John asked angrily, "What right have you to question the word of experts?"

No right. Still, I felt they were wrong and refused to back down.

John, to whom this indication of the limits of my docility came as a surprise, was startled by my firmness. "How do you explain the attacks, then?"

Not having the proper vocabulary, realizing I was on shaky ground, I said awkwardly that what I had seen mimicked a seizure; it was not the real thing. I could understand why they happened when he was with his mother (though I didn't say what I thought his thwarted impulse toward her had been). If he were to react similarly whenever we had a disagreement, a relationship between us would be impossible.

John had no further attacks. Though for some time thereafter he continued to worry about the return of his "illness" whenever he was under great pressure, petit mal was never again mentioned by him or anyone else in the family. Only the draft board, which classified him as 4F, continued to follow the Detroit diagnosis. The price of the so-called cure—for we all thought it was that when, even during the terrible summer of job-hunting, he had no seizures—was that I had left John with the feeling I thought he had been play-acting, the very thing he accused himself of in periods of soul-searching and self-doubt.

On the summer night that he ran along by the East River shouting that he couldn't go on, that no one believed in him, not even I, this is what he meant. Had I not accused him of faking the seizures?

"Faking" was his word, I said, not mine.

If he could fake seizures, could he not also fake the search for a job? He thought he was looking for one. But *was* he? After B. came to visit from England, he had said he was looking for work so they could get married. A lie. He hadn't been looking. Believing that what a writer should do was write, he had not at all accepted that he would have to earn a living some other way. Had he *still* not accepted it? Was that what was wrong? Torturing himself over this question was pushing him to the brink of madness. He would rather be dead than go on as he was.

After I dragged him away from the railing and got him to sit with me on a bench, I tried to convince him that I was certain he was doing all he could to find a job. The reason he wasn't having any success was that the kind of work he was qualified for was not available. What he had mostly been doing had been applying for jobs that didn't exist. Black as the situation was at the moment, I was sure he'd receive an offer before long. When it came, he would be able to get back to writing, would find a publisher and would become a first-rate poet. I was so sure that he would one day be famous (if not that he would soon be offered a job), that after hours of talking I was able to convince him.

If we were to survive this period, however, we would have to take precautions. He must quit the encyclopedia company and take a week's vacation from the ordeal, and from the city heat, at my aunt's summer cottage on Long Island. These suggestions he was only too happy to accept. Seeing how shaken I had been by his impulse to vault over the railing, he also promised never again to threaten suicide.

It was during this terrible night that, for the first time, I began to see the seriousness of John's psychological instability. If I had not done so before, it was not his fault. He had told me about his breakdown after he returned from England, he had told me about his "craziness" in Detroit, he had even told me he'd had an hallucination one day at Harvard. He had told me his history and I had only half listened, believing that with love and care and a reasonably orderly life he would be well. Now I saw that no amount of love and care could protect him from external circumstances, and that these could bring him to the edge of madness. What had been the cause of the symptom of fainting was still there, and could at any time manifest itself in another form.

Before our marriage, I had worried about our relationship being threatened by his "unspeakably powerful possessive adoring MOTHER." After the night on the esplanade I became aware of the presence of a tall mute shadowy figure whose features I could not make out, a figure whose power over John was as strong as his mother's. It was the specter of John Allyn Smith.

IV
PRINCETON
AND THE
BLACKMURS

Princeton seemed an earthly paradise to the intellectuals who fled Nazism and settled there in the late thirties and early forties. They unpacked the belongings they had escaped with, and in an attempt to mend their fractured lives, set to work again on the books they had been writing in Berlin, Hamburg, Prague and Paris before the advent of Hitler. Seeing these men in the common room at the Institute for Advanced Study, at concerts, lectures and parties, listening to the vigor of their conversation, one might have imagined that they had got off scot-free. But the nightmare they had left behind was so much with them that although the paradise was within easy reach, it was months, years for some, before they were able to enjoy it. By that time they had become aware, of course, that what had seemed paradisiacal was a typical American university town, more beautiful than most it was true, but unique only thanks to their presence, which transformed it into a cosmopolitan community with a density of brilliant minds— among them writers Thomas Mann and Hermann Broch; social philosopher Erich Kahler; art historian Erwin Panofsky; mathematicians Hermann Weyl and John von Neumann; physicists Albert Einstein and Wolfgang Pauli, to name a few—that was unequaled anywhere in the world.

After a season in hell, Princeton looked like paradise to John and me, too. Arriving as we did in the brilliant days of Indian summer, when the trees blazed red and gold, the air smelled of wood fires, and the only sound one heard was the whir of bicycle tires and the muffled footfalls of students (in uniform) jogging to class on leaf-strewn paths, we could hardly believe that New York was only an hour away.

R. P. Blackmur, the poet and critic, who had been one of John's heroes during his undergraduate days, had come to our rescue. Toward the end of October, long after we had given up hope of a college appointment, Blackmur wrote that if John had not already committed himself elsewhere Dean Christian Gauss would like to see him. Why didn't he come down for the day and bring me with him? The offer was firm, the meeting with Gauss a formality.

Having heard so many of Delmore's stories about Blackmur's bohemian days in Boston, when he and his wife Helen, a painter, had lived in a dilapidated building in a raffish section of the city, and having seen a photograph of him wearing a flowing Byronic tie and looking pale and poetic—"Stephen Dedalus, don't you think?" Delmore had asked, showing us the picture—I was unprepared for the academic façade Blackmur had assumed during his two years of teaching in the Creative Writing Program in Princeton. (Could this possibly be the man who, at the height of a Boston party, had sat in the kitchen, arm resting on the table, fist clenched, thumb sticking out, barking at the dancers who circled him, "Bite it! Bite my thumb!"? Had I mixed up Delmore's stories?) At thirty-nine Blackmur was neither pale nor thin. Short and solidly built, he wore a fedora with an ever-so-slight tilt to one side, well-pressed tweeds, a conservative tie and highly polished brown shoes. With his graying hair and trim gray mustache, he looked more like a college president, or the "man of distinction" in the whiskey ad, than a writer. The mustache adorned a mask, his public face, behind which, by the time I met him, the wild poet was carefully hidden. His manner was so dignified and formal, even under the influence of Dean Gauss's Old Fashioneds (the strongest I had ever tasted), that John kept calling him "sir." Occasionally his blue eyes, though not the rest of his face, smiled in amusement at something Gauss or John said.

Only later, when he took John and me to dinner at Lahière's, the local French restaurant, did he unbend. He began sternly enough: "Look here, John, no more of that 'sir' stuff."

John had not only addressed him as "sir," but had been as deferential in manner as if he had been in the presence of the Pope. "Sorry," he said. "A bad habit I picked up in prep school."

"And, Eileen, you mustn't call me 'Mr. Blackmur.' My colleagues call me 'Dick,' my men friends and all women call me 'Richard.' "

One felt that Richard was sympathetic to women, a sympathy that got bottled up inside, the way his smile got bottled up behind his mustache.

On the train returning to New York John kept saying, "I don't believe it!" The contrast between the day we had just spent—the campus aglow with autumnal colors, the graciousness of the Gausses, the urbanity of the conversation—and any day during the last five months made him feel disoriented. In September, in desperation, he had taken a job teaching Latin and English, at a Christian Brothers preparatory school in Westchester. His humor, which had made Harvard undergraduates laugh appreciatively, threw unruly adolescents into foot-stamping, whistling pandemonium. The headmaster reprimanded him for being a poor disciplinarian; his colleagues were almost as immature as the students; his office was in the men's room; he had to stay up half the night reviewing Latin and correcting papers. Richard's letter had come at the moment when he had decided he couldn't stick it any longer.

"Do you realize that Blackmur is the author of the essay in *Poetry* that changed my life?" he wrote:

'The art of poetry
is amply distinguished from the manufacture of verse
by the animating presence in the poetry
of a fresh idiom: language

so twisted & posed in a form
that it not only expresses the matter in hand
but adds to the stock of available reality.'

This "new Law-giver" from "Olympus" was the man he was going to be associating with *every day*! The contrast between the last months and the day in Princeton made John ask, "Which is the real world?"

By the next morning he was certain Princeton was, and was impatient to become part of it. He might say in conversation that it was necessary for a poet to suffer, and even believe it, but no one was more eager to be relieved of suffering than John. "Was it possible that only a few weeks ago I felt suicidal?" To have work for which by training and temperament he was suited, to look forward to the companionship of a man whose writing he had admired since his undergraduate days made him feel reborn, hopeful of the future, yes, even optimistic.

Optimism was difficult to maintain when we began to look for a place to live and came face to face with what, in our desperation to have an end to the joblessness, we had not allowed ourselves to talk about. The Princeton appointment was for just four months, renewal subject to the needs of the English department in March. (Only then would it be clear how many students would be assigned by Washington.) Richard, who in every other way eased our introduction into the community so that we knew not a moment of the loneliness and isolation other newcomers suffer in what they feel is a cliquish society, was, when it came to practical matters, a risky guide. Though he knew our current financial situation exactly and could guess at our debts (having lived a hand-to-mouth existence himself for years), he behaved as if we had inherited a small fortune and were trying to break into society.

No, perhaps he couldn't guess just how heavy our debts were. Of the confessions John had made to me before we married (his father's suicide, his medical history), the one that had troubled me most was his admission that he owed Columbia for undergraduate expenses not covered by his scholarship. He owed money to every bookseller in Boston. He owed Clare College so much they had impounded the splendid library he had acquired in London and Cambridge. The Kellett, on which he'd gone abroad, allowed the recipient to live as well as other undergraduates and travel to the Continent during the "long vacs." With this, the first money of his own, he had been improvident.

During one of our dinners together, Mrs. Berryman had warned me that John was a spendthrift. "I said to him before he left for England: 'If you return with money in your pocket, you will always have money. If you return in debt, you will always be in debt.' " Again John followed his mother's example rather than her advice. She was as unrealistic about money as she was about men. When she was working and earning a high salary, she spent more than she had. When she was jobless, she ran up bills.

This was a way of life familiar to John but foreign to me, one that might have worked for someone who earned large amounts of money at least periodically (as his mother did) but dangerous for an uncompromising poet. I had a horror of debts and was determined that we should pay off what John owed as quickly as possible. His two major extravagances, books and records, he agreed not to indulge in once we married (and apart from a few "spectacular" book bargains he couldn't resist, he kept his word). But Grove Street had been beyond our means. And now Richard was urging us to take an expensive apartment so that we could entertain properly.

"Make yourselves invaluable, and they won't be able to let you go. I've found just the place for you," Richard said, walking us from his apartment on Princeton Avenue around the corner to Nassau Street. "It's in the historic Hodder House. The woman who owns it runs the local kindergarten. A good soul, but a Christian Scientist. Therefore, no booze. She'll probably offer us tea."

She did offer us tea, and the apartment she showed us was just the kind we would have liked—if we could have afforded it. In its place, I persuaded John to take a studio the University offered us at a third the rent. It was in a four-story red-brick building with a center courtyard that could well have been in Forest Hills. "Suburban," Richard said, disdainfully. But aside from the modest rent, it had the advantage of being on Prospect Avenue (the street with the student eating clubs), within easy walking distance of the Blackmurs', the campus, the library and the town. It consisted of one room, with a Murphy bed. "I thought they only existed in comedies," John said, adding, after our first tussle with it, which reduced us to helpless laughter, "The comic possibilities are *infinite.*" There was also a tiny dressing room and bath, and the kind of kitchen a bachelor who didn't eat at home would have found adequate.

We thought we could manage well enough in this small place because John would have an office on campus and I, having found a job at the Institute for Advanced Study, would be working six days a week. To be sure, when the gramophone and boxes of records and books arrived from a Boston storage house, we felt rather cramped. But the campus housing office promised that if John was reappointed (always that "if"), we would be first in line for a larger apartment. Once we settled in, we learned that we could even wedge in a guest —if it were anyone we knew intimately enough to bed down in the dressing room—for a weekend. When Richard heard that my sister or John's brother was coming to stay with us, he said, "You two are even younger than I thought."

Our first Thanksgiving in Princeton we invited Richard (Helen was working that day) and an eccentric young mathematician John had met on campus to dinner. The grace John and I said silently was heartfelt. We had a place of our own again; we both had jobs. The mathematician kept his coat and scarf on throughout the meal (though the apartment was warm), and John played the Scott at a volume which announced to the neighbors that the new tenants liked their Mozart *loud*. By the time the meal was over, however, Richard was convinced that, while the Berrymans would not entertain in Hodder House style, neither would they be a total loss socially.

R. P. Blackmur—a characteristic pose

Richard had taken me shopping before the dinner. He wanted to be sure I went to the right greengrocer, the right butcher. At Bauman's, an old-fashioned store with produce arranged attractively in pyramids, he hefted the lettuce. "There's none to be had here like the lettuce I grow in Maine. When you come down for a visit, you'll see what I mean." He shook the melons, scorned the string beans, urged me to buy the chestnuts.

Continuing down Nassau Street at a leisurely pace, tipping his hat to Princeton matrons, stopping to greet and introduce me to a professor, dawdling at every window on the way, Richard the *flâneur* came to a dead stop before the sign that read: "Vogel Brothers." With Vogel the Younger, he discussed the weather, the news, the meat business, what the wealthy customers in the west end of town were ordering, what Mrs. Dodds (the wife of the president of the university) was having for Thanksgiving, the finicky eating habits of Helen's cats, and Mrs. Vogel's operation. (Though Richard was terrified of doctors, dentists, hospitals and injections, he had a writer's interest in the medical profession, and also liked to pretend not to be frightened of illness by dwelling on the gory details of surgery and the manifold ills to which the body was susceptible.)

What Vogel, dressed in a white apron and operating dexterously on a marble slab, made of all the esoterica he collected from Richard was hard to say. It was evident that he knew he was in the presence of a man with a classy mind—this was not your ordinary run-of-the-mill professor—so he listened while the delivery boy, who was waiting impatiently for the wicker baskets to be filled so that he could go on his rounds, shifted from foot to foot.

Richard needed people the way he needed cigarettes, rum and strong coffee. He needed conversation, he needed an ear for his monologues, he needed chat. After sufficient chat, he picked up the package that contained the bird we were going to have for dinner (the first and last bit of shopping I did at the most expensive butcher in town), tucked it under his arm, said good-bye to Vogel the Younger, stopped a few doors down at the newspaper store for *The New York Times,* before we continued on our way. At my side was the Leopold Bloom of Nassau Street, looking, listening, talking, sniffing, sauntering. And just try to hurry him!

While John and I ran into Richard almost every day, Helen we saw

only on Saturday nights. It was after midnight when she returned from
her job as a supervisor on the second shift in a factory making airplane
parts in Trenton. She'd come in the back door of their apartment
dressed in overalls and carrying a workman's metal lunch box, greet
her two Persian cats warmly, Richard and the guests coolly. Then,
dead tired, she'd curl up in her armchair with a bowl of one of the
mysterious concoctions she ate to placate an ulcer. With her shoulder-
length hair, which was graying in exactly the way Richard's was, and
her intense blue eyes framed by bangs, there was something feline
about her appearance, as there was about her walk. For many years she
had taught ballroom dancing in order to supplement their income in
the lean years when she earned little from painting and Richard less
from writing. She still loved to dance (a passion we shared), and to
"do," so when she decided to contribute to the war effort it was in
character for her to work in a factory instead of taking a desk job.
Taciturn by nature, she had a low tolerance for "all the sitting around
and jawing" in Princeton. When she did speak, what she said was blunt
and funny. Listening with increasing impatience to Richard ruminate
aloud about the Nature of Man one evening, she cut through his
monologue with, "Man? Man is just a hunk." The movement of
Richard's head, the sucking in of his cheeks and tightening of his lips
meant he was laughing with the rest of us.

Both the Blackmurs spoke with a Boston/Maine accent (Helen's the
more obvious), and used a Boston vocabulary: "package store,"
"cleanser," "beach wagon." The word "Saturday" Richard pronounced "Sarady," and where most people would have said "presuma-
bly," he favored "presumptively."

From Delmore we had learned that the Blackmurs were a wretch-
edly unhappy couple. "This marriage has insatiable, sad eyes," Richard
wrote, and both he and Helen would undoubtedly have agreed with
the judgment of friends that their union should never have taken place.
As a young man Richard had fallen in love with Tessa Gilbert, a free
spirit who said and did what she pleased, dazzling the introverted and
inhibited young poet. He proposed to her, was rejected, fell in love
with her best friend, Helen. Helen dared him to marry her. He accepted
the dare, took out a license, panicked, returned it (the fine print which
he, a reader, read, said that if not used it must be returned), and because

COURTESY OF E. T. CONE

Helen Blackmur

no one had ever done so before, caught the interest of a newspaper
reporter who wrote a story that made headlines in the Boston paper.
The story was taken up by the other dailies, giving Richard, as
Delmore said, the kind of publicity no literary effort he made would
ever get him. It also humiliated him, and Helen, in a way from which
they never quite recovered.

For four years they conducted an off-again, on-again courtship
which was brought to a halt by Richard's future mother-in-law who
said: Enough! Worn out by ambivalence, unable to think of a way
to escape, Richard and Helen dragged through a wedding ceremony
that neither wanted.

The first time we saw them together there was no missing their
incompatibility. Listening to Richard talk about Helen when she was
not around, however, we were struck by how proud he was of her
talent as a painter, and how much he admired her directness (given as

he was to circumlocutions in speech and Byzantine complexity in thought).

As they had come, in a curious way, to resemble each other, so they had also come to share many of the same tastes. Their apartment was an agreeable mélange of both their interests. In the living room, which had tall windows that gave on the street, the blond wood furniture was simple, the floors and windows bare. This severity was counterbalanced by the walls, which were covered with Helen's paintings—early ones of flower arrangements and the fields outside their house in Maine, in oil; later ones of dead owls and cardinals, in watercolors. The surfaces of tables were covered with Richard's books. At a given time there might be stacked by his chair a Roman missal, a portfolio of Rembrandt etchings, his Dante, the current *Kenyon* and *Partisan,* a collection of Tolstoy's plays, De Tocqueville, and, always, *The New York Times.* On the table in front of the couch where I usually sat were current novels sent him by New York publishers, which he'd glance at before passing them on to me. The next time we met he'd ask me about them and I'd give him a capsule review of any that were interesting.

Helen's factory job served a dual purpose. The war effort permitted her to dramatize her rebellion against the role of faculty wife: A worker in overalls does not pour tea and play hostess. While she enjoyed having a friend or two in for dinner on her day off, and went to a good deal of trouble to prepare food for them that she herself couldn't eat, she refused to entertain "people"—professors, students and others Richard felt obliged to have in, famous poets not exempted. When T. S. Eliot came to town, and Richard told Helen, somewhat diffidently, that he had invited the Great Man to dinner, she snapped, "Tell him to bring his own chop."

Richard had not only tried to persuade us to take the Hodder House apartment. He had also said that we should get our dress clothes out of storage and have calling cards printed.

"Calling cards? Is he kidding?" John asked.

I said I couldn't tell. I didn't know Richard well enough yet to judge. He had mentioned them in the same deadpan way he had said, as he walked me down Prospect Avenue to show me the eating clubs, "Whenever a virgin walks past here [Cannon Club] the cannon goes off." Not a muscle in his face twitching, he added, "Doesn't happen very often."

I decided to call Helen for advice. Helen hooted. Dress clothes hadn't been worn in Princeton since they'd been living there, and calling cards existed only in Richard's fantasies—where they were dropped into highly polished salvers in the vestibules of well-run houses.

Richard's appetite for social life, and Helen's lack of one, led him to inaugurate his Saturday evenings at home, to which he asked Dorothy and Stow Persons (our neighbors in Prospect Apartments) from the History department; Ed Cone, a composer and pianist; and, over the years, an ever-enlarging circle of academic friends, members of the Institute for Advanced Study, as well as visiting intellectuals from New York and Boston.

The expression "at home" was of a piece with the calling cards and the polished salvers in the vestibules. We soon realized that the Blackmur ménage included more than Helen's two cats (and very real presences they were). It also included the ghost of Henry Adams. Richard, who had been working on a biography of Adams since the mid-thirties, yearned for the historian's patrician way of life. When Helen rode him about "putting it on," he defended what appeared to be snobbishness as a desire for at least the accoutrements of a well-ordered society. It was a desire sharpened by the contrast between the biographer and his subject's early years. Though the two men were born geographically close to each other, their family backgrounds were as distant as their eras. Adams's father had been the United States ambassador in London; Richard's an unemployed lay-about. Adams had admired and respected his father; Richard scorned and hated his, for his father was to blame for the terrible indignity Richard had suffered growing up: His mother had had to run a boarding house on Irving Street, not far from Harvard Yard.

Though he had been his mother's favorite and much indulged by her, Richard was unhappy at home. He was hypersensitive to the meanness of his surroundings and to the warfare between his parents. (His insomnia, like Delmore's and John's, was not unconnected with his parents' quarrels.) At school he was no less unhappy. Since his father was too weak to discipline him, and his mother too indulgent, it was left to his teachers to do what they could. The education of R. P. Blackmur was a turbulent affair.

"To get out of going to school, he could raise his temperature at will," Helen said. "Richard, show them how you used to do your eyes to scare your teachers."

Richard rolled his eyes back until I begged him to stop, saying he looked like an idiot on the verge of a fit.

"Can you do it?" he asked John. John, Helen and I tried, without success. "Felix Krull could," Richard said, and was off on a monologue about Mann and confidence men.

During Richard's high school years the conflict between the recalcitrant pupil and his teachers came to a head. Richard was expelled. Just what he wanted! He was not meant to sit in a classroom with adolescent louts and pedestrian instructors. If he belonged anywhere it was with the elite at Harvard. But how to get in there? He was underage, had no diploma and was penniless. In a bookstore near the Yard, where he took a job as a sales clerk, he met and made friends with undergraduates. From them he heard which professors were worth listening to and began to audit courses. Meanwhile he educated himself, reading his way along the shelves in the store. Later, with the man who was to become his brother-in-law, Wallace Dixon, he opened a bookstore which became a center for literary undergraduates. By this time Richard knew he wanted to be a poet.

"You should have seen the way he dressed," Helen said mockingly. "Flowing ties . . ."

"Flowing ties cost no more than conventional ones," Richard said defensively.

With his handsome head full of brilliant ideas and romantic notions, he "carried on," Helen said, "as if he were Baudelaire." If his Harvard friends were rich, he was talented. Maybe even a genius. Despite the conflicts at home, and the shabbiness of his surroundings, he didn't leave Irving Street until he married. "Couldn't leave his mother," was Helen's explanation. But he rarely took anyone home, and never discussed his family with his friends.

From Richard's conversation, one would have thought that he had had no childhood or youth. His autobiography began with the period when he was hanging around Harvard and running a bookstore. The outlines of his early years, which he kept hidden, we had learned from that *Dictionary of National Biography* of our circle, Delmore. The details were filled in by Helen. Richard was so ashamed of the boarding house and so hated his father that in the twenty years I knew him he never mentioned either. It was quite by accident that John and I learned, after ten years of intimacy with him, that he had a younger brother who lived not far from Princeton. Even his mother—"Would you believe he writes her three or four times a week?" Helen asked one evening when we were talking and Richard had left the room—and his younger sister Betty, of whom he was very fond, figured little in his conversation. Tessa, his first love; George Palmer, his cousin; Rob Darrell, with George his oldest friend; Lincoln Kirstein and John Marshall, from his hanging-around-Harvard-days; the other editors with him on the prestigious literary magazine *Hound & Horn*; writers Kenneth Burke, Malcolm Cowley, Allen Tate and his wife, the novelist Caroline Gordon; his neighbors, the local characters in Harrington, Maine: These were the people who figured in his talk.

Richard was most at ease as a bachelor host. He made drinks, sat in his chair and, draping one arm over its back, a cigarette held between third finger and thumb, began to talk. He never tired of telling anecdotes about the irrepressible Tessa:

"Did I ever tell you about the time she bought a lampshade and wore it home from the store?" he'd ask, and whether he had or not, would tell us again. Tessa was so much like Molly Bloom to him that I often thought he was speaking of one when it was the other.

Or his talk might be a hymn to Maine, not fashionable coastal Maine, Bar Harbor and Blue Hill, but inland Maine around Harrington, where Helen's family owned a house. It was here that he had lived one year, recovering from tuberculosis, here he and Helen spent three months or more in the summer. It was also in Maine that he had developed his passion for gardening, and learned to love sailing:

> Who that has sailed by star
> on the light night-air,
> first hand on the tiller,
> second, the nibbling sheet

City boy that he was, he had had a good scare or two in Harrington when rats jumped out of dresser drawers, bats swooped low over the bed, and neighbors' dogs bit through his trousers when he went for the milk. His taste for the macabre incited him to embroider these stories with frightening details, especially after he caught on that, city girl that I was, I scared as easily about such things as he did.

"Eileen, I don't think I ever told you about the guest we had who awakened with a bat in her hair. Long hair it was. Very long. Helen had to cut the bat out, leaving the poor woman with a bald patch. Her nerves were never very good after that."

Richard's monologues alternated with conversation. John also talked at Princeton Avenue, but as with Delmore at Ellery Street, much less than Richard. Where Delmore, the host, had been ebullient, and he and John together created an atmosphere of intellectual gaiety, Richard was ruminative, and he and John together were likely to be more sober. Sometimes Richard's voice dropped so low it was as though he were talking to himself. At other times, if he disagreed with an unconsidered literary opinion of a member of the English department, say, who happened to be invited on a Saturday night, he'd furrow his brow, get red in the face and bellow, "For God's sakes, man! Don't talk nonsense."

Whole evenings were devoted to Henry Adams, especially during the period when John was reading the typescript of the finished chapters. Adams at Harvard, in London, in Washington, his marriage, his wife's suicide.

"What do you make of Adams' not having talked about her, not even mentioning her name, until he was an old man?" John, who found this bizarre, asked. Richard, whose way was to bury wounds, found Adams' silence completely comprehensible.

"And what went on with Mrs. Cameron?" Richard would shrug his shoulders: Who knows?

Delmore had sketched for us a play he wanted to write (and later jokingly suggested he and Richard write together) in which Henry Adams and Henry James, the only characters, have a dialogue. Adams leads James on as if he is going to reveal the motive for the suicide, with no intention of doing so. The dialogue is interrupted at a dramatic moment by the ghost of Adams' wife. "I wish Delmore would write it," John said. The question that intrigued him and Delmore was: What explained Marian Adams' suicide?

In conversation with Richard, John, who was as silent about his family history as Richard was, didn't say that he thought and read so much about suicide in an effort to understand what would bring a person to it. On one of the occasions when the conversation was about Marian Adams, Helen, who was there and one would have thought not listening to the conversation, blurted out, "Richard threatened it once in his Baudelairean days." She had been unsympathetic with "such nonsense" and told him to "cut it out." If, thereafter, he had such thoughts, he kept them to himself.

When we were the only guests at Princeton Avenue the talk was almost always literary. It might be about Richard's plan for a new magazine, a successor to the one Adams had edited to be called by the same name, the *North American Review,* for which he hoped to get financial backing. Or it might be about the books Richard was teaching in the seminar John sat in on. That first semester it was *Ulysses.* The Tuesday evening meetings with a handful of students which were supposed to last two hours often ran to four, as first Richard and John exchanged ideas about the chapters assigned, and then Richard took off on his own, the students mesmerized by the brilliance and complexity of his thoughts. He would continue as he and John walked down Prospect together, continue outside our building (until someone who was trying to sleep called out to remind them it was late), and continue on Saturday night, as if there had been no interruption, "What I meant to say, John . . ."

Through Richard's introductions we soon met everyone in Princeton he thought interesting, and in no time had a wide circle of friends. Our agreeable social life we were able to enjoy only to the extent that we could suppress our ever-present anxiety about the future. "Have I brought Hell to Paradise?" John would ask, during irritable and sleepless periods when he was haunted by the painful recent past, a past briefer but to him almost as terrible as the one that haunted the European intellectuals in town. Had his instructorship offered him security, the memory of the summer in New York might have faded more quickly, but as each passing week brought him closer to the end of his four-month appointment, and as even Richard's job seemed in jeopardy, John knew he was not worrying needlessly.

When in March word came that Richard was to be farmed out to the Institute for Advanced Study for the duration (with the promise that he would head the Creative Writing Program after the war), and John was told he would not be reappointed, his colleagues on campus said how sorry they were that he would be going. "Well, we're *not* going to go" he'd say to me, "We're going to stay right here and hang on." Unless, of course, Bennington or Briarcliff or Oglethorpe in Atlanta, all of which had written him, made him an offer. Also, he would remind me, he had applied for a Guggenheim and should hear any day. Until then he would once again wait.

A favorite subject at Richard's Saturday nights during the period when both he and John were uncertain about jobs was how a writer could best earn a living. What price did one pay for teaching creative writing?

"God, how I hate the word 'creative.' Wouldn't it be better to be a banker, like Eliot?" asked the son of a banker. "Or work in an insurance company, like Stevens? Or be a doctor, like Williams?"

"Or a lumberman?" Richard had a friend who'd come home from World War I a burnt-out case and had made a life for himself working as a lumberman in Maine.

Richard urged John to make a "literary experiment"—to try to earn his living as a freelance writer as he, Richard, had done before coming to Princeton. John should be able to earn $700 a year which, with my salary (especially if I asked for a raise) would make it possible for us to survive. This, after all, was every writer's dream. John and I were young. We were free. Why not try it?

It was at this time that John decided that, much as he enjoyed classroom teaching (if not lecturing, for which he suspected he was not fitted), he did not want to climb the academic ladder. Though he had an advanced degree from Cambridge, he didn't have a Ph.D., and had no intention of getting one. In a way he was almost as much of a freak in academia as Richard was. And, like Richard, any teaching he undertook would have to be done outside the system. Richard's literary experiment was a more appealing way to live, though John was somewhat concerned as to whether he could write on demand. There was also the possibility (Delmore's suggestion) of writing a novel and getting an advance to live on. Or—the idea he had had when he returned from England—writing a play with the hope of having it produced on Broadway. Whatever happened he was unwilling to submit himself to a period of job-hunting such as he'd gone through during the summer. He couldn't get it out of his head that if he had had the courage to hang on from June to October and wait for the Princeton appointment, he might have used those months for writing poetry and so have spared himself, and me, a summer of agony.

There was much in these discussions with Richard, and with John alone, to make me uneasy. While I could sympathize with John's lack of academic ambition, I wasn't sure he would be able to tolerate the insecurity of living outside the system. And could I take it? The literary experiment made me, if anything, more apprehensive. John writing on a subject suggested by someone else? Against a deadline? Would that really allow more time for writing verse than teaching? Also, what Richard's suggestion took for granted was that I was as eager to remain childless as Helen was. (She used to say, "Richard won't admit it but what he wants in a wife is a mother. I have no desire for another child.")

John knew I wanted a child. He also knew that if he free-lanced there was no way I could take time off from working. As for his having squandered the previous summer looking for work, he had done so, I reminded him, because Princeton had not been able to make a firm offer and had suggested he look elsewhere. Still, I understood that he had neither heart nor energy for a new round of job-hunting. Though I was less optimistic about the Guggenheim than he, I agreed that we had no choice but to sit tight and hope an offer would come in the mail.

Sitting tight produced its own strains. Every morning that I went to work and John stayed home, he felt a pang of guilt: He was allowing his wife to support him. Without an office on campus, there was no escape from the four walls of our tiny apartment. It made him feel so claustrophobic he couldn't write. "I'll never write again," he'd say every evening at dinner. "There's nothing *there.*"

Helen, hearing his complaints about not having a place to work, offered him the use of an attic studio in our building where she had painted before taking the factory job. John moved aside tubes of paint and marmalade jars full of brushes, sharpened his pencils and stared at the blank sheet of paper before him. Would he get a Guggenheim? That's what he thought about, not poetry. And would he go bald? Since he never struck me as being vain about his physical appearance, I was at first baffled by the way he suffered over the loss of hair. If I tried to reassure him by pointing out that he had a long way to go before being bald, he'd say, "You refuse to see it." (Thirty years later when he died he was still not bald). Or, if I tried to tell him how attractive I found him, he'd say, "How *can* you?" After awhile I realized that nothing I said could reassure him for long. This loss had symbolic significance. He associated it with loss of potency and—an even greater threat—loss of potency as an artist. "Almost a year has gone by and I've written nothing, not a word."

How little he had accomplished as a writer, how far he still was from having a book published was borne in on him when he learned that Richard, Mark and Delmore had been invited to read at the YMHA in New York. Public readings being uncommon in those days, the evening at the Y was to be something of an event. It was arranged that we would all have dinner together beforehand, and that Delmore would come back to Princeton to spend the weekend at the Blackmurs'.

The morning of the reading Richard had an appointment at the Rockefeller Foundation. He was hoping to convince them that they should back his new literary magazine. Later, when he and John met to go downtown to join Delmore, Richard said the board members hadn't been very encouraging to him. "I'll tell you who they were interested in though. You."

"Me? How come?" John asked.

"They wonder if you'd like a grant to do a critical edition of *King Lear*."

This was so improbable that John asked Richard if he'd been drinking.

"Old man Rockefeller, a teetotaler, put a clause in his will prohibiting booze on the premises. What one is offered in the Foundation dining room with lunch is ice water. No, John, I'm quite serious." Douglas Southall Freeman, the historian, had spotted John's review of W.W. Greg's *The Editorial Problem in Shakespeare* in *The Nation* and had called it to the attention of the Foundation. Difficult though it was to believe when one was trying, unsuccessfully, to get money out of them, they were always looking for people and projects to support. Richard said the edition of *Lear* was right up their alley.

John was digesting this astonishing news when they met Delmore. The reunion, which John had been very much looking forward to, did not go well. Delmore accused the two Princetonians of being "strange."

What may have been strange to Delmore was the relationship that had developed between Richard and John, a relationship Delmore knew about through the two men's letters but experienced for the first time when they appeared together. He felt that his two old friends had become close in a way that excluded him. Richard and John read and criticized each other's writing in the way Delmore and John had done at Harvard ("Slow? There never was a man as slow as Richard," John said, "but my God, what a reader!"). And although, because of the difference in generation and Richard's natural reticence, they never developed the kind of intimacy Delmore and John had shared, they saw each other far more often, and were, at the time of this meeting, as close intellectually as two men could be. What had begun on John's side as awe had changed into admiration and affection.

Delmore also claimed that John had changed. "You're wearing a new suit," he said accusingly. John was amused at first. It was a suit he had bought soon after arriving in Princeton (gray flannel, the local uniform), the first new one he had had in years.

The real way in which John had changed was in the pleasure he now took in social life. Since we had been in Princeton I had often thought how little Delmore would have recognized the recluse of Appian Way, and even of the early days on Grove Street, when he had had to prod John into accepting invitations. This change (as John said the following day when we were discussing it) Delmore couldn't have seen. So what did he mean? Before there was a possibility of finding out, Delmore began to attack Richard and his friends at the Rockefeller Foundation (John Marshall, Richard's friend from Harvard days, was on the board).

"They've turned down *Partisan Review*'s request for a grant. It's because of *Partisan*'s politics, isn't it? Admit it," Delmore demanded.

Richard said mildly that the board had been put off by the "abusive book reviews" *PR* had recently been specializing in.

"Whose reviews? Mine?" Delmore became more and more excited and, on the way to dinner, hammered at Richard. By the time they met Dorothy and Mark Van Doren at the Charles Restaurant in the Village, where I joined them, the three men were gloomily silent. The meal would have been a fiasco but for Mark. His diplomatic manner had such a soothing effect on them that by the time the meal was over everyone was in good spirits. During the taxi ride uptown, Delmore had so lost his feeling that John had changed that he was again confiding in him about his private life. "She's beautiful, brilliant—but alas! John, so far my love is unrequited."

Literary New York was assembled in the auditorium on upper Lexington Avenue. It was John's first visit to the Y. He read off the names in bold gold letters above the proscenium: DAVID MOSES ISAIAH. To the right, after JEFFERSON (the order interested him) were SHAKESPEARE DANTE GOETHE. Wooden chairs were arranged on the stage on either side of a lectern. On a table was a pitcher of water and glasses. The poets filed in and took their places.

Mark, the most experienced performer, was first. I had heard so much from John about Mark's Shakespeare class at Columbia that I had especially looked forward to hearing him. His flat, uninflected voice disappointed me. Rather than recite, or even read, he said his poems in what seemed to me a self-deprecatory manner. He had developed this style, John said, as a reaction to the rhetorical, melodramatic, even "hammy" readings he had heard when he was a young man.

Richard, reading poems from *From Jordan's Delight* and others that would appear in *The Good European,* was serious and impressive, though John thought his well-concealed nervousness made him less good than he had been in rehearsal with John the previous day. Delmore looked pale, was physically restless and had such difficulty controlling his voice that he was at times inaudible. "He's tossing his poems to the audience as if they're pennies," John said.

After the reading, in what is now a familiar pattern, there was a party at the apartment of a wealthy and hospitable patroness of poetry. There were drinks and a great many eager young women who treated the performers, I told Helen the next evening, as if they were movie stars. Delmore, moving restlessly around the Blackmurs' living room, interrupted my account to say, "I've slept with five of those 'poet followers.' As Philip [Rahv] says, 'Poets get all the girls.'"

Delmore's bragging remark was so uncharacteristic that we were all shocked. All but Helen, who said, mockingly, "Only five?"

He rounded on her. She was a fool to be working for the war effort. She should quit her job and go back to painting. Or, "Better still, why don't you have a baby?" To me he said, "You should have one, too."

Richard, who had had a trying day with his guest (more attacks on the Foundation), had obviously decided that the only way to get through the evening was to drink deep draughts of Myer's rum. He sat in his chair, his head bent to his chest, turned inward on himself. The only indication he gave that he had heard Delmore's incendiary remarks was to say "Hmmmmmm," which meant that he had many reflections to make on this subject but not the energy to do so at the moment.

John, whose morale was very low—no job, no money, no poems to show for the time since he had stopped teaching—was struggling with his reaction to an earlier remark Delmore had tossed him to the effect that he, Delmore, had four months free in which to write lyric poetry should he feel like doing so. Was this ache he felt envy? John, examining his hypertrophied conscience, asked himself. If so, how unworthy his feeling was when he should be glad for Delmore.

That left Helen and me to respond to Delmore. Certainly he knew that Helen didn't want a child, and that I did. He may also have known or suspected how ambivalent John's feelings about paternity were. Helen, the only one in the room with a cool head, finally broke the silence. She fixed Delmore with her catlike eyes, laughed her mirthless laugh and said, "I never know how much we who are childless should congratulate our unborn on what they're missing."

The next day when Delmore and the Blackmurs came to us for lunch, a very subdued Richard complained that he could feel the outline of his liver quite clearly. Delmore, looking red-eyed and haggard even though he had slept until noon, was, if less inflammatory, still so scrappy that by the time we put him on the train we were all giddy with relief. "What's *wrong* with Delmore?" John asked, as we drove away from the station in the Blackmurs' beach wagon. We couldn't just go home and worry about him, Richard said. The weekend needed a coda. He invited John and me to dinner at Lahière's, after which we went to the Garden Theatre to see *Jane Eyre.* The movie was unintentionally funny. Richard and John glossed the dialogue so audibly and wittily that when the lights came on the student audience gave them a round of applause.

A few weeks after the Y reading, John received a letter from the Rockefeller Foundation, confirming Richard's report of their conversation with him. If it would interest John to work on *Lear,* they would like him to write a proposal for the board's consideration. To be sought after in this way, at a time when he was so desperately casting about for a means to earn a living that he even considered taking a job in the factory where Helen worked (the one place he could be certain not to be rejected), threw him off guard. So seductive was the Foundation's warm embrace that for once he didn't ask himself: Will the work I'm taking on be dangerous to my art? What he did ask himself was: Have I the makings of a Shakespearean scholar? One time he'd return from an interview in New York convinced that he could train himself to the role; the next time he'd feel that he was a fraud. When he heard that he would have to pass a physical examination, he felt fraudulent in another way.

"What if they find out I have epilepsy?"

"You don't. Remember?"

Although he hadn't had an episode in over two years, he was never free of the fear that one day his "sickness" would return (by which he meant not so much the fainting attacks, but a more general fear of insanity). Since he was as concerned about the rejected diagnosis of schizophrenia as by the label of epilepsy, I suggested that he see a specialist in New York for another opinion.

The suggestion that there could be another opinion, that he wasn't stuck with the Detroit diagnosis for life, relieved him so greatly that he got over his jitters and came through the examination successfully. "The doctor says I'm well enough to do research. Very funny. How well do you suppose that is?"

What the doctor also told him, and he suppressed for months, was that he had a partial hearing loss in one ear. He was afraid, and with reason, that I would say, "So *that's* why you play the Scott at an ear-splitting volume." (John liked to tell the story about his grand-mother, a spry old lady by the time I met her, with a face as wrinkled as a withered apple and a tongue as tart as a greening: When she consulted an otologist with the complaint that she didn't hear as well as she had, the doctor said, "Don't worry about it, Mrs. Little. Most people hear too much, anyway.")

Since Bennington, Briarcliff and Oglethorpe had all fallen through, since, after weeks of waiting for the mail every day, the letter from the Guggenheim began, "We regret to inform you . . ." John was so relieved to hear that the Rockefeller Foundation had accepted his proposal that he suppressed whatever concerns he had about the under-taking and was grateful for a one-year grant with a stipend of $2500.

This income would allow us to stay in Princeton and even permit us to move to a larger apartment.

With the proposal out of the way, John tried once again to use the time he had free before the grant began to write verse. Verse stubbornly refused to come, as I could tell when he started to talk excitedly of returning to the play on the Irish rebellion he had begun in Boston. He talked about it so much I suspected he was willing it into being, for I had learned that the chances of a project coming to fruition were in inverse proportion to the amount he discussed it. This was especially true if the talk was high-keyed, and, to my ears, forced, which meant to me that it was make-work, busy-work, anxiety-relieving work— always plausible, always interesting to hear about; not, however, the real thing.

Then, abruptly, Connelly and Pearse dropped out of his conversation. He was impatient to get to the attic in the morning, worked all day, was preoccupied during dinner, and returned to the attic again in the evening where he remained until three or four in the morning. Not a word about what he was doing. It was surely not a lyric he was

John, amused

working on, for it was taking too long. A novel? When he complained at dinner about how "ungainly and uncontrolled" fiction was by comparison with verse, I suspected so. And hoped not. I had a feeling John was no more a novelist than Richard was. I had read Richard's two unpublished novels—one about a physiologist, the other about a lawyer—and while I found them interesting (especially for the insights they gave me into the author's personality), it seemed to me that they were highly competent exercises in novel-writing. I was afraid John's would be, too.

At the end of two weeks, he told me that *Kenyon Review* had announced a short-story contest and handed me a manuscript he planned to submit. What did I think of it?

In "The Lovers" an adolescent boy's infatuation with a girl his own age is contrasted with the feelings of a man, a friend of his parents, for the boy's mother. It is from this man, a writer, that the boy first hears the word "work" pronounced with the special emphasis that makes it clear that what a writer does is of greater importance and interest than the work other men such as his father do. The locale was the Long Island town where John spent summers during his South Kent years. The adolescent love was his first love.

I wondered as I read the story if its subject had been suggested to him by a rereading of his letters to his mother (which she had recently returned), and hers to him, written during his stay in England. In response to his announcement that he was in love with B., his mother had sent him a stern reminder that if he wanted to be a poet he would have to make sacrifices, with the strong implication that a relationship such as he had embarked on with B. would distract him from his goal. At that time, and again when he and I married, John hoped he could have both—"work, a wife and work."

The mother in the story is shown in soft focus—beautiful, blameless, so young-looking she and her son are taken for sister and brother. (It was all right for others to think that; it made the boy feel more grown up. Very different from a mother claiming it to be so.) The mother is attentive to her son, to her house, to her garden, innocent of any effort to attract the writer. Here John is describing his mother in the way he remembered her during his prep-school days—this at a time when her actual behavior was causing him acute embarrassment. He had just discovered that during the period when he had been waiting to hear if he would be reappointed at Princeton, she had written to her old friend Franklin d'Olier, who was on the board of trustees of the university, asking him to put pressure on the English department to keep John on. Since the head of his department was not letting John go because he was dissatisfied with his teaching, but rather because there were going to be few students to teach, John was convinced that his mother's meddling had had the effect of suggesting to those to whom d'Olier spoke that he, John, was d'Olier's natural son.

"Well? What do you think of it?" John, who had gone for a walk while I read the story, wanted to know. I said I thought it was terrific. But I hoped he wasn't counting too much on winning with it.

"There's no chance of that. The magazine has received a thousand submissions for the contest."

Just before we left for Cape Cod, on our first vacation, John Crowe Ransom wrote that while "The Lovers" had not won the prize, he considered it "brilliant" and wanted to print it in *Kenyon*.

This was John's first publication (aside from a review or two) in so long that I was elated. "Eileen is delighted," I would hear him say, as he told Richard and other friends that the story had been accepted. Not a word about how he felt. It was the first instance I had of being a surrogate, a role that as his literary successes and failures followed on one another more closely, I was to play with increasing frequency.

V
LEAR
AND
RANDALL

Enter *Lear.*

The king had been loitering in the wings for years. John's interest in Shakespeare, which had begun in a serious way in Mark Van Doren's class at Columbia, had broadened and deepened in Cambridge during his preparation for the Oldham competition. Thereafter Shakespeare was never far from his mind. "Why do we ever read anyone else?" he'd ask, rereading one of the plays. Textual criticism began to attract him during that uneasy spring in Boston after he heard that he would not be reappointed at Harvard. Too unsettled to write verse, he turned to textual work as another man whose attention could be more easily engaged might turn to crossword puzzles. The game was so intriguing it allowed him a respite from anxiety about his future. When he wrote his review, "Shakespeare's Text," for *The Nation,* and pointed out the need for a critical edition of *Lear,* it did not occur to him that he might be the person for the job. Or rather, it occurred to him so peripherally that only after the Rockefeller query did he realize that he had said to himself: Were I not a poet, I might make a not-bad Shakespearean scholar.

The out-of-work poet had been relieved to be given the grant. Why, then, after the first Rockefeller check arrived, did he stall? Each

day he said, "I must begin." Each day he put it off. The scope of the
project was intimidating. What was more troubling was the realization
that, knowing himself and the intensity with which he tackled any job
(even teaching Latin in a prep school), he ran the risk of becoming
obsessed. A serious risk.

"Will *Lear* crowd verse out of my brain? Will *Lear* devour my
writing time? Can I control my bloody obsessiveness? Ha! I have it."
What he had was the bright idea of dividing his work space, renting
the attic studio next to Helen's for writing, asking the university for
an office in the library for *Lear*.

What the university came up with was a closet of a room, the Ball
Room (named for Professor Ball, not a joke about its size), in the
basement under Chancellor Green, and reachable by way of a long,
dark tunnel through which ran asbestos-covered hot-water pipes. John
soon became impatient with this circuitous route, especially after he
had been locked out once or twice at night. When the library was
closed, he entered and left through a ground-level window above his
desk just wide enough for him to shinny through if he rounded his
shoulders. The campus proctors who policed the grounds looking for
disorderly students soon became accustomed to picking up in the beam
of their flashlights the agile and eccentric bookworm who crawled in
and out of his cubby hole at night.

During the first year of the grant the division worked surprisingly
well. There were periods during which he chronically misplaced the
key to the Ball Room, behaving, as he said, "as if the Devil dwelt
there" (and as if he didn't have his own easy access). With one trick
or another, he was able to fight becoming obsessed, and had a very
good year (another man would have said a happy year). He was
earning a living at work that absorbed him, and he was writing. After
his reviews appeared in *politics,* the *Sewanee Review* and the *New York
Times Book Review,* people began to stop him on the street to talk to
him about them, as if, he said, he was a writer! A new and heady
experience, to which he sometimes responded with diffidence, sometimes with pleasure. When Erich Kahler, a social philosopher known
in this country for his book, *Man the Measure,* praised "The Lovers,"
he did it so skillfully that John was frankly delighted.

It was through Richard that John had been introduced to the
Kahler-Broch household on Evelyn Place. Erich had followed his old

friends Thomas Mann and Einstein to Princeton. He bought a commo-
dious house (around the corner from where we lived) in which he
installed his aged mother, an immense library, the few paintings from
his collection that he had been able to bring with him and the remnants
of a rich man's wardrobe. Lili Loewy, a Viennese art historian who
later became his wife, came to look after his mother. Hermann Broch,
the fourth member of the ménage, lived in the studio apartment on
the top floor, where he was at work on *The Death of Virgil*.

At Evelyn Place once a fortnight a group of men—the composer
Roger Sessions, the mathematician Hermann Weyl, the philosopher
David Bowers, the economist Friedrich Lutz, as well as Richard and
John—met for an evening of serious conversation. The subject might
be the poetry of Hölderlin, the works of Kierkegaard (which were
beginning to appear in Walter Lowrie's translation), the economy of
postwar Europe or the form of punishment that should be meted out
to the Nazis.

What John enjoyed more than the conversation group (in which he
felt somewhat inhibited because of the age and fame of the other men)
were the evenings when he and I were invited as a couple. One stepped
off a Princeton street and was plunged into Europe. Erich, dressed in
a well-worn velvet smoking jacket, pulled back the portieres on a
room in which a circle of chairs had been arranged around a large oval
table. On its inlaid surface had been set out a crystal decanter of sherry,
Bavarian wineglasses and a plate of Viennese cakes baked by Lili. There
were leather-bound books everywhere, as well as copies of *Du* and
Die Neue Rundschau. Since Erich loved company, and made his house
a meeting place both for refugee intellectuals and new American
friends, more and more chairs were brought in to enlarge the circle
during the course of the evening.

It was at these evenings that we met all of Erich's friends, all that
is, save Einstein, who preferred to visit Erich when there was no one
else present. On one occasion Einstein had just left when John arrived.
Soon after John returned home Lili telephoned frantically. Had John
by any chance taken the professor's umbrella? The world-famous
physicist, who was even more absent-minded than the obscure poet,
had left his in the hall rack, and the poet had unwittingly taken it
(leaving behind his almost identical one); the physicist's secretary had
spotted the loss when her employer returned, rain-drenched, from his

walk, had called Lili, who called me, who checked to see, and sent John
hurrying back to make the exchange, lest it be thought—"Horrors!"
—that he, like so many admirers, had been after a souvenir of the
Nobel laureate.

At Erich's evenings, Hermann Broch, tall and stooped, with a face
as long and fine as a Saluki's, descended from his studio to join the
group around the table when coffee was served. Why he was so
attractive to women it is not easy to say, but attractive he was. He
would go around the circle, saying something gallant to each one
present, then take his chair. Pulling on his pipe, he might talk in a
rather preoccupied way about "twilight consciousness," or be very
down-to-earth about a *New Yorker* cartoon. It was not how well one
understood philosophical ideas in a foreign language that measured
one's comprehension, he said; it was one's grasp of the humor. *The New*

COURTESY OF ALICE VON KAHLER

Erich Kahler

Yorker was the weekly test he gave himself. Failure to understand even one caption made him gloomy. He would show it to John and me, and ask us to explain what to him was incomprehensible.

On one occasion Broch gave me a lesson in English. When Erich and I returned from a movie one bitter cold evening (Erich dressed in his fur-lined overcoat with mink revers), it was Broch who let us in. "How is it out?" he asked. Shivering, I said that it was "freezing." He looked surprised and said, "Surely it's colder than that." Since the thermometer registered closer to 5° than 32°, Broch was right. I had used the word sloppily. From then on I was more precise.

It was on the evening of the English lesson that Broch told me the story of his secular road to Damascus. It had occurred in Vienna, on the route he traveled every morning in a chauffeur-driven car to the textile factory of which he was the director. He was forty years old at the time and had taken it for granted, as had everyone else, that he would live his life as a businessman, though a businessman who spent his evenings discussing philosophy and literature with intellectuals at the Café Zentral. On this particular day, which had begun like any

Hermann Broch

other, he felt a sudden compulsion to tell the driver to stop, to turn back. He never again returned to the factory, and thereafter devoted his life to writing.

Except for a rare evening such as this one, Broch was something of an apparition, appearing and disappearing mysteriously. It was Erich who was the center of the household. At sixty, he had a young man's enthusiasm for new ideas and new friends. Though I didn't realize it at the time, when we met him he was coming out of a severe depression and was beginning to enjoy living again, with a capacity for enjoyment rare at any age. In Europe he had led the life of a rich intellectual, writing and reading during the day, going out in society at night. When, years later, John was asked to contribute to the Festschrift in honor of his old friend, he wrote the poem "The Mysteries":

> I accost you on a summit of your honour
> Erich Kahler for you shoot like a tooth

Shoot like a tooth he did, intellectually, but John also acknowledged Erich's party-loving side:

> . . . you who were a dancing man

The best waltzer in Princeton (and the only one who knew how to reverse), Erich would have liked nothing better than to entertain in the old style. His fortune having been confiscated by the Nazis, it was all he could do to keep Evelyn Place going by selling paintings. When, at age sixty-five, he was given a visiting professorship at Cornell, he said, "How proud my father would have been to see me earning my living! At an age when others retire, I have taken my first job."

Erich, an only child, had suffered from being isolated while growing up. It was this, he thought, that made him crave company as an adult. Unlike many only children, he was capable of great intimacy with men and women alike. He was also one of those rare people who can maintain a relationship over a long separation. Though he and I wrote to each other infrequently during the four years I lived abroad during the sixties, on my return we took up our friendship where we had left off. When I was an overnight guest at Evelyn Place, Erich and I would have breakfast together, and over tea and a boiled egg discuss the Beatles or the book he was currently at work on, or I would get him to reminisce about Thomas Mann or the circle of Stefan George.

John had sought Erich's opinion from time to time, for he valued his judgment as a critic, so he was pleased by Erich's excitement over his second story, which appeared in the *Kenyon Review*. With the *Review*'s announcement of another short story contest, John abandoned the library in favor of his attic study. For weeks there was no more talk of quartos, folios, collations, emendations, cruxes, nor a repeating of the litany of distinguished English textual scholars: Greg, Dover Wilson, Chambers, McKerrow, Granville-Barker. At mealtimes he complained about how little talent he had for narrative.

Four years after the episode in Union Square, in which John had been drawn into the "savage" argument, he was reworking the material he had originally tried to cast in verse form. The judges of the contest thought he had sufficient talent for narrative to give him the first prize for "The Imaginary Jew." He enjoyed my elation at the letter of congratulations, but when the proofs arrived he was so disappointed by what he had written that he seriously considered withdrawing the story. Only after a good deal of rewriting, and considerable persuasion on my part, did he return the proofs to *Kenyon*.

Erich was deeply moved by the story. Believing that it should have a wider circulation than *Kenyon* could give it, and that it should be read abroad, he asked if he could translate it for *Die Neue Rundschau*. This marked the first appearance abroad of anything John had written.

With his book of poems he still had no success. Harcourt Brace turned it down a second time. It was a measure of his stability in this period that he recovered from this rejection fairly quickly by reminding himself that Harcourt wasn't the only publisher in New York. He would try another, and also Faber & Faber in England. He finished "Canto Amor," the poem in terza rima he had been grappling with for two years, and sent it to Allen Tate, then editor of the *Sewanee Review*, who accepted it for publication. John also included it in his book, which he now sent to Henry Holt.

For the first time since we had married, we didn't begin at the end of the winter to worry about how we'd live in the fall. With a renewal of the Rockefeller grant almost certain, we were able to enjoy the most beautiful spring either of us had ever seen. Princeton, with its profusion of blossoming trees—dogwood, flowering Judas, magnolia, catalpa—

was as lush as a Southern town. On Saturday afternoons after I left the office, John and I explored the countryside on bicycles.

From time to time the Blackmurs took us on outings further afield. In their beach wagon, Helen at the wheel, we drove over to Andover, New Jersey, to see Richard's old friend, the critic Kenneth Burke. Kenneth, a short, intense man with hair that stood up straight from his high forehead as if electrified by the activity in his brain, greeted Richard with a bear hug. He introduced us to the other guests, Ralph Ellison, the author of *Invisible Man* (who was later to become a friend of John's), and Mrs. Ellison.

Even before he had finished making drinks for us, Kenneth began to talk exuberantly about an article he was writing on literary criticism. The word "cloacal" turned up repeatedly. I must confess that, whether because of the stiff drink, or the complexity of his reasoning, I was unable to make sense of his theory.

After an enormous lunch, our host took us on a walk along an abandoned railroad track. The overcast sky and eerie landscape were in marked contrast to Kenneth's high spirits as he led the way, entertaining us with Bennington gossip about doomed romances between writers on the faculty and their students. He was full of stories about the absent-mindedness of his old friend, William Carlos Williams, during a recent visit to the Vermont campus. Addressing the Bennington girls with a speech he'd already delivered to aspiring writers at Yale and Harvard, without making the change in gender necessary for his audience, Dr. Williams had squeaked at the girls, his voice high with passionate conviction (and Kenneth's rising even higher in imitation of it), "If you want to write poetry, you've got to be men! You've got to be men!" The young women, first puzzled, then resentful, slid deeper and deeper into their seats. "Why are they all so sullen?" Williams, who was used to having women of all ages find him attractive, asked Kenneth afterward.

With the Blackmurs, Dorothy and Stow Persons, and one or two other friends from Richard's inner circle, we also went canoeing on Sundays. On these outings the Blackmurs were more relaxed with each other than at any other time. Richard commented on the flora and fauna as we paddled along, while Helen sketched. We feasted our eyes on the new green leaves and picnicked in the dappled sunlight on the banks of the canal.

In the evenings the group of friends we had grown close to enter-

JOHN BERRYMAN

Nela Walcott's "rather good portrait" of John, which he used in lieu of a photograph

tained one another at dinner. Or we went to parties at the house of Nela Walcott, a painter, who was doing a drawing of John—a rather good portrait of the way he looked at the time—which he used in lieu of a photograph for the Oscar Williams anthologies. The end of the war in Europe (which John had followed closely, full of concern not only about the fate of Europe but about B. and his English friends) had put him, had put all of us, in a celebratory mood.

Nela had an independent income that permitted her to run up bills at the local liquor store. It took very little urging for her to allow Helen and me to clear her studio for dancing. "Enough jawing!" Helen would say. She and I supplied records and coaxed the timid to the floor. John was not one of them. Though he pretended to have outgrown his enthusiasm for dancing, he was the only partner Helen and I could always count on to whirl us around. Richard, on the other hand, danced only when he had had quantities to drink. An awesome sight it was. The Wild Man of Delmore's Cambridge stories we only caught a glimmer of from time to time. (One night when we were invited to dinner at Brenda and Monroe Engels', their seven-year-old daughter —hair at the nape of her neck curly and damp from her bath, her white nightgown patted smooth at her sides after she had wiggled into the place on the sofa between Richard and me—looked up at Richard expectantly. He didn't disappoint her. Making his Felix Krull eyes at her, he said, "Let's tell lies," at which she clapped her hands in delight. Or, out of the blue at a very proper dinner with people we didn't know very well, he'd say in full voice, "John, have you ever noticed that while many women have bottoms like cellos Eileen's is like a viola?" John, delighted by the introduction of so enlivening a subject, would take it up, and the two of them would be off on the subject of bottoms.)

It was only during dancing parties that I realized Delmore's stories had not been exaggerations. Richard would catapult himself from his chair, and circle the room two or three times, stalking his prey. Pouncing, he would grab his victim in a viselike grip, then push, pull, twist, jerk and spin her around, grunting and grimacing like a samurai, while his partner made frantic gestures behind his back, begging for a release. If no one intervened quickly enough, it was only a matter of time before the two of them, locked in combat, fell to the floor. On one occasion Richard so frightened a new faculty wife by stripping to the waist as he approached her that she fled the party, and was said to cross the street whenever she saw him in town. On the dance floor only Helen could tame him. If she saw the distress signal, she'd cut in and, taking the lead, partner him as if he were a patient at a mental hospital social hour. "As a teacher," she said, "I learned to dance with all kinds."

It was at Nela's that we celebrated Richard's fortieth birthday. It was there too, at the last big party before we broke up for the summer, that Richard misjudged his capacity for rum and passed out cold. At 2:00 A.M., when Helen and I left, John, who was deep in conversation with one of the other guests and by no means ready to leave, promised to see that Richard got back to Princeton Avenue.

It was dawn when John came in. Daybreak was the hour he and Richard favored for going to bed. Victims, both, of nightmares and night terrors, they felt that only when light began to show in the sky (the hour when parental quarrels finally wore themselves out?) could they safely go to sleep. John got into bed giggling. He had awakened a very docile and contrite, if not yet coherent, Richard. As they walked to Princeton Avenue, Richard, after a silence so long that John won-

dered if he was asleep on his feet, said, "Think about the rats, John."
"What rats?" John asked. "The rats on the sinking ship."

The external pressure John felt from editors and friends to continue
writing stories after he had won the *Kenyon* prize was easy enough for
him to resist, for he was convinced that his talent was for verse, not
fiction. He looked upon "The Lovers" and "The Imaginary Jew" as
freaks, and doubted that he would write another story. The internal
pressure to finish *Lear,* however, was irresistible. It wasn't that the
Foundation would ask to see what he had done. It was that as the end
of the grant came in view the obsession he had fought so hard took
over.

Quartos, folios, collations, emendations, Greg, Dover Wilson,
Chambers, McKerrow, Granville-Barker: During the final six months
of the grant he thought of nothing else. About social life he laid down
the law. We had entertained his brother, his mother, my sister, Dorothy and Mark Van Doren, Bob Giroux, Bernard Haggin, former
students from Harvard as well as our many Princeton friends. We had
gone canoeing and bicycling, had danced at Nela's, stayed up half the
night talking at Richard's, and had enjoyed it all. *"No more!"* John said,
severe as a deacon. "Until June, I can allow myself only one evening
off a week. The rest of the time it must be work, work, work. Do you
hear?"

For six months I was married to a phantom who emerged from the
Ball Room periodically to speak a language that would have been
comprehensible only to Greg, McKerrow, et. al. In the kitchen, preparing dinner, I sang, parodying Delmore: "All scholars' wives have rotten
lives."

"Weren't scholars' lives famous for being slow-paced and low-
keyed?" I asked. I had imagined Greg at Oxford, leaving his house in
the morning at a reasonable hour to work in his office methodically
and with little excitement—except for an occasional leap of the heart,
an "Aha!" as he resolved a crux he had been puzzling over for years
—breaking for lunch with a colleague, then an afternoon walk (in a
drizzle, very likely) to clear his head, before going back to his study,
home for dinner, a pipe and reading before bed. A dull life. It would
not have done for a man of John's temperament. Still, the contrast
between my fantasy and the way John was living made me wonder

if what was making him work as he did was not merely that the end of the grant was in sight, and that he wanted desperately to finish. Was it possible that he was driving himself in this way for another reason?

For more than a year he had lived a life without turbulence. Had he not been so afraid of the word, he would have admitted that he had been happy. He had seemed, even, to accept my wish for a child. Such a life had great appeal. "Who does not wish for personal happiness?" he would ask. But happiness was dangerous. As he felt himself tempted by it, he pulled away and buried himself in his underground office. For someone untrained in textual work to try to complete the *Lear* in two years, indeed for anyone to attempt it in that time, was absurd, as he knew. Yet this was the goal he imposed upon himself.

Only the consideration of how he would earn a living in the year ahead intruded on his obsession. For the first time there was an embarrassment of possible riches. With the war ended, the universities were returning to normal; publishing houses were back in full swing. Allen Tate, who was leaving the *Sewanee Review* to go to Henry Holt, offered John the editorship of the *Review*. It was a tempting offer at a salary larger than he had ever earned. Richard, still longing to have his own magazine to run, urged John to grab it. Delmore at *Partisan,* John at *Sewanee,* Richard at *North American*: what could be better? Then while John was waiting for a formal offer from the University of the South, Dean Gauss, who had appointed Richard Resident Fellow in Creative Arts, offered John a job as Richard's assistant. Richard now wanted John very much to stay and work with him.

At the end of May, for a party Margaret Marshall of *The Nation* gave to introduce Randall Jarrell (who was to replace her as literary editor while she was on leave), John came up from underground. He and Randall, who were the same age, had corresponded at the time *Five Young American Poets* was published, and knew each other's work intimately, but had never met. John was so eager to talk to the poet he admired, the poet-critic he thought was the most original of their generation, that he broke his rule about no social engagements.

He knew a great deal about Jarrell from the Tates. Knew, for instance, that he had been born in Tennessee and had spent his youth in Hollywood:

Randall in Princeton

> When I was twelve we'd visit my aunt's friend
> Who owned a lion, the Metro-Goldwyn-Mayer
> Lion. I'd play with him, and he'd pretend
> to play with me.

Randall was senior to his one brother by the same number of years John was to Bob. After his parents had divorced, Randall was looked after by grandparents and a great-grandmother who doted on him. Later he went to live with his mother in Tennessee and attended Vanderbilt College, studying there with Ransom and Tate. He followed Ransom to Kenyon College and began his teaching career, which was interrupted during the war when he joined the Air Force.

Having been told more than once that Randall and John resembled each other, I looked for similarities between them when Randall and I were introduced at the party. I found none. Randall's features were more regular, and he was darker—dark eyes, dark hair and mustache, and an almost sallow complexion. There was something vaguely Latin about his appearance. Tall and slim, he looked even slimmer than John because he didn't have John's shoulders.

That Randall was proud of his slimness I discovered when we knew each other better and we invited him for dinner one evening. He came into the kitchen while I was cooking and leaned against the refrigerator door. I thought: As a boy he used to shadow his grandmother while she cooked. But the boy had grown into a man, and the man was studying my figure in a way that was difficult to ignore. To be watched as I cooked made me uncomfortable; to be scrutinized with the cold-eyed stare of a judge at a bathing-beauty contest was unnerving. Also surprising. Until this moment Randall had treated me as a person rather than a woman (as I think he treated most women). "What *is* it, Randall?" I asked.

"I bet my waist is smaller than yours." He was so solemn I burst out laughing. "What's your size?"

My size? I didn't know.

Still solemn, he said, "Let's measure." He took off his belt and gave it to me to see what notch I would wear it in. With a triumphant smile he said, "You *see!* My waist is half an inch smaller."

This slimness, together with his characteristic stance, one knee

locked into the other and slightly flexed, gave him a willowy silhou-
ette.

The surprise of *The Nation* evening was Randall's speech and his
voice. The author of those killer reviews, which set the literary world
buzzing whenever they appeared in the quarterlies, studded his conversations with italics and out-of-date expressions like "Gol-ly!," "Gee
whiz!" and (my favorite) "Ba-by *doll!*"—all delivered in a high-
pitched twang. It was difficult to believe that this was the same man
of whom John said second-class poets were so afraid that they thought
twice before rushing into print, the critic who made even first-class
poets fear for their skins. Would it not be better to remain unpublished, one's dreams of glory intact, than to see one's name in a review
entitled "Bad Poets," and to read that those subsumed under this
heading had expressed your "hard lives and hopeless ambition"

> more directly and heart-breakingly than has ever been expressed
> in any work of art; it is as if the writers had sent you their
> ripped-out arms and legs with "This is a poem" scrawled on them
> in lipstick.

Or that one wrote "well-meaning gush" and was

> like someone who keeps showing how well he can hold his liquor
> until he becomes a drunkard . . . [ending] like a man who will
> drink canned heat, rubbing alcohol, anything.

Of all the poets gunned down, probably only Auden, the author of
the "well-meaning gush" who would "become like a man willing to
drink canned heat," etc., had the last word. Making a lightning recovery after reading Randall's article, he said to Stephen Spender, "Jarrell
is in love with me."

On the way to a restaurant after *The Nation* party, a professor
tagged along, trying to push the work of one of his former students
whom he said Randall should publish. When Randall heard the young
poet's name, he screwed up his eyes, drew his lips back over his teeth
in a spasm of pain like a man who had been stabbed between the
shoulder blades, and said, "Oh, *him.* I know his work. I wouldn't think
of publishing it. He's . . . dopey." To a man as brilliant and

as uncompromising as Randall, many, many people were dopey.

Not wishing to be numbered among them, I proceeded with caution in our conversation as we sat next to each other at the restaurant. I had heard of the young woman, Southern, who told Randall at a party that she "just loved" a poem of his that had recently appeared. Randall, who didn't enjoy parties, came to life. "Gee! Did you *really?"* he asked her. Thinking that anyone who loved a poem must have read it carefully, and many times, he questioned her about what specifically she had liked, how she had understood line five, and on and on, while the tongue-tied girl gulped down her drink and prayed for deliverance.

That Randall didn't drink or smoke, disapproved of gossip and sexual innuendoes in conversation, and had no tolerance for small talk —didn't even know what small talk *was*— I had also heard. On the other hand, he knew a great deal about psychology, which had been his undergraduate major. Having decided during the months when John was underground that I needed an occupation that would interest me in the way my nine-to-five job at the Institute did not, I had applied for admission to graduate school to prepare myself for a career in psychology. With Randall that evening, as later, psychology was our subject. His knowledge of the father of psychoanalysis—"a man/sick of too much sweetness"—was broader and deeper than that of many analysts. He knew pages of Freud the way he knew Yeats, Proust and Tolstoy—by heart.

If John was an electric wire, Randall was a whip. You know more or less what to expect from an electric wire. It is alive, it may send out sparks, it may explode, depending on its condition and the demands made upon it. A whip looks benign when it's standing in a corner. But when it's cracked—watch out!

Only once during the years that I knew Randall was I afraid he'd crack the whip at me. An amateur graphologist, he consented to take a test for me if, in return, I'd give him a sample of my handwriting. We took turns being examiner and subject, and agreed that, as neither of us had as yet achieved professional competence we would not interpret our findings for each other. My handwriting was so different from what Randall had expected, however, that he couldn't resist an analysis. His face took on that pained stabbed-in-the-back look, as if I had given him a bad poem. Had I misspelled a word I wondered? (I had been a dyslexic, as John had diagnosed, and spelling remained a weakness of mine, especially if I was hurried or inattentive.)

"Gol-ly!" Randall said, shaking his head in disbelief, "You don't have any lyric *e*'s or *d*'s in your writing . . . and . . . I just can't believe what I see. . . . You're . . . why, Eileen, you're . . . you're . . . optimistic!"

About the lack of lyric (i.e., Greek) *e*'s and *d*'s, I had nothing to say. Since "optimistic" was obviously a pejorative term in Randall's lexicon, and since I didn't believe this characterization to be exact, I said that while I was certainly not pessimistic in the way he and John were, I was also not an optimist. Perhaps an optimistic pessimist would describe more precisely what I was. Randall shook his head: no, no, no. He had seen what he had seen. It was *there* in the handwriting. What difference would this revelation make in our relationship? I wondered. As far as I could tell it made none. Randall seemed to forgive me my grave defect as soon as he had identified it.

If John and Randall had moments of difficulty in their relationship later on, their exchanges at their first meeting were so easy and good-natured that, though it meant missing the train John had said we must take home, we lingered over dinner so they could talk about tennis. And how they bragged! John, who ached to play well (but was temperamentally rather than physically unsuited to the game), bragged that he had once been ballboy for Helen Wills at Forest Hills. Randall could top that and did. They recalled games they'd seen, exchanged stories about memorable shots. Listening to them was like watching a match. They served to each other and plock, plock, plock, plock, back and forth went the ball, while the rest of us at the table swiveled our heads from one to the other.

When Miss Marshall urged us all to go back to her house for dancing, John, who had thrown off his scholar's robes and was rejuvenated, said, yes of course, we'd go along. Did Randall dance? You bet he did. In his two-toned shoes, he moved around the floor like a figure in an early movie, speeding up and slowing down to a tempo only he could hear. Since he maintained only tangential contact with his partner (in a style now commonplace, but in those cheek-to-cheek days uniquely Randall's), one fortunately didn't have to follow closely. John caught my eye as Randall and I skidooed by and signaled with his eyebrows, "Wild!"

It was so late when we finally left Miss Marshall's that John grabbed

Randall skidooing

my hand, ran me to a taxi, from the taxi through Pennsylvania Station, down the steps to the platform just in time to take the last car of the last train to Princeton Junction. After we had caught our breaths, and begun a post-mortem of the party, John told me that because the gossip had it that he was the new editor of *Sewanee,* he had been congratulated almost as much as the guest of honor. Mary McCarthy told him she had heard for certain that he had accepted. When he protested that he hadn't yet made his decision, those who knew the University of the South, and the town of Sewanee, like Robert Lowell (who had had to leave before dinner), told him we'd feel buried alive there. One saw the same homogeneous group of people, most of them considerably older than we were, for lunch and dinner, day in and day out. One made genteel conversation, played bridge and drank. "Sounds like exile to me," John said.

So he would teach at Princeton again. Now that the decision was made, he couldn't wait to get out of town. Close though he was to completing the *Lear,* he would not finish by the time he received the final check from the Foundation. There was a way in which he was relieved. If he had finished and published his work, wouldn't he have felt compelled to go on with scholarship? He had already taken too much time from poetry.* For the moment he was too tired to do anything. He needed a vacation. Robert Lowell had asked us to visit him and his wife, Jean Stafford, in Maine in July. Had Lowell been serious? I asked John. Or had it been party talk? It had sounded, John said, like a firm invitation. They had a house with plenty of room and were hungry for guests; it seemed there was no one to talk to in the town where they lived. Since their place was not far from the Blackmurs' and Nela Walcott's (both of whom had invited us to stay), what about stopping at the Lowells' before going to the Cape?

I was all for it. John was so overworked I had suggested he take the summer off. For the first time since we married, I was free to go away for more than two weeks because my job at the Institute was finished and I wouldn't be looking for part-time work until I began graduate school in the fall. If we sublet our apartment, and visited friends, we could afford to stay away until the beginning of the academic year.

So it was off to Maine.

---

*John put his work aside and his edition of *Lear* remained unfinished at his death, but he continued to feel a strong pull toward Shakespearean scholarship. In the years that I knew him he never ceased turning over in his mind the unsolved problems in the text of *Lear.* From time to time, out of the blue, so it seemed to me, he'd shout, "Ha! I have it," which meant that he thought he had worked out another crux.

VI
DAMARISCOTTA MILLS: JEAN AND CAL

The village of Damariscotta Mills looked as though it had been scrubbed and polished, so bright was the light, so transparent the air, on the July afternoon when a taxi left us at a white clapboard house with green shutters, the home of Jean Stafford and Robert Lowell. Though we were not late, having left Nela's house in Blue Hill in good time, Cal (as he was called) greeted us as if he had been impatient for our arrival. Jean was down at the general store shopping, he said. He would take us up to our room. Our suitcases, heavy with books rather than clothing, he picked up as if they were no burden, and with an appealing gawkiness, loped up the stairs two at a time, his shirttail hanging out in back, his shoes loosely tied, his hair tousled. He was taller than I had remembered, with a sturdy back and strong arms.

We had met only twice before, briefly at *The Nation* party and before that in Princeton when the Lowells had come down to see their old friend the novelist Caroline Gordon (Tate) who had arranged for us to have lunch together. At the Peacock Inn only Caroline had been at ease. The poets, who already knew and admired each other's work, were diffident, Cal scowling and whispering, John holding his head as if his neck was in traction. Jean and I were only a little less wooden.

In the two years since then, Jean's novel *Boston Adventure* had been published, had had a critical success and had been a best seller long enough to allow her to buy the Maine house. The luxury of owning a house, her first, could best be enjoyed by sharing it with friends, for which the previous months of snow, isolation and hard work—Jean finishing *The Mountain Lion,* Cal making the final revisions on *Lord Weary's Castle*—had made them eager. John and I were the first of the summer "influx of poets" and their wives to occupy the pretty guest room at the front of the house, one of the windows of which looked onto the quiet street, the other across a meadow to an imposing mansion.

After we unpacked we joined Cal in the living room. If from the back he had looked like an untidy prep-school athlete, slouched in a chair he appeared slighter and almost delicate, partly because of the contrast between his pale complexion and his dark, tightly curled hair. I was surprised at how handsome he was now that he wasn't frowning. Without eyeglasses (which he had replaced with contact lenses) he had the look of a choirboy: "Oh, there's a terrifying innocence in my face." The impression of innocence vanished in the coming days as the wily poet came out of hiding. Thereafter his good looks seemed more like those of a movie actor or, as John put it, a "matinee idol."

Cal's reputation as a poet was confined to the readers of literary magazines interested enough in his work to have sought out a copy of the limited edition the Cummington Press (a small private house) had published of his slim book of verse, *Land of Unlikeness,* as well as to the high opinion of his mentors, notably John Crowe Ransom and Allen Tate. The years of association with these two Southerners, and with classmates at Kenyon College, explained why it was that this Boston Brahmin spoke with a Southern accent.

What he was saying in his soft voice was that the mansion I had seen from the upstairs window was called "Kavanagh." It had been built by an Irishman, James Kavanagh, who had settled in Maine in about 1800 and had made his fortune from lumber mills and shipyards. Since Jean had not yet returned, and there was time before dinner, if we liked he would show us around the town.

What I remember best about Damariscotta Mills is the sight and sound of water. The village was much like others in Maine that had not yet been discovered by tourists. There were no shops or antique stores, only a post office, a depot and an old-fashioned general store.

COURTESY OF ROBERT GIROUX

Robert Lowell—the good looks of a movie actor

What made it unique was the sound of its industry, the very agreeable noise of the rushing water that furnished power for its mills. Cal showed us the mills and millpond, the river-fed Great Salt Bay that ran seventeen miles to the Atlantic, and Damariscotta Lake. From the lake one saw the rear elevation and octagonal cupola of "Kavanagh." It was in the Federal style and a beauty. Though it looked empty, Cal said it was inhabited by a descendant of the original family, and that in the morning I might catch a glimpse of the owner sitting on the front lawn in her high-backed and hooded wicker chair. We walked through the cemetery that had been part of the property and read the tombstones. James Kavanagh had had seven children. After he and his wife had died, an unmarried brother and sister had lived on in the mansion. Another girl had married a Mulligan, thereby joining the two most prominent families of the community. These prosperous Catholics had given the land and furnished the money for the building of the local church. Jean and he went to Mass at St. Patrick's on Sundays. They would take me with them.

Cal wondered at my interest in the local gentry. His interest was literary (though he didn't say so at the time). Mine was genealogical. I found it extraordinary to be in a village that had been founded by what must have been a branch of my own family. My father's people were Mulligans, my mother's Kavanaghs. We even spelled the name the same way (not the way it's usually spelled, and as Cal spelled it in *The Mills of the Kavanaughs*). I would have liked to know more about these people, to have seen them, in order to look for resemblances to faces I knew from photograph albums. They didn't know their neighbor, Cal said, and had never been inside the big house. Whatever gossip there was about the Kavanagh/Mulligans, Jean would certainly be able to tell me, for she knew the talk of the town.

Dinner was almost ready when we got back. It was time for a drink. In those days it was either rum, the only hard liquor available because of the war, or an inexpensive domestic sherry. In his courteous, even formal way, Cal asked, "Can I offer you a Cuba libre, to celebrate your arrival?"

Jean was eager for news from "the outside world." How was Delmore?

"Fed up with Harvard," John said. "Eager to get out of Cambridge."

We had left Princeton in a light-hearted mood and had broken our trip up to Maine by an overnight stop with Delmore. His mood had been as low as ours was high. As we sat in the Athens Olympia eating shrimp in lemon and oil, he alternately praised John for his writing and scolded him for mismanaging his career. John had made a grave mistake not to take the *Sewanee* offer. He would get stale in Princeton; he'd already been there too long. "You've given up a position of power for one you imagine will give you more time to write. Have you forgotten how you squander time on students?"

As for the way we had planned our vacation . . . There would be trouble. It was well known that the Blackmurs couldn't manage guests. They quarreled all the time.

"We know all about their quarrels," John said. "We've practically lived with them for three years."

"In Maine they're different. You'll see." Delmore looked like an Old Testament prophet of doom.

Nela—whose house was to be our next stop, Delmore knew from extensive underground reports—was drinking heavily.

The Blackmurs and Nela we felt we knew at least as well as Delmore did, so we refused to be put on guard. About the Lowells, however, he could be authoritative. The previous winter they had shared his Ellery Street apartment, where, as Cal recalled years later, they had been woefully incompetent at managing their domestic affairs:

> We couldn't even keep the furnace lit!
> Even when we had disconnected it,
> the antiquated
> refrigerator gurgled mustard gas
> through your mustard-yellow house . . .

As usual in such literary households, the arrangement, which had been entered into sanguinely, had proved unworkable. There had been a quarrel. In Delmore's view, it was Cal who had been to blame.

Jean, who seemed to have forgotten the quarrel, was laughing about Delmore's apartment. It had been up to her to keep the place in order, and the tub, which she had scrubbed until her hands were raw, had defied her efforts.

As she talked, I remembered Delmore's having told us that Jean had been very pretty before the accident. (He hadn't known her then, but had heard it from others who had.) Shortly before Christmas, in 1937, she and Cal had gone on a date to the Crawford House, a nightclub in downtown Boston. On the way home Cal, who was driving, had careened into a stanchion. When Jean regained consciousness she was in a hospital, her face swathed in bandages. A surgeon built her a workable nose, but there was no disguising that it had been badly broken. And one could see signs, as she wrote of Pansy Vanneman in her story "The Interior Castle," that her face had been "darned."

ARNI, COURTESY OF ROBERT GIROUX

Jean Stafford—"eyes that looked permanently welled-up." The book-jacket photo for her novel Boston Adventure

Had I not been told of the accident I would not have guessed that her face had been so badly damaged. Nine healing years had passed since then. Besides, it was her eyes, rather than her nose, or the darns, that struck me. They seemed to be bathed in an excess of fluid, so that they looked permanently welled-up, giving the impression that she had been crying or might do so at any moment. It may have been this, as well as her expression in repose, that made her look sad. The sadness vanished as she talked, when, depending on what she was saying, she looked sly, shrewd, or mischievous, as she twisted her mouth and blew out her cheeks with suppressed glee at the wickedly funny things she said.

At dinner she entertained us with stories about the neighbors, an Episcopalian nun and a bishop's widow, who lived across the street and

frequently invited her to tea. Since they were like characters out of
Trollope, or were on their way to being characters in a Stafford novel,
they should have interested her, but she found that when she was with
them she had a powerful thirst for a beverage stronger than the one
they offered. She was more comfortable with the sheriff, who also
owned the local taxi, the one she hired when she wanted to go to Bath.
Bath, the nearest city, had an importance for her which we were not
to understand until later.

"I have the voice of an undertaker," Jean said. "Don't you agree?"
It's true that it was low and came from deep in her throat. As a
storyteller she was as masterly at pacing and timing as a professional
comedian, holding onto and letting go of words to squeeze the maxi-
mum effect from them, gesturing as she talked with a large capable-
looking hand, palm side up, which she bounced gently as if she were
hefting a small flat stone such as one might scale over water. Her
conversation was studded with sassy expressions children used to use,
and which she continued to use in her stories. Disbelieving what
someone said, for example, she'd counter with a disdainful, "In a pig's
valise." She weighed the phrase to make it sound as if she'd run through
all the animals in the ark, and their valises—the giraffe's, the snake's,
the parrot's—before settling on the pig's as the one that would best
carry her meaning. And when she said "It's none of your beeswax" in
answer to what she thought was a nosy question from Cal, she put on
an expression as rude and anarchistic as Lotty Gump's in "Bad Characters."

John, whose speech had been as formal as his poetry and his style
of dressing when I first met him, had been dismayed by my slangy way
of talking. To please him, I modified my language—up to a point.
When he was being difficult, or when I wanted him to pay attention
to something I was saying, I reverted to pungent college idioms and
phrases from the twenties and thirties (quite different from Randall's)
that my friends and I had sprinkled through our conversation in the
mistaken notion that they made us sound worldly. After a while John
began to use them himself, in italics. Later he not only removed the
italics, he took over the phrases. "No kidding!" "And how!" "That's
the ticket!" "You can say *that* again!" began to sound characteristically
his. Jean's way of talking, her cheeky expressions (which he had not
heard when growing up) delighted him.

That first evening we stayed up late, talking and smoking. Only when we'd run out of cigarettes were we willing to go to bed. In our room, John spun me around and said, "Aren't they *delicious?* Aren't you glad we came?" He was elated the evening had gone so well, especially because I had had second thoughts about how four comparative strangers would get on over a long weekend. And Delmore had hinted darkly— at what? I wondered as I fell asleep.

The next morning in the large sunny kitchen ell that had been added on to the old house, we continued the conversation where we had left off the previous evening. On the way up to bed I had noticed that Jean was setting the table for breakfast and asked if I could help her. Somewhat embarrassed, she said it was an old boarding-house habit she couldn't break. Her father, a writer of Westerns under the nom de plume of Jack Wonder and Ben Delight . . .

"Jack Wonder. Ben Delight. What marvelous names for a writer!" John said.

"Certainly livelier than John Allyn McAlpin Berryman," Cal, said, teasing John about the way he had signed his early poems.

"Or Robert Traill Spence Lowell, IV," John teased back.

"How about *The Transmogrified Calf* for a book title?" Jean asked. Berryman and Lowell would have to think long and hard to come up

Visiting the Lowells in Damariscotta Mills

with the equal. Books with such titles had earned her father so little
money that he hadn't been able to support a wife and four children.
Boulder, Colorado—where they lived—being a college town, her
mother (like Richard's mother) had opened a boarding house. Jean, the
youngest of four, loathed cleaning for and serving others, had resented
her family's poverty and had felt kinship only with her brother Dick,
to whom she was very close. While at the University of Colorado,
where she earned extra money posing for life classes, she made up her
mind that as soon as she could she would "light out" for the East.

How old had she been when she knew she wanted to be a novelist?
John asked.

"I knew it from the time I could read, although I began, age six,
as a poet. Want to hear my first poem? It's called 'Gravel.' I've just
given it to my character Molly in *The Mountain Lion.*" In a gravelly
voice, Jean recited:

> Gravel, gravel on the ground
> Lying there so safe and sound,
> Why is it you look so dead?
> Is it because you have no head?

"From a six-year-old, it shows promise, don't you think?" Cal asked
John.

"More than the science-fiction novel I wrote when I was twelve and
thought was, as Eileen would say, 'hot stuff.'"

Her escape from Boulder had been made possible by a graduate
fellowship to study philosophy at Heidelberg.

John (who was a year older) had gone to Heidelberg for the spring
"vac" from Cambridge. Could they have been there at the same time?

By then Jean had returned to the United States and was teaching
at Stephens College. When I asked her how she liked teaching, she
made a face like a gargoyle and drawled, "I'd as lief go to hell in a
handbasket." Teaching interfered with writing. She had a novel under
way when she left Stephens and went back to Boulder to attend a
summer writing school. At the school she met Ford Madox Ford.

"Ford was very important in our lives," Cal said. "He introduced
Jean and me. It was also he who introduced me to the Tates."

Cal had come under Allen Tate's influence at a crucial moment in
his life. As early as his prep-school days at St. Mark's (where, because

of his scruffy habits and rebellious pronouncements, he'd been nick-named Cal, after the monstrous Roman emperor Caligula), he'd known he wanted to be a poet.

"At South Kent, the terror of any boy who was bookish, and didn't go out for sports was that he'd be called 'she.' You can bet I didn't read and I played football," John said. "You obviously didn't mind your nickname."

"It was certainly better than being called 'Bobby,' my name at home. And I must confess that I wanted to be on the football team as much as I wanted to write poetry."

"So did I. Or at least my mother convinced me that I did. Crew, I finally discovered, was my sport. Myopia no problem there."

The myopics, one wearing horn-rimmed glasses, the other contact lenses, commiserated.

Harvard was no more congenial than St. Mark's had been to Cal. Home was less congenial than either. He didn't say so that night, but John knew from Tate that as a child, "unseen and all-seeing," Cal had overheard his parents' nightly quarrels, as Delmore, Richard and John had heard theirs. Like them, too, Cal had been torn between a powerful mother and an ineffectual father. In self-protection, Cal had wanted to get away from home and escape from the kind of life his parents led.

"Cal's mother put on white gloves every morning and ran her fingers over the mantle and table tops to see if the maids had dusted properly," Jean said, puffing out her cheeks. "For cocktail parties she hired 'accommodators' who passed the hors d'oeuvre and served the drinks. At a signal from her that the party had gone on long enough, the accommodators swooped down to remove all the glasses (I kept a firm grip on mine) and flicked the lights off and on, to announce that it was time for the guests to go home."

Beneath this ridicule of Mrs. Lowell's domestic practices one felt that the Boston life Cal had wanted to escape was exactly the kind of life Jean, in Boulder, had dreamed of moving into. She didn't object to the listing:

> Lowell, Mr & Mrs Rob't T S Jr
> (Jean Stafford)   H' 39
>   Ken 40

in the Boston *Social Register,* which she kept on her desk next to Fowler's *English Usage* and the Merck *Manual.*

Cal's announcement to his parents that he was planning to leave college to marry Anne Dick, a girl some years his senior, had provoked a violent dispute with his parents, in the course of which he struck his father:

> I knocked my father down. He sat on the carpet—
> my mother calling from the top of the carpeted stairs,
> their glass door locking behind me, no cover . . .

The Lowells, who had become increasingly worried about their son, were now convinced he was crazy and should be locked up. Dr. Merrill Moore, a sonneteer/psychiatrist and friend of the family's, persuaded them that it would be more therapeutic to allow Cal to go South in the company of Ford Madox Ford to visit the Tates.

The hospitable Tates, whose Tennessee house "Benfolly" was already crammed with family and friends, told Cal that if he wanted to stay more than a few days he'd have to pitch a tent, never for a moment dreaming that he would do just that. He camped on their lawn not for days or weeks, but for months.

"It was a wonder I even got any writing done in those days," Caroline said, reminiscing to me years later. "What I spent my time doing was feeding poets."

In the fall, Cal transferred to Kenyon College, to study under Ransom and, informally, with Jarrell (who was three years his senior). Near the end of his time at Kenyon he went to Boulder with Ford and there met Jean.

"Cal's parents were no happier about me than they had been about Anne Dick," Jean said. "Mrs. Lowell, introducing me to her Beacon Hill friends, would say, 'Tell us, Jean dear, where *is* it you come from?' Rolling the word around in my throat, and using my undertaker voice, I'd say, 'Colorado,' at which the assembled guests would turn to each other and murmur—as if I'd said I was from the upper reaches of the Orinoco!"

That she was also the girl who had been with Cal in the automobile accident didn't endear her to her future mother-in-law. Although Jean must have suffered greatly as a result of the smash-up, she talked about it with clinical detachment, as if what was of interest were the medical details. Or she made a joke of the lawsuit she had brought against the Lowells' insurance company. "I sued for twenty-five thousand and got a measly four thousand. The lawyers forbade us to meet until the case was settled. The prohibition gave a certain piquancy to our clandestine rendezvous; we saw each other more than ever."

After Jean had recovered and was back in Colorado, she received a telegram from Cal, who was then at Louisiana State University. It read, "Have job. Come at once."

"What I didn't understand . . ."

Cal interrupted, shouting, "Calumny! Here comes the black tongue!"

". . . was that the job he had was for *me*—to be secretary in the office of the *Southern Review*." With her salary, and Cal's small income, they were able to marry while he was in graduate school.

The following year, when they moved to New York, they both had jobs at the Catholic publishing house, Sheed and Ward. "Once," Jean said, "when the Sheeds invited us to the country for the weekend, I packed a typewriter case, the only thing we had which could pass for luggage, with two pairs of pajamas, unironed, and two toothbrushes. As our taxi pulled into the driveway, the butler came down the stairs, opened the door and before I could stop him, whisked away the typewriter case. After being greeted by the Sheeds, we were shown to our room. There was the typewriter case, open on the luggage rack. The toothbrushes were in a glass in the bathroom. The two pairs of unironed pajamas were neatly arranged, one on either side of the bed. Cal thought it was a scream. You can imagine, Eileen, how I felt— *un* ironed."

The Bears were born the following year. They were a family of imaginary animals whose exploits Jean and Cal invented and told each other about. They had come into being when the Lowells lived with the Tates in Tennessee in a remarkably productive household—Caroline writing *The Women on the Porch,* Jean, *Boston Adventure,* Cal, *Land of Unlikeness* and Allen, *Jefferson Davis.* Since the Tates had not yet been converted, the Lowells went to Mass alone. To get to the church required a trip by bus, a long wait, and another bus. The Bears helped them pass the travel time. John and I never heard a full episode (the Bears were very private), but there were many references to their activities, past and present. One very important Bear wore contact lenses. Another, female, had a black tongue.

Throughout the weekend literary talk ran in counterpoint to autobiography. Not since Delmore had John found a contemporary who was as obsessed with poetry as he was, and who felt that next to the greatest joy of all—the "tortured joy" of writing poems—was the joy of discussing them. Cal, like Delmore and John, believed that in heaven, or paradise, or "the chambers of the end" (as John later called it), poets would spend eternity in one another's company, exclaiming, explicating, parsing, doing what Cal and John were doing now—talking about poetry. They began with their own generation: Schwartz, Jarrell, Dylan Thomas, Ted Roethke, Elizabeth Bishop, Karl Shapiro. Each had his favorites, and urged them on the other. Randall was Cal's; Delmore, John's. They worked backward to their mentors: Tate, Ransom, Van Doren, Blackmur, Hart Crane. Tate's influence on both of them was immense. John had been his student in a summer school course at Columbia and had had "the top of my head blown off" by Allen's brilliance and erudition. The summer after John returned from England he stayed with the Tates in Connecticut, showed Allen what he had been working on, and decided that there was no better reader, no one from whom he could learn more about composition.

Having anthologies by heart, John and Cal had no need for books as they moved abroad to Spender, MacNeice, Auden. John, who had met Auden in his tutor's rooms at Cambridge, and again at a New Year's Eve party in London at which Hedli Anderson (MacNeice) sang Britten's setting of Auden's "O tell me the truth about love,"—which John, in falsetto, sang a stanza of for us—told the story of his having gone from Detroit to Ann Arbor to hear the English poet lecture. "It was one of his first public appearances in the United States. The hall was filled to capacity: Auden fans in a high state of excitement. Wystan (as of course I didn't call him) appeared, looking as disheveled as an unmade bed, draped his great height over the lectern, rested one foot on top of the other and began to talk. In a few minutes it was clear to the fans that they were going to understand little that he said in his high-pitched, nasal voice, apart from an occasional name like Mann and Kafka (which he pronounced in an Audenesque way, with an exaggeratedly flat 'a'), and a few unimportant words like 'actually,' pronounced 'icktually.' There were those who wondered if he was speaking Icelandic."

When they reached the giants of the twentieth century—Yeats, Eliot, Pound—Cal, knowing that John had been even more power-fully influenced by Yeats than by Auden, asked him if he had ever met the master.

"You can imagine I was mad to see him." While at Cambridge John had summoned the courage to write Yeats. Receiving a letter in reply, he set off on a pilgrimage to Ireland. "I arrived in Dublin to find he *wasn't there!* He'd gone to London."

"You'd written you were coming?"

"Never occurred to me. I was so concerned with my own arrange-ments that I hadn't given a thought to what Willie might be up to. I imagined that all I had to do was go to his house and knock on the door. After a few days of paralysis, during which I couldn't think what to do, I recovered sufficiently to enjoy Dublin. I went to the Abbey Theatre one night, went backstage, commented on the performance, offered suggestions to the actors (the modesty of the young!). The troupe took me under its wing, showed me around, introduced me to Yeats' daughter, Anne, at the Cuala Press." To Cal, John said, "Did you ever fancy yourself in love with Anne?"

"Didn't every young poet?"

"Having imagined her as a dazzling beauty, I saw myself as Yeats' son-in-law. I was crushed to find she was quite plain."

On his return to Cambridge John took the trouble to do what he should have done before setting out for Ireland. He wrote Yeats, asking for an appointment and received an invitation to tea at the Athenaeum. Dylan Thomas, whom John was seeing a good deal of at the time, had

> Scorn bottomless for elders: we were twenty-three
> but Yeats I worshipped: he was amused by this,
> all day the day set for my tea with the Great Man
> he plotted to turn me up drunk.

"Dylan had this idea that all serious poets should be serious drinkers. He found my Cantabrigian sherry-sipping 'effete.' "

The meeting had gone, John said in answer to Cal's question, the way meetings with famous men usually go. John had looked forward to it for so long, and had expected such oracular pronouncements, that

Dylan Thomas as he looked when John was seeing him in London

disappointment was inevitable. It was Yeats the Public Man, the Senator, he'd seen, the mask clamped on so tightly there was no getting behind it.

"How did he look? What was he wearing?" Jean, the novelist, wanted the specifications.

"Impressive. Very. Surprisingly tall, carefully dressed in well-cut tweeds, wearing a bow tie."

(Ah ha! I thought. So that's where John's habit of wearing bow ties came from. I hadn't known before.)

"The flowing white hair looked even whiter against his dark skin. He was very dark. Not at all Anglo-Irish in complexion. I wondered if he had a touch of jaundice."

What did they talk about?

"Poetry, of course. But not *enough* about poetry. Yeats got off on [Oliver St. John] Gogarty, his friend and fellow-Dubliner [Joyce's erstwhile friend, the Buck Mulligan of *Ulysses*]. He urged me to read Gogarty's memoir, *As I Walked Down Sackville Street.* I rushed out to buy it as soon as the audience was over, read it at once and found it to be of no interest *whatever.*"

"What do you think are Yeats's greatest poems?" Cal asked.

"Out of the early work, 'The Folly of Being Comforted' and 'That the Night Come.' The supreme achievement, in *The Wild Swans at Coole,* is the title poem, together with 'Major Robert Gregory' and 'A Deep-Sworn Vow.' That's what I believe at the moment. It changes of course."

"What are his three greatest lines?"

"Greatest lines? Must we select?" John fought this narrowness.

"Cal gets that from Randall," Jean said, not quite sotto voce and looking as if she'd swallowed her tongue. "Randall has a passion for The Three Greatest. Cal's caught it."

Cal, scowling with concentration, looking again like the man we'd met in Princeton, wouldn't be deflected: They must find the three greatest lines.

John said, "I'll give you six instead:

> Unwearied still, lover by lover,
> They paddle in the cold
> Companionable streams or climb the air;
> Their hearts have not grown old;
> Passion or conquest, wander where they will,
> Attend upon them still."

The giants of the twentieth century were taking so much time that the poets clearly would not finish with them, despite the single-minded and nonstop talk, by the time the weekend was over. One necessary interruption was Sunday Mass. John the Apostate stayed home while I went with Cal, in a proper suit, hair brushed and shoelaces tied (at Jean's prompting) and Jean, hatted, with missal in hand, to St. Patrick's, a pretty country church designed by Nicholas Codd, the architect of Kavanagh, with a bell said to have been made by Paul Revere.

For me it was an unusual and agreeable experience to be accompanied to Mass. John and I didn't know any Catholics, and many of our friends were openly antagonistic to religion. John was not. Although he was unable to believe, it was very important to him that I should. As I admitted to him, I was a little in awe of converts, for they had chosen a discipline I so often rebelled against. And, having been instructed as adults, they were far more knowledgeable about theology and ritual than I.

On the way to Mass Jean said that, looking for an antidote to her mother's Scotch Presbyterianism, she had received instruction and joined the Church while in college. What she didn't say, but what I felt, was that she had been growing cool toward Catholicism and might have been on the point of giving it up had it not been for Cal's conversion at the time of their marriage. Privately she told me that Cal was a puritan at heart. He had become increasingly and rigidly devout, focusing on the things in the Church she found least attractive: spiritual exercises, retreats, good works. And what was "maddening and enervating" was that he insisted she follow him in them.

My having been what Caroline Gordon called a "cradle Catholic" interested them as much as their conversions interested me. Even more, they were intrigued, as Delmore had been, by my having been an orphan. I thought at first that Jean's questions about my childhood came from a novelist's avidity for details. Then I realized that she felt I had lived out one of her childhood fantasies. She had wanted desperately to be an orphan. If she bristled when Mrs. Lowell pointed out that she came from a barbarous section of the country, and from parents "one hadn't heard of," Jean also cringed because her own judgment coincided with her mother-in-law's. If she wasn't a Mexican like Rose Fabrizio in *The Bleeding Heart,* or a "rube" like Emma in *Children Are Bored on Sunday,* or the child of foreigners (the mother a domestic) like Sonia in *Boston Adventure,* she felt that she was. Sonia longs to be adopted by Miss Pride, Rose by the cultivated and fatherly looking gentleman she sees in the library. I hadn't been adopted, but as Jean saw it my orphanhood had given me an enviable freedom. What happens to those who free themselves from parents and choose substitutes is a theme she treated with irony in her fiction.

Cal, too, had wished for the freedom to choose his parents. He had left home and camped on the property of the parents he would like to have had, Caroline and Allen, returning to them with Jean after marrying. (Allen was not pleased when he heard that Cal referred to him as "Father Tate.") Anne in *The Mills of the Kavanaughs* is an orphan who is adopted by Harry Kavanaugh's mother. Randall Jarrell, reviewing the book, said of the poem, "Yes, Robert Lowell would act like this [like Anne] if he were a girl . . . but whoever saw a girl like Robert Lowell?"

After Mass Jean repeated what she had said the previous evening: John and I mustn't think of leaving as originally planned. We must stay, Cal said. How could John even consider going when they hadn't discussed "Lycidas"?

It didn't take much coaxing. We were having such a good time we were dying to stay. And we felt they were pleading with us not only because they, too, were enjoying our company: It was also because they wanted not to be alone—although why we couldn't have said.

My concern was over the labor it would be for Jean. She was a conscientious hostess and a housekeeper so meticulous that her mother-in-law's glove would have been spotless after an inspection of her rooms. She loved the furniture she had carefully selected, the vases she kept filled with flowers, the painting of Chartres by Biala (Ford Madox Ford's wife), all of them bought with *Boston Adventure* money. Sometimes when the poets were talking about Hopkins, or Keats, or Wordsworth, she'd take an oiled chamois out of the drawer of a small commode next to her chair and caress its highly polished surface. With little fuss she conjured up three meals a day from the limited stocks of the general store, rows of S.S. Pierce cans from her pantry shelves, vegetables from local gardens, and insisted on doing it all herself. For such a hostess two guests meant a good deal of work. We agreed to delay our departure for Cape Cod on condition that Jean allow me to help with the preparation of meals. John and Cal, or Cal and I, would take turns doing the dishes.

Once it was settled, Jean worried that we might run out of "hootch." The bottle of rum opened when we arrived was almost empty. Cal said we could do without liquor; John and I drank little and he wasn't drinking at all. "Maybe *you* can do without it," Jean said, "but it gives me the wimwams to be in a house that's bone-dry." The next morning when I asked the neighbors' permission to telephone to the Cape, Jean called her friend the sheriff and arranged to be taken

to Bath. In Maine, liquor was sold at state stores. The closest one was
in Bath.

The days of our visit, which stretched from a weekend to two weeks,
fell into a casual order. Although neither Cal nor John was supposedly
working, there was never a time when they were not working. After
breakfast and a good long recitation:

> Bitter constraint, and sad occasion dear,
> Compels me to disturb your season due;
> For Lycidas is dead, dead ere his prime,

and explication of "Lycidas," which they had no trouble agreeing was
one of the greatest poems in the language (though there was the usual
push/pull over the Three Greatest Lines), or another poem that one
or the other had come out of sleep thinking about, Cal went up to
his room. Sprawled on the bed like a big kid, he read and wrote until
noon. At a small desk in the guest room, John sat immobile for long
periods, one leg snaked around the other. He pulled on his beardless
chin, pushed his glasses back up on the bridge of his nose with his
spatulate middle finger, tapped his teeth with his pen preparatory to
putting a word on paper.

Jean, whose desk was in the downstairs hall between the kitchen and
the parlor (a position I would have thought too exposed until she
explained to me that she worked best when she had a view out of as
many windows as possible, so that she could keep an eye on the
comings and goings of her neighbors), was working on a new novel.
Or trying to. She was not unhappy to be interrupted by the postman
who often brought her fan mail, which she read avidly and answered
immediately. "Listen to this," she'd say, calling to me out on the lawn
where, lounging in a canvas deck chair I was preparing in a desultory
way for graduate school, and read me a sentence or paragraph that
tickled her fancy.

Periodically Cal, shoeless, appeared at the side of her desk with a
draft of a poem for her to type. Draft after draft after draft. This
astonished me because I couldn't imagine John asking me to type for
him. For one thing he was better at it than I; for another, he never

showed Richard, or me, or anyone else, a poem until the penultimate version. Jean claimed that Cal was the world's champion reviser, sometimes with startling results. "A poem which had begun with the title, 'To Jean: On Her Confirmation' . . ."

"Don't listen. She lies. She lies." Cal tried to shout her down.

". . . finished by being called, 'To a Whore at the Brooklyn Navy Yard.' "

The typing chore Jean seemed to accept as a wifely duty. That Cal was a "mechanical moron," who couldn't play a phonograph, much less type, was only another sign of his massive incompetence in dealing with everyday life. Were it not for her, she said, he would go for days without eating, sleeping or bathing. She would have liked to go to Boston or New York from time to time, but how could she leave Cal to look after himself and the house?

I had moments of worrying about the same thing with John. Less obviously dependent than Cal, John nevertheless required a good deal of attention. As usual with him, ambivalence made his wishes confusing, to himself and to me. After a period of resistance, he had seemed to accept the idea of my going to graduate school. But hadn't he also seemed to accept my wish to have a child? Stifling my uneasiness, I returned to studying, and to enjoying what John, looking back on the summer of 1946, called his "last summer of innocence."

Writing, reciting, reading, studying, talking. Our sedentary life we interrupted in the afternoon for a walk to the mills or a swim in Damariscotta Lake. That is to say, Cal and John and I walked and swam. Jean, who knew the name of every tree, bush, flower and weed, ventured out infrequently, preferring to observe nature through the window. Aquaphobia, which she'd suffered from since childhood, kept her from swimming or boating. She confessed that as a child taking a bath had made her so anxious she had been able to manage only by organizing an elaborate ritual around it (like Molly in *The Mountain Lion*).

At 6:30 or so we'd have a drink on the lawn, weather permitting, as it often did on those lovely long July evenings, followed by dinner, which might consist of ramekins of crabmeat (a specialty of the house) and summertime dishes like corn on the cob and strawberry shortcake.

If it was Cal and John's turn to clean up, Jean and I would hear them reciting to each other—Hopkins, Donne, Marvell, Crashaw, or recent Lowell and Berryman—Cal in his soft Southern voice, John, taut, passionate, with the vestiges of an English accent. At a poem a plate, the work went slowly.

When it was my turn with Cal, we might begin by talking about J. F. Powers, Dorothy Day, Jacques Maritain or Emanuel Chapman (the philosopher my sister had studied with at Hunter College, whose work Cal knew and thought more profound than Maritain's). Often our kitchen duty ended in clowning and hilarity. John, sitting in the other room with Jean, whose somber mood was growing more obvious every day, wondered what could possibly be so funny. After one such session he startled me by asking, with his "mad charm" smile, "You're not falling in love with Cal, are you?" In the five years we had been together this was the first sign he gave of jealousy (at least of a romantic sort; he could be extremely jealous of my sister and especially of her children, though he loved them and was, for the most part, a devoted brother-in-law as well as a highly entertaining uncle). Cal was certainly very attractive, and far more fun than I could have guessed from our pre-Damariscotta meetings. But I couldn't imagine being in love with anyone but John—as I thought he knew. He did, he said. Then why had he asked? Just checking. He had a feeling . . . he wasn't sure . . . he'd tell me later.

Since I never again saw Cal quite so buoyant, and saw him afterward often when his mood had swung dangerously high or low and illness had robbed him of his youthfulness, it's difficult to recapture his light-hearted playfulness at the sink. What was a chore for others was clearly a game for one who wasn't ordinarily called upon to help out. If he washed, there would be soapsuds and water all over, down his trousers and on the floor, as he gestured during one of his imitations —he was a wicked mimic—of Randall or Allen. If I washed, he played the boss of the job, handing me back a pot and saying, "Ah leen, Ah do believe you could put a little more elbow grease on this." One had the sense that he was enjoying a rare period of equilibrium. That summer, before the publication of *Lord Weary's Castle,* with the fame he had dreamed of in sight, he was still free of the demands fame brings.

When we joined the others in what Jean called the parlor, and Cal called "the soft room" (the chairs there being more comfortable than those in the dining room), we'd settle down to more talk, this time not about poetry but about people. It was a custom the Lowells had picked up, Cal said, from living with the Tates. After a hard day of writing, they all felt there was nothing so refreshing as gossip. Isolated as they had been in Tennessee, they had provided their own entertainment, delighting in the "amiable venom" with which they went over their friends and acquaintances. Each night, sitting around the fire, a drink in hand, Allen or Caroline would say, "Let's see, who should it be tonight? What about John Berryman?"

John winced. He could imagine the scene clearly, having been with them when they said, "Let's do the Lowells" (which was how he had learned of Cal's fight with his father and much else besides that Cal would have been distressed, though hardly surprised, to know had provided the subject for an evening's entertainment). The summer John stayed with the Tates in Connecticut, he was so disoriented by his return to America after two years abroad, and so distraught over his relationship with his mother and the separation from B., that he had not been an easy guest. He could well imagine the comedy his behavior could make in the Tates' retelling.

In any case John was not completely comfortable with gossip. His position stood midway between Randall's and Cal's. While he enjoyed it if it was about people he didn't know or didn't like, he was very protective of his friends. He was passionately loyal toward them, and wanted them to like one another as much as he liked each of them (and was crushed that they seldom did). He wished that Cal and Delmore admired each other as much as he admired both, and was saddened that there had been a rift between them. John was only willing to discuss Delmore up to a point in the evening gossip sessions. He didn't say that we had noticed Delmore was drinking too much when we had stayed with him in Cambridge (Delmore, who only four years earlier had told us Jews didn't drink). Nor did he say that there had been an obvious deterioration in the way Delmore was living, and that he seemed increasingly suspicious of the motives of others. Though John roared with laughter—one couldn't have resisted—at Cal's imitation of a Blackmurian monologue on the subject of blueberry bogs, in which the bogs were treated as seriously and analytically as Henry

James might have been, he would not have considered gossiping about
our visit with the Blackmurs.

The visit had been a disaster. We had been charmed by the studio in
which the Blackmurs lived, and found the view from their lawn all
Richard had promised. In Maine he looked healthier than he had
during the winter, and was free of his nagging sinus trouble. From their
bedroom above ours, we could hear his bellow of joy as he got up in
the morning. He was in Maine, in God's country, and could breathe
again. In a blue work shirt and corduroy trousers—"Here men wear
natural colours, mostly blue"—he looked younger and trimmer. His
eyes were as blue as the water of a Maine pond. Even before breakfast
was over, however, we wondered if we had interpreted the bellow
correctly. Helen, whose property it was, and who loved Maine at least
as much as Richard did, was more taciturn than usual. Although they
had invited us to come (or had it been Richard alone who had
extended the invitation?), and had set the date, Helen hinted that we
had arrived at an inconvenient time. The workmen were putting in
a new well. It was Richard's fault that the job wasn't finished. If he
was going to dawdle over the newspaper again this morning . . .
Richard, hiding behind the paper, pretended deafness. He was addicted
to newsprint. In Princeton he could kill a morning over *The New York
Times,* fighting the conscience that told him he should get to the
typewriter. In Maine, the local gazette seemed equally engrossing.

Helen explained to us, for Richard's benefit, that Harrington workmen were contemptuous of a householder who didn't supervise them.
They had been dragging out the job, doubling its cost, because he
wasn't attentive. As soon as we could, John and I excused ourselves to
go for a walk, thinking that, left alone, Richard would join the men
outside. Instead, he got up from the table only to move to a more
comfortable chair and continue reading, so Helen said when we returned.

While she and I cleaned up after lunch and dinner (a lengthy process
because we had to pump the water and heat it), Helen complained
about Richard. He had turned down a Rockefeller grant (news to us)
which would have allowed him to live year-round in Maine and write,
preferring instead to "sell out" to academia. "I married a writer, not

Helen and Richard at a happier time

a professor," she said grimly. "I hate Princeton. It suffocates me. Richard does nothing but sit in that damn Balt [a cafeteria on Nassau Street, opposite the campus, where his cronies on the faculty hung out] and jaw. That book on Henry Adams will never be finished. It's being killed by talk."

When we joined the men after dinner, and I was listening with relief to John and Richard talk about *The Golden Bough,* or some other book John had picked out of Richard's library and was rereading, Helen would wrest the conversation from them to go over the same ground again, this time attacking Richard directly. Why hadn't he accepted the Rockefeller grant? Why didn't he finish the Adams?

John, too, wondered about the Adams. Knowing how close it was to completion, he had asked himself what was holding Richard back. Was it that Richard had never been to Europe? It would be difficult to write about Adams without having seen London, Paris, Chartres,

Mont-Saint-Michel; yet Richard showed no impatience to go abroad.
Aside from suffering from severe inertia, which made him reluctant
even to go to New York, he was troubled about not speaking a foreign
language. One could teach oneself to read French, and that he had
done. One could not teach oneself to speak it. This was one of the areas
in which he suffered from a lack of formal education. John had pointed
out to him that few American writers, no matter how well-educated,
could speak a second language—"It's their Achilles' heel"—because of
the absurd way languages are taught in this country. "Any debutante
with a year in a Swiss finishing school is more fluent than most
American intellectuals."

That there were probably more complicated reasons why Richard
didn't finish, John knew well, for nothing about Richard was simple.
When professors on campus taunted him—"Well, when are we going
to see your opus, Dick?"—as if he were a graduate student and the
Adams book a dissertation, John became infuriated: How dare they
patronize a critic of Richard's stature? What the hell did they know
about his kind of writing? And now, when Helen attacked him, John,
though sympathetic with her point of view (Richard *should* have taken
the Rockefeller grant), felt he must defend a fellow writer. So he tried
to head her off. To no avail. She kept it up, and kept it up. Richard
answered her in abstractions, or merely said, "Hmmmmmmm." Whatever his response, it enraged her, making her attack harder and harder
until she provoked a counterattack.

Even if John and I had been more adroit socially, we would not
have been able to divert them. They had been waiting for an audience
to say to each other things they didn't say when alone. The following
morning Richard would be mulish, Helen sullen, the workmen lethar-
gic. The evening we went over to Blue Hill to have dinner with Nela,
in a moment alone with her I appealed for advice. Nothing I said
surprised her. The bickering went on whenever the Blackmurs had
house guests. I should not listen to Helen. Although everything she said
was undoubtedly true, it had been going on for sixteen years. John and
I should turn a deaf ear to their scenes. We tried, without success.
Privately we sided now with one, now with the other, were angry now
with one, now with the other. We squirmed and ached to see two
people we loved suffer so much at each other's hands.

One night John, keyed up by an horripilating quarrel (reminiscent of the quarrels between his parents?), stayed up late reading because he couldn't sleep. He found himself thinking over the geography of the Blackmurs' property—the lawn, the sheer bluff, the water in the middle distance, and in the far distance the island P'tit Manaan:

> . . . it occurred to me
> that *one* night, instead of warm pajamas,
> I'd take off all my clothes
> & cross the damp cold lawn & down the bluff
> into the terrible water & walk forever
> under it out toward the island.

What I had not understood when I had extracted the promise from him not to threaten suicide, and did not take in for some time even after he told me, as he did the next morning, that he had had a premonition of death by suicide, was that behind the theatricality of his threats was something far more dangerous. Suicide threatened him. He felt it as a kind of undertow, sucking at him, sometimes feebly, sometimes with terrifying strength, always, always there:

> he feels his death tugging within him wild
> to slide loose & to fall:

Once I saw this, and learned to distinguish the play-acting from the genuine terror, suicide became my adversary. No clearer in my mind than he was in his about what constellation of events would be strong enough to allow him to succumb, I lived with a low-grade apprehension that periodically flared up. As far as I knew, the premonition in Maine was the first waking threat.

On our morning walk, his nerves raw, John said he couldn't take any more of the Blackmurs' quarrels. We must leave. I tried to think of a graceful way to go. There was no way that wouldn't wound them, John said, though after we left they would be united by our offense. We decided that, since Nela was expected for lunch, we would ask if we could return to Blue Hill, to begin our visit with her earlier than planned. We packed our bags in haste when, full of sympathy, she agreed and we made an awkward departure, feeling utterly miserable.

No, this was not the kind of story John would tell the Lowells. When Jean began to question him about the Blackmurs' marriage, saying she'd heard a good deal of gossip about how badly they got on, he changed the subject: What writers had been at Yaddo when she was there? "The star," Jean said with heavy irony, "was Carson McCullers." One knew from the way she pronounced the name that the author of *The Heart Is a Lonely Hunter* would furnish us with more than one evening's entertainment in the parlor.

Philip Rahv, the *Partisan Review* editor, a Marxist and literary essayist (who was one of the critics responsible for the Henry James revival), had with his wife Natalie rented a house not far away from Damariscotta Mills. One evening, by way of diversion, the sheriff came over in his old Buick to drive us to their place. En route Jean warned us about the Rahvs' cat. Jean also had a cat whose intelligence and grace she boasted of in the way a fond parent boasts of a child. It was very much her cat, but occasionally Cal picked it up and played with it, imitating the way Caroline Gordon talked to her dachshund. Instead of talking to the dog, as most dog owners do, Caroline amused herself by pretending that the dog talked to her. It called her "Mama," and commented trenchantly on their house guests, especially visiting poets.

Hart Crane was memorialized in a Gordon/dachshund dialogue. In 1925, when the Tates were living in Patterson, New York, and were very broke, they had taken in the even more impoverished Crane. As the winter wore on, there were many disagreements between them. (During periods when they weren't speaking, they communicated by slipping notes under each other's doors.) On one occasion, when Caroline reproved Crane for being inconsiderate, he made the mistake of defending himself by saying he was "nervous and sensitive," and shouldn't be held to the standards of behavior demanded of others. Afterward, Caroline would hold her dachshund up in the air, as Cal now held Jean's cat, and have it say to her, "I'm nervous and sensitive, aren't I, Mama? Like my Uncle Hart Crane." The nervous and sensitive young poets who had stayed with the Tates, and had learned to fear

Caroline's tongue, were so relieved that it was Crane, and not them, whom she mocked in this way that whenever they heard this story they fell into fits of laughter.

(Although he sometimes played with Jean's cat, I don't think Cal was interested in animals, except perhaps in birds, but I shocked him one evening when I struck out at a luna moth. Never having seen one before, I was frightened and sought, reflexively, to protect myself. Cal explained what it was, and said I musn't kill it. Jean later told me that he had remonstrated with her for setting traps for the mice whose gnawing behind their bedroom wall had kept her awake on winter nights. "Why not let them live?" he'd said, "there's food enough for all of us." "This, mind you, from a violent man!" Jean added.)

The Rahvs' cat, according to Jean, was scary. It was likely to reach through one of their lattice-back chairs with a prehensile paw and grab at one's arm. Also, she suspected it was a snoop and a spy. It eavesdropped on the conversation, and, like Saki's Tobermory, slunk off to its room to record what had been said. Certainly the cat, if it was listening, got an earful of literary gossip that night. I was on my guard against being grabbed (the cat *did* look dangerous), and was less attentive to the conversation than usual. When Natalie saw my uneasiness, she took her pet in her lap and stroked it, which led Philip to expound, in his rich Lithuanian accent, a theory he had: A woman who says she wants a child would, if she understood herself better, realize that what she really wanted was a cat.

A *cat?* It certainly wasn't what I wanted.

"Think how much suffering in the world such self-knowledge would save!" Philip went on, better and better pleased with his theory.

Surprised at finding himself in a "roomful of Catholics" instead of Marxists, Philip questioned Jean closely about the religious ladies of Damariscotta Mills, whose activities he seemed to feel must be a cover for an underground life Jean had not yet discovered. Hooding her eyes and adopting Philip's conspiratorial tone, she reported him as having said, when he spotted Sister Geraldine walking on the street outside her house, "Look! Look! There goes Sister in her nun's clothes," as if he'd caught the nun in one of her disguises.

A few years later at a New Year's Eve party at Nancy and Dwight Macdonald's, Philip recalled our evening together in Maine, and asked me what I thought of the recent conversion of the Tates and of the

Lowells' defection from the Church. As we sat side by side on a couch, Philip gave me a friendly nudge in the ribs and asked, "Do you write?" I said I did not. "Then I don't get it. I see why they become Catholics. They're looking for new metaphors. But what do you get out of it?" I'm afraid my speechlessness made Philip put me down as what he would have called "a dumb broad."

Either the night of our visit to the Rahvs', or soon thereafter, Jean and John stayed up talking, and were still up when Cal and I came down to breakfast. We had become increasingly aware that Jean was suffering from insomnia, aware also that she made more frequent trips to Bath than were necessary to supply John and me with a predinner cocktail. Cal's discreet attempts to control her drinking had led her to stow a glass of sherry behind the cookbooks in the kitchen, and to keep a hidden supply so that the house would never be "bone-dry." She made a joke to John and me about the capacious shoulder-strap pocket-book she bought in which she could hide a flask, so that when she visited the religious ladies she could duck into the bathroom and have a nip.

Her appearance, too, gave her mood away. She wore the same hound's-tooth checked slacks and baggy black sweater every day, disguising her model's figure as effectively as if she was wearing a habit. She let her ash-blond hair hang limp, or covered it with a pointed hat such as Lolly Gump might have fancied. What vanity Jean had was for her house.

Delmore, the intriguer, had hinted—yes, now I put it together— that she was interested in another man (himself perhaps?). He had even insinuated this to Cal, whereupon Cal had socked him. The fistfight that ensued brought the Ellery Street winter to a dramatic close, and explained the coolness between the two men.

If Jean had been in love with another man that winter, by summer it was her house that had become the object of her affection. And yet the house, which for so many years had been a dream, had become a subject for nightmares. The idyll of a long, silent spring in the country, with uninterrupted days for writing, had made her feel locked in and isolated as spring delayed and snow continued to fall. She and Cal had been too much alone.

We thought at first that Jean was suffering from the letdown writers feel on finishing a book. She told John the night they sat up together that although there was a letdown, as well as the usual anxiety that accompanies the publication of a second novel after the first has been a success, what was even more disturbing was that she was having trouble with the third novel. The new book had to do with the period when she was in college. She and another girl, as rich as Jean was poor, had been in love with the same man. What was to be the central episode in the novel was the suicide of the other girl. Since these events had occurred ten years earlier, Jean had thought she was far enough removed from them to be able to treat them fictionally. She was not. Writing the novel had revived painful memories and guilt. She felt she had been responsible for the suicide.

John, who later sang out his feelings about his father's suicide and his own guilt for any reader of his poetry to hear, was no more willing to talk about his family than Cal was willing to talk about his terrible quarrel with his father. In that all-night session with Jean, John said nothing about his father's death. Nor did he try to reassure her that she was probably not responsible for her friend's suicide, knowing how useless that would be. Instead he suggested she put the novel aside and work on something else. (Later, she tried many times to continue with the fictional account of the triangle without success, though a section of it appeared as the short story "The Philosophy Lesson.")

To me Jean talked about how difficult it was to live with Cal now that he wasn't drinking. "I fell in love with Caligula and am living with Calvin. He's become a fanatic. During Lent he starved himself. If he could get his hands on one, he'd be wearing a hair shirt. He so exaggerated his drinking habits to his confessor just before Easter that the priest suggested he take the pledge for a year. And he did. For a *year!*"

Neither one of them had fully recovered from the period when Cal had been in jail. He had tried for a commission in both the Navy and Army, and had been rejected because of poor vision. By the time he was called up by the draft in 1943, he had decided he couldn't in conscience serve, as he wrote President Roosevelt and his draft board, because of the Allied bombing of European cities. Made to stand trial after his "manic statement," he was sentenced to serve a year and a day in a federal prison (and was paroled after five months). "I was married," Jean said, "to a jailbird." She couldn't be funny about it long. In many ways she felt it had been a more difficult period for her than for Cal. "You won't believe this, but Cal is crazy. That made it easier for him."

Only once, on a day when Jean was in Bath, did Cal talk about the period of his incarceration. It was obvious from his change in manner that the memory of those months was still painful to him. He became again the scowling, whispery voiced head-hanging Cal we had met in Princeton. What his feelings had been during this period, he didn't say. Instead he talked about his fellow inmates, among them notorious criminals seen at a distance, including:

> . . . the T shirted back
> of *Murder Incorporated*'s Czar Lepke,
> there piling towels on a rack,

and about those who had attended the evening class he'd taught. (One wondered what they made of his assignments from books like *The Cloud of Unknowing*.) By the time we were doing the dishes again that evening, though, his solemn mood had lifted. It was difficult to imagine this clowning plate-slinger as a jailbird, impossible to believe he was "crazy."

CHARLES PHILLIPS REILLY, COURTESY OF ROBERT GIROUX

Cal, Jean and Bob Giroux in Damariscotta later that summer

By now, the poets had worked their way through their private anthologies of American and English poetry and were reciting Shakespeare:

> . . . the good days
> when we sat by a cold lake in Maine
> talking about the *Winter's Tale*
> Leontes' jealousy
> in Shakespeare's broken syntax.

We had our last walk to the millpond, our last swim in the lake, our last Cuba libre. We had come to know one another more intimately in two weeks than would have been possible in two years of meetings at dinners or parties. We embraced, promising to write from Wellfleet and to meet in New York in September.

Although we did see Jean and Cal in the fall, and for years to come, the last time we saw them together was as the taxi drove off, and they waved us good-bye. Two months later their marriage had broken up and they were on their way to a bitter divorce. At the close of the summer Cal had fallen in love with a guest who, like Minnie in Jean's story "An Influx of Poets," had made a dramatic arrival on the lake by aquaplane. He had left Jean, left the Church, and was living on his own in a tenement above a kosher butcher on the Lower East Side. (To get to his apartment one had to duck behind a slaughtered sheep that blocked the street entrance.)

Jean was in Payne Whitney, the psychiatric division of New York Hospital. She spent the enforced exercise time walking with other inmates in an enclosed garden she called, her comedic sense not failing her even in illness, "Luna Park." The Bears were dead. The dream house in Damariscotta Mills was up for sale.

VII
ANALYSANDS
ALL

Sometime after the publication of *Lord Weary's Castle,* and the appearance of Randall's and John's laudatory reviews of the book, Cal called from New York to ask if he could bring Randall to Princeton. Come early, John said, to allow time for a good long talk before dinner. They appeared at our door in the early afternoon, Cal looking as sturdy as a woodsman beside a wan and willowy Randall. The previous evening they had attended a cocktail party for Cyril Connolly at which everyone, Cal included, had overindulged—everyone except Randall, who, as usual, had drunk not a drop. It seemed hardly fair that the teetotaler should be the one to suffer from a hangover. From the canapés! Cal couldn't imagine anything funnier.

Randall was not amused. He felt so ghastly he asked if he could lie down. I installed him on the couch in the living room with pillows and a comforter. He participated only listlessly in the conversation, and when dinner was ready said he couldn't face food; he doubted that he would ever be able to eat again. With his pale face against the pillow, the comforter pulled up to his chin, he reminded me of a Mary Petty cartoon I'd cut out of an old *New Yorker* that I'd found in a secondhand magazine store and pinned up over John's desk, to rib him about the way he carried on when he was ill. In a Victorian bedroom, in a high bed, buried under a mound of covers, one sees the figure of a man. His head, with its peaked face, is framed by snowy white pillows. A doctor, looking grave, says, "You're a very sick poet."

If the sick poet had lost his appetite, he soon found his tongue. Leafing through a book of English ballet photographs John had taken out to entertain him while we were eating, pictures of dancers John had seen perform in London and still thought highly of, Randall would call over the back of the couch, "You don't really like X, do you? She's *so* awful." Or, with mock compassion, "Poor old Y. She was no *real* good."

Music proved no more soothing than ballet. It was not this late Beethoven quartet John should have played, but that one. Randall, who was also a Haggin fan, couldn't find grounds for agreement with John about Haggin, much less about Mozart, Haydn or Bach.

Cal, trying tactfully to find a subject that would jog Randall out of his peevish mood, turned the conversation to poetry. John, who had thought Randall's review of *Lord Weary's Castle* better than his own, congratulated him on it. Randall grumped a thanks, and began to make up wickedly witty parodies of Cal's poems, full of sabbaths, sermons, graveyards, ancestors and, not to leave out the religious theme (though it was now out of favor with Cal, the Apostate), the Mother of God.

By the time the taxi arrived to take our guests to the train, Cal and John were also looking peaked. They were suffering from what Cal called Randall's disconcerting habit of not distinguishing between what he said to one's face and behind one's back. All the way to New York, Randall kept up his attack on John, convincing Cal that, far from bringing his two friends together, he had driven them apart.

Cal would have been surprised to learn that the three-way meeting had plunged John into gloom. The visit was such a monumental flop (and so memorable that after Randall's death both Cal and John wrote about it), that as John and I did the dishes, we went over the sequence of events, trying to see what had gone wrong. Could everything be explained by a poisonous canapé? As we took turns imitating Randall the waspishness was diluted, leaving an anthology of mannerisms that seemed hilariously funny. The following day, however, and for a week thereafter, John suffered from an emotional hangover he at first couldn't understand. Unable to work, crushed by doubts, he asked himself repeatedly: *Am* I a poet? Despite Randall's parodies of Cal's verse, his admiration for Cal was patent, as was Cal's for him. Together they projected such a façade of iron self-confidence that John had felt like a gatekeeper who has let in a tank disguised as a pleasure vehicle and is crushed against a wall. (Was this, he wondered, the way Delmore had felt the day of the Y reading, when Richard and he had gone to pick up Delmore?) To avoid another such crisis of confidence—there were quite enough caused by events beyond his control—John decided that in the future he would do what he could to avoid seeing Cal and Randall together.

One hears so much talk about the competitiveness of poets that I've often wondered: Are they any more competitive than astronauts, art collectors, assistant professors, jockeys, hostesses, ballet dancers, professional beauties? I doubt it. In the years during which John and his contemporaries were making their reputations, what impressed me was the generosity with which they offered one another advice, praise and encouragement. Cal, recalling this period, wrote, "We [John and he] hated literary discussion animated by jealousy and pushed by caution." This was what one felt listening to them talk. As those of their generation neared the finish line and saw how few there were left in the race, they kept a close eye on one another's positions, of course, and rivalry undoubtedly became as keen with them as with any other finalists. With only a few prizes worth having, how could it not be so?

> Does then our rivalry extend beyond
> your death? Our lovely friendly rivalry . . .

The rivalry between Randall and John, which at times was also "lovely friendly," was a rivalry not between poets (as it was between John and Dylan Thomas), but between critics—critics of ballet dancers, of composers, of performing artists, critics of poetry. Since, in their early idealistic years, they disapproved of any rivalry as being unworthy of a writer's calling, they tried to govern their feelings, with results that were sometimes comical. Once, when they were discussing a new poem of Cal's and disagreeing about one of his stanzas, which John argued was needlessly obscure and Randall claimed was not, John, tired of worrying the point and pushed into a corner by Randall's tenacity, said, "Well, Eileen found it difficult." Randall's eyes opened wide with astonishment as he said, "Really? Mackie [his wife] found it *easy.*"

Jean Stafford, who wanted a full account of the Lowell/Jarrell visit, had her own explanation of why it had gone badly. Cal had undoubtedly forced John's learning, if not his talent, down Randall's throat so insistently that Randall had arrived in Princeton at least as sick of Berryman as he had been from food poisoning. "Enough of Randall. How was Cal? What did he say about me?" Cut off from her usual sources of information, Jean was eager for intelligence about her estranged husband.

Jean had received us in the lounge at Payne Whitney and taken us to her room. Both might have been at the Barbizon Hotel for Women, the difference being that to reach these rooms one had to be piloted by a matron through two locked doors. "Everything's locked," Jean said, "even the closets and dresser drawers." Aware that we hadn't taken in what this meant, she added, "Suicide precautions." Still, if one had to have a breakdown, Payne Whitney was a swell place to have it. The staff was solicitous of one's comfort. "Can you believe it? There's even garlic in the salad dressing."

As a result of a high-protein diet, vitamins, sedation and, above all, a prohibition against alcohol, Jean looked far better than she had in Damariscotta Mills. Her psychiatrist kept after her about her appearance, she said, so her hair was carefully groomed, and instead of the baggy sweater and hound's-tooth checked slacks, she was wearing a blouse and a skirt. "For dinner I put on pearls—like a Smith College girl." She puffed out her cheeks at this absurdity. Though she made fun of the rules, of the objects she and the patients made in "o.t." (occupational therapy) and of their walks in "Luna Park," she was relieved to be hospitalized and looked after. If she minded the restraint of not being able to come and go as she pleased, she felt comforted after each outing by the security of the "loony bin."

Except for her unrealistic hope that she and Cal would be reconciled, she had seemed so well that we believed her when she said the doctors were considering discharging her very soon. On learning that her mother was dying of cancer, she was so overcome with remorse about her angry feelings toward her in the past that she checked out of the hospital and flew to Oregon, arriving in time to attend the funeral. Contrary to the doctors' expectations, and ours, she didn't begin drinking again; in fact the week out West seemed to have done her good; although when it was time for her case to come before the hospital board, it was decided that she was not yet well enough to be discharged.

Being confined when her book was published did not seem to spoil her pleasure in the excellent reviews that Bob Giroux (who was Cal's editor as well as her own) brought her. The *New Yorker* critic, for instance, said *The Mountain Lion* was "a second novel that is hard to

COURTESY OF ROBERT GIROUX

Jean photographed with the mountain lion at the Bronx Zoo, 1947

match these days for subtlety and understanding." Nor was she displeased when *Life* asked to photograph her, although she had a salty thing or two to say about being posed in front of a mountain lion's cage at the Bronx Zoo.

Cal's success was even greater. He was, as John said, "blazing." With the publication of *Lord Weary's Castle* he became famous in the literary world in much the way that Delmore had with *In Dreams*. But Cal, unlike Delmore, also had public recognition. In the spring of 1947, he received the Pulitzer Prize, and following the announcement of the prize, he, too, appeared in *Life* in a prominently placed article. (For both measures of success, about which these friends were periodically contemptuous, John would have to wait twenty years.)

Instead of being able to enjoy Cal's fame, as she would have done in the days before their separation, Jean was filled with bitterness, as she told us when she came to spend a weekend that spring. She knew now that there was no chance of a reconciliation. Cal had asked for a divorce. He was going to remarry. What would her life be like now that she was on her own? She was full of apprehension. What a mistake it had been to marry an intellectual! She was fed up with them. A woman needed a husband like Mrs. Wilkenson's (a patient she'd met at Payne Whitney and with whom she had become friendly), one who would look after her. She hated the idea of living alone and was frightened of not having money. While *The Mountain Lion* was a critical success, it was not going to be a best seller like *Boston Adventure*. Cal wasn't going to give her a bean. And he was planning to marry that woman! He was crazy. Why wouldn't anyone listen when she said so?

"Crazy" was not the word I would have used to describe Cal when, shortly after Jean's visit, he came to Princeton again, although his mood was certainly elevated beyond what it had been at his most ebullient in Maine. That was to be expected, was it not, of a poet who at thirty-one had won the Pulitzer? At an outdoor party we took him to (one of the many that season that I didn't enjoy), he drank quarts of beer, took off his shoes and tossed them up in the air, while John, who had drunk an equal amount and had climbed a sycamore tree, tried to catch them. The sight of poets disporting themselves in this way may have entertained the other guests, but I was feeling that excess of alcohol made even these brilliant and attractive men tiresome.

Before going to bed that night Cal drank as much milk as he had beer, his way of sobering up and avoiding a hangover. At breakfast the next morning he confirmed, soberly, that he planned to marry Gertrude Buckman as, for some months, we'd been hearing he was going to do. He knew his friends thought they were unsuited to each other. Nevertheless, he was determined. John did not try to dissuade him. Instead, he urged him to go slowly.

Cal gave John almost identical advice as they walked to the station together. The "ease and light" Cal had found in John's company in Damariscotta had by midwinter been replaced with irritability and depression. In the spring his mood changed to one of false gaiety. By the time of Cal's visit, the gaiety had turned into hysteria.

On our return to Princeton after vacation, John and Richard again taught together. The two men saw each other daily, talked about literary matters and about students, as in the past. John was particularly excited by the work of Frederick Buechner, who had shown him part of a novel, and by W. S. Merwin, who was writing poetry. Both of them were "the real thing." Such students made John feel he had made the right decision in staying on in Princeton, although there was unquestionably a change in his relationship with Richard. Since neither ever referred to the fiasco in Harrington, what had occurred there remained between them like a moat. Formerly, if I had been away overnight and John had been at loose ends, he would have walked around the corner and spent the evening with the Blackmurs. But the memory of Helen and Richard's quarrels, and the apprehension that in his company they would begin again, kept John away from Princeton Avenue—except on Richard's Saturdays, at which there was now always a roomful of people. He could have gone to see Ed Cone, who had become a close friend, or Irving Howe, another friend and neighbor. But he knew that Ed and Irving, like other members of the faculty, worked evenings. On nights when I had a late class over at Rutgers, or had to stay in the library, John drifted into the company of a group of undergraduates. The postwar students were no longer "boys," as he had called them at Harvard. But for the years they had lost in the service they themselves would have been teaching. Some were married and had children.

After the months during which he had driven himself day and night to finish his *Lear,* I had imagined John would continue this pattern and would hardly be aware how busy I was in graduate school. While I was in the Rutgers library, he would be in the Ball Room; and so he should have been, for he had agreed to write an introduction to Pound's selected poems for New Directions, and a biography of Stephen Crane for the American Men of Letters Series, published by Sloane Associates.

The Crane advance of $1,000 would not be enough to live on in the coming year, when his job with Richard would be over. In February and March, when he had again to face how he would earn a living beginning in June, John announced that he was fed up with teaching—"I'm a writer, damn it, not a nursemaid"—and that even if he received an offer, he would decline it. Yet "Vain Surmise," the story he began at this time, did not reflect such a pose. On the contrary, it revealed a desire to teach so well that he would be able to change his students' attitude toward poetry. In the story a professor assigns his class "Lycidas," a poem he loves and knows from experience his students hate. He prepares for class with great care, marshaling his energy, intelligence and patience for a lesson he hopes will make his students hear the poem for the first time. Thinking of his dead friend, a colleague and fellow poet (Bhain Campbell) who, like Lycidas, had died young, he tries to recapture the care and attention his friend and he gave to teaching. If the professor succeeded in making the students hear "Lycidas" as it should be heard, would there not be hope of educating a wider audience to poetry?

Dissatisfied with the frame for the lesson, John put "Vain Surmise" away, taking it out to rework it off and on for years. (It was published posthumously under the title, "Wash Far Away.") His "I'm not a nursemaid" sounded at least partly defensive as time went by and no offers to teach came in. Offers, as we were beginning to learn, came two at a time or not at all.

For a while John hid his apprehension about being unemployed behind a busy-work plan to begin his own literary magazine. I doubted that John would succeed in getting backing where Richard had failed, but Richard and others encouraged him, so he talked to people he thought would be helpful. And he hung on, waiting. I could hear Delmore saying, "I told you so." If John had taken the editorship of *Sewanee,* he would have had a new scene, some years of financial security instead of the annual spring crisis about how to earn a living and hours free every day for his own work. Instead he was in Princeton, which he was sick of, and he was jobless.

What I grossly underestimated at that time was John's susceptibility to loneliness. One long, solitary evening would do it. He came down from his studio, or home from his office, and I was not *there*. It reminded him of the time before we married. No matter how many books there were to read, or how many records to listen to, the empty apartment made him feel desolate. The objection he had raised at first to my becoming a psychologist had been based, I thought, on my having to go to graduate school (which he objected to on principle). But since, because he taught intermittently, I was going to have to continue working, wasn't it better for me to have a profession of my own, so that I would be able to earn more money and also have work that engaged my interest? If he had understood his own feelings, he would have said yes, it would—*if* it didn't engage my interest too much. I promised that my being a student would make no difference in our lives, as I had promised about having a child. I would read what he wrote, run the house, entertain—do what I had always done. And so I did. Nevertheless, for the first time I was also away one or two evenings a week, and on weekends was busy writing papers and preparing for classes.

John found himself with a wife who wanted a child he was afraid to have (though he didn't know it; nor did she), a wife who was on her way to a career that took attention away from him, which he resented (though he didn't know it; nor did she). While he was a man who took no great pride in being rational, he would have thought it absurd to complain that he felt abandoned; yet that was how he felt. Abandoned, with no idea how to earn a living in the coming year, his book of poems once again rejected, unable to get going on the Crane, sinking into his old "vice of reading" and his new "vice of squandering time with students" who were always free when he wanted company: This had been his state of mind when, sometime before Cal's visit, he became infatuated with the wife of a Princeton graduate who was living in town.

"Lise," who was a few years younger than John, had an air of self-assurance, insouciance and vitality that he found compelling. Infatuation turned into an obsession as his love for her was only intermittently requited. During the weeks when she was away from Princeton on vacation with her husband and son, the obsession allowed John a respite. He questioned the genuineness of her feeling for him, and in brief moments of clarity, his for her. Did she love him? One day she seemed to, the next day not. When she did, was it him she was attracted to, or the poet who would immortalize her in the sonnets he was writing?

As for John, was it Lise he wanted? Or the sonnets Lise inspired, as Yeats had been inspired by Maud Gonne? "If Miss Gonne had called Willie's bluff and gone to bed with him, she wouldn't have filled his days with misery. No misery, no poems. You can bet your life that what Yeats was after was *poems*," John used to say when asked what he made of their relationship. Was a new subject for poems what he too was after? Or were Lise and the sonnets an elaborate device to keep him from the Crane, which in a moment of madness he had agreed to write but now dreaded writing and couldn't back out of?

Tormented by doubts, tortured by guilt, John began to behave so alarmingly that the anguish I felt at what I suspected was happening was soon smothered by the fear that he would have a breakdown. He was alternately hysterical and depressed, couldn't sleep, had violent nightmares when he did and, most disturbing of all, was drinking in a frighteningly uncharacteristic way. After one all-night party he had a hallucination. It was too terrifying to describe, he said, holding his head and rocking back and forth in his chair. "It's the old illness coming back. I'm going mad."

While waiting for him to come home, I had decided, as I paced the living room in a rage, to confront him once again with my suspicion and force the truth from him. But seeing him bathed in sweat and trembling, in a state of anxiety so intense it was catching, my anger was replaced by panic—this was not play-acting; he really *was* going crazy—as I tried to think how to calm him, what doctor to call for help. There was no time to nurse my wounds which, for all I knew, were imaginary. Whatever was going on it was certainly not an ordinary love affair and couldn't be treated as such. With the help of a sedative the anxiety attack finally passed and he fell asleep. In the morning he agreed to go away to a friend's farm for a week or so, in the hope that he would be able to rest and get control of his nerves. On his return he seemed calmer, but after a few days in Princeton all his symptoms had flared up again. This was the state in which Cal was seeing him. Should he, when I begged for candor, confess that while he loved me he was in love with Lise? he asked Cal on the way to the station. When he wrote:

> Once in a sycamore I was glad
> all at the top, and I sang,

one of the things he meant was that at the top of the tree he had a moment of escape from the world below, and especially from the two women who were, with Cal, down on the ground. Cal, convinced that the obsession would burn itself out, advised John to lie to me and wait six months. If at the end of that time he still felt the same way, he should tell me. (This, as so much else about the affair, I learned only later from an accretion of detail, from John himself and from others.)

The affair was short-lived. For the obsessive love, which turned into obsessive hate—Lise's self-assurance now appeared to him as arrogance, her insouciance coldness, her vitality destructiveness—to run its course took exactly the time Cal had allowed. In between John underwent a crisis so profound that he never recovered from it.

It began with a series of parties given by undergraduates. Never had there been so many parties—afternoon parties, evening parties, house parties, long long parties with short strong drinks. John, who until this period had drunk little, didn't see the danger in lunch-time daiquiris, before-dinner martinis, late-night stingers. The others seemed to have no commitments that required them to get up the following morning. They slept late and were ready to go again. For John, who awakened guilt-ridden and exhausted from a battle with demons, a "brilliant" martini became the cure for a hangover, a nightcap or two the cure for insomnia.

Cal's visit, reminding me of the single Cuba libre before dinner in Maine, as well as his self-protective antidote (milk) for the poison he had drunk, pointed up the change in John. So little did John see it that, when I threatened to leave if he didn't stop drinking, he said, "You needn't worry. I have no intention of becoming a drunkard."

"Drunkard" was a word from a melodrama. Certainly I would not have used it to describe what John had become. Although I, too, did not see the full seriousness of the change, what alarmed me was that what had so recently been a pleasure had now become a need. John

John

needing a drink? The night of the hallucination I recalled the far-off but vivid ending to our engagement party and the effect the vodka had had on him. No, I would not be reassured when he promised to be more moderate, not unless he agreed to see a psychiatrist.

At an earlier time he would have protested, suspicious as he was of anything that meddled with the psyche of an artist. But "living on the thin edge" for so many months had forced him to entertain the possibility even before I insisted on it, as I knew from the second stanza of "The Lightning," the one poem he showed me that summer, a gift for my birthday:

> Analysands all, and the rest ought to be,
> The friends my innocence cherished, and you and I
> Darling—the friends I qualm and cherish and see.

Although the poem ends on an optimistic note: My love loves chocolate, she loves also me,/And the lightning dances, but I cannot despair," despair, except for moments as brief as a flash of lightning, was what he had been feeling for so long that if I could find a competent analyst, he would be relieved to go to him.

Obsessive hate freed John from the sonnets (or as he put it to me at the time, from the sequence of poems he had "squandered" the summer on, and didn't feel were good enough to show me), allowing him to turn his attention to other work. One of the fruits of his early months in treatment was that he became somewhat more realistic about money. With no salary check coming in from teaching, the advance on the Crane dwindling, the psychiatrist to be paid, he realized he had to *do* something. He would take a more active interest in publishing. Publishers paid advances, however small, for poetry, did they not? Deciding that he could no longer hold out for his long-time dream of having Bob Giroux as his editor, he sent his book to Sloane Associates, his publishers for the Crane. To his astonishment and delight, Sloane accepted it, offering an advance of $250. (Not ten days later, but too late, John had a telegram from Bob: He was now in a position to offer John a contract at Harcourt. "So it goes," John said.)

With dreams of Broadway, John returned to a play about an eighteenth-century criminal, Katherine Nairn, who had committed adultery and murder, which he had started and set aside. On his twice-weekly visits to New York, he began going to the theater regularly. What he saw did not encourage him in his hope that the kind of play he was writing would interest a New York producer. In any case, a play took time to write. What he needed was work for which he would be paid promptly. He made the rounds of magazines, talking to editors about possible articles.

Having heard that *Partisan Review* had raised its rates, John went to the magazine's office. There he found Delmore, now an editor, unshaven and dispirited. When Delmore discovered that John had also been to see Hannah Arendt, an editor at *Commentary,* he threw off his lethargy and, gesturing like a tragic actor, shouted, "John, you have a sacred obligation to write for us. It's your literary and financial duty."

Delmore's work was not going well. The truth was he wasn't able to work at all. He was paralyzed. If one wrote, one published. If one published, one was reviewed. *Genesis* had been treated so harshly by reviewers he couldn't bear to expose himself to further blows.

Was it not possible for him to make an agreement with himself not to read reviews? John asked.

"Not read them? Only you, John, would have such a quixotic idea."

"Why not simply measure them the way Conrad did?"

Delmore was suffering too much to find this funny. He, too, was having treatment. His analyst, a woman, was very bright. Bright but ugly. "How can I make a transference to an ugly woman?" this Freudian expert moaned, as if the whole system broke down unless one had a therapist who looked like Ingrid Bergman in *Spellbound.*

Before leaving the office, John agreed to write an omnibus review of poetry. In what was to be an unnerving pattern for both of us as for whatever editor he was dealing with, he delayed and delayed, missing one deadline after another, partly because he aimed so high. With considerable pulling from Delmore and pushing from me, he handed in at the final hour of the final deadline not a review but an essay, "Waiting for the End Boys."

It had been worth the wait, Delmore said. When it appeared in early 1948, the enthusiasm of other readers so encouraged John that he imagined he could earn a living by writing articles, imagined also that they would take less time than teaching. Besides, it was *writing*. And after receiving a generous letter of praise from Randall about the essay,

John said, "If I can excite Jarrell by what I write, anything is possible."

As a result of John's activities, and my graduate work at New York University, we were spending more and more time in New York. Whereas formerly we had gone in so seldom that there had been time to see only family, we now also saw friends, especially Nancy and Dwight Macdonald. Dwight had left *Partisan Review* and was now putting out his own magazine, *politics,* with Nancy as business manager. They were the center of a group of intellectuals we had met on the Cape while staying with Joan Colebrook, an Australian novelist who had recently arrived from England. We had come to look forward each summer to the bracing ocean-swimming and the equally bracing change in milieu. Whereas (in John's characterization) Princeton was academic/suburban/bourgeois, Wellfleet and Truro on Cape Cod were literary/radical/bohemian. Aside from the Macdonalds and Joan, with both of whom we stayed, there were also Mary McCarthy and Edmund Wilson, Nicola Chiaromonte, an Italian anti-Fascist writer of political essays and theater criticism (who had been in André Malraux's air squadron during the Spanish Civil War) and his wife,

COURTESY OF NANCY MACDONALD

An evening in New York. Clockwise from left: *Bowden Broadwater, Lionel Abel, Elizabeth Hardwick, Miriam and Nicola Chiaromonte, Mary McCarthy, John, Kevin McCarthy, Dwight Macdonald*

Miriam; the novelist Waldo Frank; Paul Goodman, a writer, literary critic and old rival of Delmore's; the composer Gardner Jencks and his wife, Ruth.

The first time Joan took us to visit the Macdonalds, we heard Dwight before we saw him. He was with one of the many contributors to *politics* who came to see him each summer to discuss possible articles, and was talking in a rapid and penetrating voice, agreeing enthusiastically, disagreeing vehemently and, as we saw when he came into view, gesturing with his head, arms and shoulders like a great bird. As Mary McCarthy looked the way I thought a woman novelist should look, coiffed like Virginia Woolf, her black hair in a bun at the nape of her neck, setting off her classic features, so Dwight, wearing eyeglasses and a goatee, looked the way a radical should look. With the Macdonalds, the Chiaromontes, Joan Colebrook and others, we swam, picnicked, went clamming and gathered in the evening for conversation.

The discussions were often so heated, the fight to have one's say so boisterous, that often Nicola, whose tonsured head made him look like

Dwight and Nancy Macdonald on the Cape

a monk in a sixteenth-century painting, was appointed to the chair. In an attempt to keep a semblance of order, he, the most urbane member of the group, often had to impose a time limit for those who asked for the floor. Politics, domestic and foreign, Marxism, psychoanalysis, the poetry of Louis Aragon—there was no lack of subjects, nor of fuel to heat the arguments. How different these evenings were from those John had attended at Erich Kahler's in Princeton! A disagreement was expressed judiciously at Evelyn Place, hyperbolically on the Cape. John would shout, Paul would shout, especially Dwight would shout, "WHAT? My God! You believe *that?* You must be crazy."

At the end of the first summer, the Macdonalds asked us to be sure to call them when we were in New York. John sat in a phone booth in Pennsylvania Station, ready to dial the number. "I can't do it," he said. "Suppose Dwight says, 'Berryman? Who the hell is Berryman?' " Dwight would hardly have forgotten who he was so soon, I pointed out. No use. John had lost his nerve. Why didn't I call Nancy? I did and Nancy asked us to come for dinner. From then on we saw them winter and summer. After John's psychiatrist recommended that he not stay with his mother when he had to be in the city overnight (or even see her, at least for some months), John often slept on the Macdonalds' couch.

When we were in the city, we also saw Jean Stafford, who was now well and had an apartment in a brownstone off Central Park West. Giving me an extra key so that I could use her typewriter between classes to type up my notes, she said, "You'll never guess who's living downstairs." Drawing out the name as if it were too delicious to pronounce all at once, she drawled "Sax Rohmer." As I went in and out that year, I hoped I'd run into the author of the Fu Manchu series (whom I rather expected to look like his protagonist), but our paths never crossed.

Far from being lonely, as Jean had been afraid she would be when she was discharged from the hospital, she was being lionized. This delighted her—though clothes were a problem. She was confident about her taste in decorating, she said, but she didn't know how to dress for dinner parties. And what should she wear to receive the National Press Club award? When she had dinner one evening with her friend and playmate, Jamie Caffrey, he teased her about what she was wearing. "Where did you buy *that?*" Jean said she had bought it at Lane

On the beach at Wellfleet

Bryant or McCutcheon's, she couldn't remember which. No wonder! Lane Bryant catered to overweight, middle-aged women, and McCutcheon's was where one's mother bought linens. Jamie took Jean in hand. Together they did the department stores. This one, not that, he'd say, as she modeled for him. Under his guidance, she was "dolled up" in a pretty blouse, a taffeta skirt held out by a flounced petticoat and a waist-cincher. On her very good legs, she wore black lace stockings. (The glamour faded as she plucked the lace and snapped it. "See? It's elasticized.") Her spirits had not been dampened by the gossip, which she ferreted out in long-distance telephone calls to Boston, Washington and Sewanee, that Cal was not going to marry "that woman" after all!

About his decision, Cal said not a word, even when John went to Washington to read at the Library of Congress, where Cal was serving as Poetry Consultant. Throughout their weekend together they spent every waking minute talking about poetry. As in Damariscotta Mills, John fought Cal's anthologizing mania, and would not agree that "Thomas has four, maybe five poems." Again John tried to push Cal to a greater appreciation of Delmore's work, while Cal pushed for Randall's.

In the impressive study at the top of the Library that was the

Consultant's office, John made a recording. They listened to Ransom's reading of "Philomela," a favorite of John's, and to Randall's "Lady Bates." In John's imitation of the record it sounded as though Randall was about to burst into tears.

With great sadness John also imitated Ezra Pound, whom he and Cal visited at St. Elizabeth's, the psychiatric hospital to which Pound had been committed when he was brought back to this country after the war. St. Elizabeth's was not like Payne Whitney. There was no denying that it was, to use Pound's term, "a bug house"—the real and chilling thing.

From the moment John agreed to write the introduction to Pound's selected poems, Pound began to bombard him with post cards, firing off sometimes two a day, full of recommendations, orders, miscellaneous bits of esoterica, jokes, epigrams—the words so abbreviated, so dressed up or down with capitals, exclamation points and parentheses that it was a puzzle to make them out. Pound talked much the same way. At one moment he was so clearheaded, witty and sharp it was difficult to believe he was schizophrenic; the next moment there was his anti-Semitism (at the same time that he said he admired "The Imaginary Jew"), and his conviction that his nickname for President Truman, which he took it for granted John must know, and therefore didn't mention, was sweeping the country. Logorrhea being one of his symptoms (as later mutism would be), he talked all the time. While doing so, he twisted his hands, drummed his feet on the floor and, on one occasion, stood up abruptly, went to his room and returned with two bananas, both of which he ate when his visitors refused them.

On another occasion, when they were alone, John asked Pound how he was feeling. Pound turned the question aside. Psychiatrists hounded him with that question every day. He preferred impersonal conversation (though he was touchingly sympathetic when John said I had been ill with the flu), was pleased to answer John's questions about Yeats and to reminisce about the past. In a rich brogue, he sang a parody of Yeats's epitaph, the first line of which went "Under bare Ben Bulhen's bum," that John thought very funny. No matter how long he stayed, Pound always asked if he couldn't stay longer.

After their joint visit, Cal and John went back to the Library and read each other's poems. Cal looked over the carbon of the book John was preparing for Sloane, while John studied a sheaf of manuscripts

Cal gave him, especially "Mother Marie Therese." John thought it brilliant, the best thing Cal had so far written. (No sweeter praise: They always hoped the last thing they'd written was the best.) From this weekend, the most satisfactory time they had had together since Maine, John returned inspired by Cal as, in the days at Harvard, he had so often been inspired by Delmore. It wasn't, he said, that Cal had encouraged him about his book. He had barely looked at it. ("I made the mistake," Cal later wrote, "of thinking John was less interested in his new poems than in mine . . .") It was that Cal had made him feel again that poetry must be the ruling passion of his life, and that he would never settle for anything less than the best he was capable of producing.

A month or so after the Washington trip, John came down from his studio happier than I had seen him in a year. "I have a wonderful first stanza for a new poem." It was about the seventeenth-century poet Anne Bradstreet. Some weeks later he had another stanza. He would undoubtedly have continued with the Bradstreet poem had it not been for his absorption in the forthcoming publication of his book. He made countless revisions of early poems, wrote three new ones, one of which gave him his title, *The Dispossessed,* and fought with his editor over the jacket copy, which he was determined must not say anything "idiotic."

To one who had waited so long to appear, whose first book was coming out when he was thirty-four—thirty-four!—the publication had immense importance. It would decide his future. In the morning John was convinced that the book would make him famous; by evening he was sure it would be ignored. Both attitudes generated tension that left him bristling with irritability, which erupted during a post-seminar get-together at the Nassau Tavern, where he attacked the guest of honor, Yvor Winters. "Yes, *of course* I realize he's one of the critics who may review me," John said the next morning, so full of compunction he decided he was "unfit for human society."

The reviews, that's what was harrying him. If they were bad and affected him as they had Delmore . . . No, he couldn't risk that. He would follow the advice he had given Delmore. Since John couldn't pretend that he didn't care what the reviewers said, his hedge was that I should read and digest them for him. Richard couldn't believe John would keep to this arrangement, though he knew John to be capable of not answering the telephone no matter how persistent the ring, or not opening the mail no matter how attractive the envelopes. When John questioned Richard about his practice, Richard admitted, after reflection, that he had never been able to read a review of his work from beginning to end. His eye skipped here and there, sliding over whole paragraphs, so that when he finished he often didn't know exactly what had been said. "Hardly your customary way of dealing with a text," John pointed out.

On publication day there was no celebratory party, no mail, no phone calls, no copies of *The Dispossessed* in the bookstores. The only evidence that it existed was the copy John had inscribed and given me, which I kept on the table next to my chair. When, after what seemed an interminable delay of three months, a review appeared in the *New York Times Book Review,* I reported the externals: It had been given to a serious critic, Dudley Fitts. It was well-placed, carried a photograph and measured fifteen inches. Fitts admired the poet's craft, sensibility and wit. About the book as a whole he had reservations.

John's system worked only moderately well. He was struggling to accept his disappointment over my report when friends in Princeton and New York congratulated him on the "rave." He was baffled. Had I misread it? What Fitts had said was that John was a poet of "discriminating sensibility and a saving wit; yet there clings about all but the very best of his work an aura of academic contrivance, a certain mussiness that is as hard to define as it is to ignore."

"Academic contrivance"—a rave? Hardly. The explanation, we decided, was that to those outside the literary world any review in an important publication, accompanied by a photograph, was a rave, no matter what the reviewer said.

More disappointing than Fitts's opinion was the silence from poets to whom John had sent complimentary copies. Pound fired off a post card: "Thanks for values rec'd." Wallace Stevens' graceful way out was: "I am a bit careful about reading other people's poetry because it is so easy to pick up things." O.K. One was insane, the other was busy running an insurance company. What about his own generation, his friends? John wondered. Silence from Cal. Silence from Randall (who it turned out was going to review it in *The Nation,* where he criticized the "slavishly Yeatsish grandiloquence" of the early poems, said of the later ones that their style was "dissonant, darting, allusive, always over or undersatisfying the expectations which it is intelligently exploiting . . ." and ended "looking forward with real curiosity and pleasure to Mr. Berryman's new poems"). Silence from Delmore. If these three men had nothing to say to him . . .

When he had given up hope, Delmore called, full of apologies. He hadn't written, still couldn't write because he was crippled by inertia. Although he knew the poems as well as John knew them, he had read them again, and had all kinds of generous and extravagant things to say, such as that if there were a decent committee, John should get the Pulitzer. What pleased John most was that he singled out the new poems for praise, especially, "The Dispossessed" and "The Lightning." They were "moving in a new direction."

As so often in the past, it was Delmore who sustained John, Delmore who knew exactly what to say to keep him going.

Never mind the early poems. "Damn right I'm moving in a new direction," John said, taking heart. "I have my two Bradstreet stanzas. Ha!"

In an attempt to take a philosophical attitude, to put *The Dispossessed* behind him so that he would get on with other work, he repeated to himself what Pound had written many years earlier: "It is extremely important that great poetry be written but it is a matter of indifference who writes it." John said he should have this message printed in large letters and hang it over his desk where he would see it every day. "A little less ego, Berryman. That's the ticket!"

Listening to John talk one could have been persuaded, as he was, that he was virtually unknown. So it came to me as a surprise to learn, as I did from time to time, that in the literary world he had already built up a considerable reputation, based on the poems, criticism and fiction he had published in literary magazines, as well as on the passion and learning he brought to any conversation about literature. Together these had convinced his contemporaries, and his mentors, that he was a serious poet who one day would be well-known. Despite his feeling that the publication of *The Dispossessed* had made no difference whatever in his situation, he was offered two teaching jobs, one at Princeton and the other (which showed his reputation was spreading to the universities at large) by Paul Engle at the Writer's Workshop in Iowa. His book also won the Guarantor's Prize given by *Poetry* magazine, and the Shelley Memorial Award. Not the Pulitzer by a long shot, but, as even John admitted, *something*.

The celebrated Gotham Book Mart party. Back row, left to right: *Marya Zaturenska, Horace Gregory, Tennessee Williams, Richard Eberhart, Gore Vidal, José Garcia Villa, W. H. Auden* (on ladder), *Elizabeth Bishop.* Middle row, left to right: *Stephen Spender, Sir Osbert Sitwell, Dame Edith Sitwell, Marianne Moore.* Front row, left to right: *William Rose Benét, Charles Henri Ford, Delmore Schwartz, Randall Jarrell*

"Here's fame," he said, waving an invitation to the Gotham Book Mart cocktail party for the Sitwells, a party that became famous because of the guest list as well as for the commemorative photograph taken by a photographer from *Life*. Literary New York was there, all save Oscar Williams, the anthologist, who was hiding in a cafeteria across the street, in terror of Edith Sitwell. He claimed that she had threatened to claw his eyes out over a disagreement about the selection he had made from her work. Oscar had heard that where Miss Sitwell was concerned no threat was idle.

Spender, Auden, Elizabeth Bishop, Delmore, Randall are among those who posed for the photograph. Cal and John are not in it, Cal because he was in Washington, John because, hating to have his picture taken—and with reason: The camera rarely caught him truly—he was nowhere to be found when it was shot. (Or was the true reason that, trying for a little less ego, he had swung so far down he felt he didn't belong with the others?)

Delmore, photogenic as always, looks as though he was in good spirits that day. If he was, it was an exception to his general mood. He felt so little able to cope with practical problems that he asked if John would go to Cambridge with him, to help him pack up the apartment he was vacating. While Delmore slumped in a chair, John filled carton after carton with books and prepared them for the movers. Delmore complained that he was hopeless about taking care of himself, that he was terribly lonely. He was thinking of remarrying. Who was the woman? John asked, lassoing a cardboard carton with a length of rope.

Who? It was not a question of who, but which one? Playing marriage broker to himself, Delmore took out four photographs, and described the virtues and defects of each candidate. Reporting this conversation to me, John said, "Predictably, the one for whom he had the highest praise is the one not in love with him. I begged him not to act precipitately."

T. S. Eliot, although in the country at the time, was not in the Gotham photograph, nor was he at the party. He was in Princeton. The previous year, when he had been in New York, Bob Giroux, his friend and editor, invited John to join them for tea. On the train to the city, John was only a little less nervous than he had been before meeting Yeats. But once the three of them were talking about poetry and publishing, he was far more self-possessed than he had been in the days when he had been "a monk of Yeatsian order" meeting the High Priest. At Bob's apartment:

> The poet hunched, so, whom the worlds admire,
> Rising as I came in; greeted me mildly,
> Folded again, and our discourse was easy,
> While he hid in his skin taut as a wire,
> Considerate as grace, a candid pyre
> Flaring some midday shore; he took more tea,
> I lit his cigarette . . .

John was impressed with Eliot's gravity and honesty. About each writer whose name came up, Eliot said neither more nor less than he thought. Cal's work he felt "had the real punch." While staying with Bob, Eliot had been working on two lectures he was going to give in Princeton. For days before his arrival the academic community was in a state of excitement that reached fever pitch when word went through the campus, into the Balt, down Nassau Street, through the students' clubs that T.S.tstststs was arriving on the 12:10. Alexander Hall was packed and aquiver that evening—not, however, as John said drily, because of the speaker's subject: poetic diction. Unlike other famous writers from England who had come to Princeton and, patronizing an American audience, delivered what John called "kindergarten lectures on poetry," Eliot aimed what he had to say at the listeners with the keenest interest and the widest knowledge of his subject.

In November of 1948, when Eliot returned for a two-month stay at the joint invitation of the University and the Institute, he was at first left so much on his own, no one daring to invite him to dinner, that he ate at the Nassau Club every evening. It was when Richard, who was seeing him frequently for lunch at the Institute, caught on to this that he had proposed to Helen that they invite Eliot for dinner and she had said, "Let him bring his own chop." Other women didn't feel the same way. When word got out that one hostess had invited the year's Nobel Prize winner for Literature, others hurriedly followed.

Once Eliot began to be lionized John was reluctant to invite him, and he might never have done so but for the Macdonalds' visit. Dwight had been one of the people in the United States whom Eliot had been most eager to meet. He had become a fan of *politics* during the war years, when he felt that its reporting on the war was uniquely free of cant. Bob had taken him down to the Macdonalds' apartment, where the conversation had gone so well that Eliot was eager to continue it. When John called to invite him for a drink, and to see the Macdonalds again, he said he would be delighted to come. To avoid any resemblance to a cocktail party, we invited only one other person, Paul Goodman, who happened to be in town for the day.

Mr. Eliot gave the impression of being so tall he had to stoop to get through the doorway of our apartment. The changes in his face brought about by age, the deep creases around his eyes, nose and mouth, were so much in the direction of its original character that at sixty he was recognizably the good-looking man with the slicked-

T. S. Eliot at the Institute for Advanced Study

down black hair (now graying) of the early photographs. His manner was as formal as his dress, the conservative dress of an English banker. Shyness had been disciplined into courtesy. On being introduced he made an effort not to avert his eyes, as one felt he would have done as a young man. Instead he faced one directly, and took a moment longer over the exchange of greetings than was usual even with people whose graciousness is studied.

When John congratulated him on the prize, and added, "High time!" Eliot said, "Rather too soon. The Nobel is a ticket to one's own funeral. No one has ever done anything after he got it." John protested: It was not so. "All of Yeats's great poetry was written after he received the award. Can't one therefore look on the prize as a recognition of promise?" Eliot was delighted and said, "That's how I shall try to look on it."

With Dwight, whose manner remained unchanged no matter to whom he was speaking, Eliot seemed at ease. When the talk turned to poetry readings, he said that although he was willing to lecture, he looked upon a man's reading his own verse in public as "indecent exposure." With no effect that we could see, he drank off five martinis. ("Did you count five, too?" John asked afterward. "If I hadn't seen it, I wouldn't have believed it.") When Paul Goodman, a premature hippie, arrived—his hair flying in all directions, his clothes ripped and stained, his shoes muddy—and John made the introductions, Paul leaned toward the guest of honor and said, "I didn't get it. What's the name?"

"Eliot. Tom Eliot." He seemed amused rather than offended, as he was amused by the noisy verbal cross fire that Dwight and Paul and John fell into whenever they were together.

(After Eliot left, Dwight remonstrated with Paul, "Goodman, my God! *What manners!* You knew damn well who he was." Paul, all innocence, blamed his myopia.)

Eliot excused himself for having to leave early. His acceptance speech was not yet finished and he was flying to Stockholm in a few days. At the door he asked John how he had found Pound on his last visit to St. Elizabeth's. John, who talked with Mrs. Pound whenever she was there about what one could do for her husband, said to Eliot, "Won't you try to get him back to writing verse?" Eliot shook his head. "If one could get a word in . . . Do you?" Rarely, John responded, sad to think that these two old and close friends could not communicate. Seeing his guest to the taxi, John asked, "Do you think Pound will ever finish the Cantos?" "If he does," Eliot said enigmatically, with a farewell wave, "he will die."

VIII

"THE COLOUR OF THIS SOUL"

"*Stephen,* not Hart. Christ! Why can't people get it straight?" John asked with exasperation, clapping his hands over his ears. "Was that my first mistake? If I were writing about Hart Crane how much easier it would be! Maybe I should call Sloane and ask to change. No kidding. That would be one way out."

The confusion in the minds of acquaintances, even friends, about what John was working on was of a piece with the difficulties which beset him over the book he had agreed to do for the American Men of Letters Series. The invitation to write on Stephen Crane had come in almost as roundabout a way as had the grant for Shakespearean scholarship. Congratulating Mark on his *Hawthorne,* one of the early publications in the Series, John mentioned in passing that he had recently been rereading Crane with excitement. Mark, in his untiring efforts to be helpful, showed the letter to his editor, who in turn wrote John asking if he would like to write a critical study of Crane. Without seriously considering what was involved, John agreed. He had always wanted to make a thorough examination of Crane's work; this would give him the occasion. When, later, he cried out, "How did I get into this?" I reminded him that there had also been the advance—the $1,000, that had been tempting to one who saw himself once again without a job. Recalling that Dylan Thomas had drunk up a $500 advance for a book about Wales before putting a word on paper, John had been cautious enough, in the spring of 1946 when he signed the contract, to ask that the money be withheld until the following year when he would begin work in earnest.

He had not gone far in his research before he realized that while other contributors to the Series had been able to "knock off" their books in a year, he would not be able to do so. He was again in the position of having too little time for a project that he was temperamentally incapable of treating in a superficial and graceful way. Thomas Beer's biography, on which he had thought he could depend, turned out on the first rereading he'd given it since undergraduate days in Mark's class, to be, as he later said in his introduction to the book, "agreeably incomprehensible." In an effort to suppress the scandal that had attached to Crane's name, Beer had expurgated material that would have shocked readers of the twenties.

It was the realization that in order to understand Crane's work John had to know the truth about his life, and that it would be up to him to find out what the truth was—in short, to write a biography—which overwhelmed him. With characteristic ambivalence he wanted to back out and was determined to go ahead. What he did instead was stall. And then, in the summer of Lise, write sonnets. There followed the autumn of psychotherapy and the beginning of a profound interest in psychoanalysis which forced him to examine his own life, and Crane's, in a new way.

Deadlines came and went. The editors of the Series, losing patience, issued an ultimatum. If the manuscript was not ready by February 1949, it would be dropped from the list. With end-of-the-year euphoria, John said on New Year's Eve 1948 that he *would* finish. The new year would allow him a fresh start, a magical rebirth, freeing him from the defects of character that had crushed him with guilt and paralyzed his will for months. Our marriage had survived a "nightmare." Now that he was beginning to understand his incomprehensible behavior— his drinking, emotional turmoil, stalling about work, irresponsibility about earning a living—he felt sure we would be able to recapture the happiness of our first years together. We had been happier than any couple we knew, and would be again. He would give his full attention to the Crane, finish the research and write the book "like a shot."

One didn't have to be a pessimist (*pace* Randall) to feel a certain reserve about John's ability to meet the deadline despite two months of work so grueling it required stimulants to get him going in the morning and sedatives to put him into an all-too-brief sleep at night. Dexadrine and Nembutal, neither of which he had used before, became as much a part of his diet as coffee, cigarettes and martinis, as the days and nights, interminable yet fleeting, moved inexorably toward the due date. There was not only Sloane's impatience to prod him. There was also Knopf's announcement in *Publishers Weekly* that another biography of Crane would be ready soon. Its author, Schoberlin (*"Who?"*) was probably lying to his editor about being nearly finished. What writer didn't? Besides, biographies of Crane were announced and abandoned year after year. Still, it would be just his luck, John said, for the Knopf biography to be completed before his.

At a moment when writing was as agreeable to John as going to the dentist, one of his wisdom teeth screamed in pain. To whom should he go? As I had discovered about his relationships with doctors, if he was with the right person he was "a lamb," as his mother would say; if with the wrong one, a lion. Years of neglect meant that whomever he consulted he would have to see frequently and over a long period. After considerable thought, I decided to risk sending him to my dentist. "Difficult," the word most often used to describe John when he was acting up socially, was the word I used, fond though I was of him, to describe my dentist. John and he would either hit it off or there would be fireworks at the first session.

During my childhood, Dr. Glickman had practiced around the corner from where I lived. He was a friend to all the children in the neighborhood, but especially to my sister and me. To have been orphaned he thought (incorrectly) was the greatest catastrophe that could befall a child. He didn't approve of the way our relatives were raising us, and felt it his duty not only to care for our teeth but also to advise us about how to cope with Life.

He, too, had suffered an early loss, as he told me while I was seated in his chair. His father had died while Glickman was in high school, which put an end to his football-playing days (although not before the snowy Saturday when, running down the field for a touchdown, he "got creamed by a thug from Evander Childs High School" and came out of the game with a profile almost identical to the one I later saw in Piero della Francesca's portrait of Federigo di Montefeltro). He was devoted to his tyrannical mother, and supported her as soon as he finished dental school. A sister with teeth so terrible he despaired of ever finding her a husband was a cross he carried less willingly.

What I must do, as soon as I grew up, was get away from my "guarrdine" (guardian) and get married. "With teeth like yours, you'll have no trouble finding a rich guy, Red—*if* you use dental floss."

When I told him I was going to marry John, and invited him to the wedding, he asked about John's bank balance. Small. On the other hand he taught at Harvard. "Harrvod," Dr. Glickman said, making fun of the name but obviously impressed, "Well, at least you got yourself a smart guy."

To me he remained Dr. Glickman even after I grew up; to him I was always "Red." John came back from his first visit, saying they'd settled on "Henry" and "John" as forms of address. So the meeting had gone well. Ordinarily John bridled at being called by his first name ("a loathsome American habit based on a naïve view of democracy"), but Henry had been so skillful in his operations, and so interesting to listen to, that the patients had piled up in the waiting room for the two hours that John remained in the chair. "Three quarters of the session for talk; one quarter for dentistry." Henry had a captive audience, and he held forth while John, the blue-white neon light shining in his eyes, his mouth full of cotton, clamps and rubber tubes, gestured and grunted agreement or disagreement, saving his more complicated responses for the brief moments after he had been allowed to spit and before the drilling began again:

> The drill was after or is into him
> Whirr went a bite.

Dr. Glickman's subject continued to be, as it had been during my childhood, Life. After a tour of duty in the Pacific and an unsatisfactory marriage that produced two spoiled children, he was gloomier and more misanthropic than the man I had known as a girl; full of "plights & gripes."

Glickman and Berryman: Each saw something of himself in the other, and both delighted in trading prophecies of doom, as John would report when he returned from the city, and over dinner enter-

tained me with the latest Henryisms. "Criminals?" the dentist would
say, apropos of a quarrel with his wife (and an impulse to strangle
her?), "I know all about them. See this thumb?" John, in telling me
this, would hold his left thumb the way Henry had, reminding me how
fascinated I had been with seeing it at eye level as a child: The first
joint was twice the size of the one on the right thumb. "That's a sign
I've got criminal tendencies. You? You're a poet, but you've got them
too. The only difference between us and the guy who commits murder
is we control ourselves." Henry puffed out his chest, proud of his
control.

John would grunt agreement.

"You take it out in poetry. Me, I take it out like this." The dentist
would pick up the pliers and twist his wrist sharply. Interrupting this
train of thought to prepare a filling, he'd say, working the metal with
his criminal thumb, "What I don't get about a guy like you is why,
if you're so smart, you can't afford inlays. Poetry—where will it get
you? Why don't you give up that Hiawatha stuff? Go into the stock
market. With your brains, you'd make a killing. Pay your bills. Mine
for instance. Buy Red a mink coat. Shakespeare: What did he get out
of it? A two-car garage? With teeth like yours, Mr. Poet, you're going
to need dough. Lots of it. Red now, she's got a perfect jaw. I've fixed
her teeth since she was a skinny little thing. A good kid. What does
she know? She thinks you're a gen-i-us." (He'd string out the word
with a combination of mockery and awe.)

"If you hit the best-seller list, I know what'll happen. You'll forget
all about Henry. Go to some Park Avenue guy for your inlays."
(Henry's office, as aggressively un-Park Avenue as he could make it,
was clean but scruffy. The bell only rang if you hit it the right way,
the waiting-room chairs were either too hard or too soft, the magazines
were battered, the walls blistered and peeling.) "Why should I worry?
If you stick with poetry, you'll never be able to afford anyone but
Henry Glickman, D.D.S."

So Henry lectured John. To me he'd say, "Red, you've got a
gen-i-us there. He's crazy, of course. Cra-zzy. He'll never give you a
home life. You know that, don't you? If that's what you wanted, you
should have married a smart Jewish dentist. Like me." He'd try on a
leer, but as he ruffled my hair in a way he'd done when I was a child,
he'd remember that his feelings toward me were paternal and the leer

would slide off his face. (Though he hinted at being a great man with the ladies, I suspected that his infidelities were as half-hearted as the leer.) "Look at that lazy, good-for-nothing *shiksa* I married. She's got everything. A mink coat. A cleaning woman. Money to buy éclairs. Buys them by the box. What does she care if her teeth fall out? She's married to a dentist, isn't she? You, Red, you've gotta look after your teeth. Don't forget the dental floss."

In 1953, after John and I separated on our return from Europe, I broke the news to our dentist the first time I saw him. Dr. Glickman permitted himself a moment's sadness. "My friend the poet," he said wistfully. With a more familiar astringency, he went on, "That's Life, Red. What did I tell you? I knew I'd never make inlays for him. He'll go to some goy in the Middle West, who knows from nothing, and forget all about his old friend Henry."

I don't think John forgot his old friend. Although he found a new dentist in Minneapolis, it seemed to me, reading *The Dream Songs,* that one of the figures shadowing the protagonist of these poems, "an imaginary character (not the poet, not me) named Henry, a white American in early middle age" was Henry Glickman, D.D.S.

The day the Crane book was due John handed in a manuscript he hoped would demonstrate that he had been working in earnest. From his point of view it was little more than a first draft. He could call it whatever he liked, the editors said after the month or so it took them to read it, so long as it was returned with the revisions completed in two weeks. John might have been crushed by the new deadline had he had any spirit left after rereading his draft. So far was he from something he could bear to put his name to that he couldn't imagine the amount of time he would need to bring it to publishable form. Again he wanted to give up. Again he forced himself to push on. Morning, noon and night he went to his study to do battle with the "violent indolence" that had him in its grip. Trying to fight off guilt and panic, he dragged through one chapter after another, some days rewriting one page, other days two or three, saying yes yes yes to Sloane Associates, he would have it ready soon, as the months rolled by and his editor importuned him with letters and telephone calls; while I, less and less able to tolerate the tension over the book, buried myself in study and preparation for a career.

Study also became a defense against John's infidelities. Often it was only suspicion that made me wretched. On the occasions when he philandered openly, and I blew up in rage, shouting and weeping that I was fed up and was going to leave, he'd beg me to stay, saying, "Surely you must see that there is little pleasure to be had from all this. It's a disease, an *illness.*" The unbearable impotence and frustration he felt over his work drove him to seek compensatory gratification in women. It made him loathsome to himself but was beyond his control.

At one point he said, with a touching lack of reproachfulness, "Do you know you've begun to treat me like a patient?" I was about to deny it when I realized it was true. It was my way of putting distance between me and his "illness," a way of managing while I brooded over what action to take. Each time I decided that I could go on no longer and would have to leave him, the husband I had known would reappear, and be so unmistakably the man I loved that I was lulled all too willingly into believing that the illness had been cured. Even in the worst moments he could hold me fast by saying, as if crying out a prayer, "As long as you do not give up on me, I am not lost."

There was also the promise of a cure through treatment. When John's psychiatrist tried to tell me how unlikely this was, I heard only the ways in which John had made progress. What John really wanted from therapy was insight that would be useful for his work. Not the Crane, the *real* work. And, as would soon become apparent, he was getting it.

During these terrible months John had brief moments of pleasure, which I shared. They came from reading and rereading Crane, and being excited anew by his brilliance and originality. There was also the thrill of playing detective, of piecing together the episodes in the life that Beer had suppressed—discovering, for example, that Crane and the woman he called his wife had not been married, and that when he first met her, in Jacksonville, Florida, she was running a combination nightclub and bordello called—"What a name! Crane must have loved it"—the Hotel de Dream.

There was also pleasure to be had from the letters of Mrs. Frances Scovel Saportas, the seventy-five-year-old widow of Crane's friend Sylvester Scovel, who wrote John about the period during which her first husband and Crane had been war correspondents in Greece. Her letters were so engaging, sometimes so girlish ("The springtime weather makes me want to swing from tree to tree") that on a day when he received one his spirits lifted. Mrs. Saportas was his living tie with the past. She sent him a photograph of Crane he put above his desk (and later used as a frontispiece for his book), and one of Crane's cuff buttons. For long periods John sat staring at this relic, wishing it was a crystal ball in which he could see the past.

There was a respite when a heavy cold kept him from his study; during it we read together the memoir written by Joseph Conrad's widow (the Conrads and Cranes were friends in England), and howled with laughter at the malicious remarks Mrs. Conrad makes about her husband. "Getting back at him," John said, "for the hell he had put her through." Thereafter, whenever he wanted to remind me that there were worse husbands than he, he'd quote the remark Conrad made to his wife after she had set out a meal for a table full of unexpected guests. Coming up behind her, he'd whispered, "A damn bad tea, my dear. A damn bad tea."

There was also a March day when he took a break to visit Crane's grave in Elizabeth, New Jersey. Afterward, having lunch, John said he knew this book was "hell on our marriage," but he would be finished soon, and we would have a life together again. He was yearning for it almost as much as he was yearning to get to work on the Bradstreet poem. The poem was *there,* waiting for him to be free. On the train going back to Princeton, he was like a man whose furlough was over. For a moment in the restaurant he had been able to imagine a tolerable future. The closer we got to home the more oppressive became his feelings of frustration and impotence, the more acute his fear that he wouldn't be able to control his material (in telling the truth about Crane he would make him appear unattractive), the more over-whelmed he was by how much work he still had to do.

Early in May, when he broke down and confessed that he was much less far along than he had led me to believe, and that he "felt friendly to suicide," his fatigue and despair were so palpable that I said no book was worth it. He must call Sloane and tell them that, since there was no way he could possibly finish in any reasonable time, he was going to give up.

"What about the advance? I'll have to repay it."

Ah yes, the advance. We'd spent every last penny of it. We'd have to ask the bank for a loan. I was becoming inured to being in debt.

Immensely relieved to see that I was not "crushed" by his admission, and to be shown a way out, John decided not to take it. He'd gone so far it would be crazy to give up now. If only he could imagine a reader for whom he was writing, one who would see Crane as his biographer meant him to be seen.

"What about Dwight?"

Yes, Dwight was the audience he would like to interest. Or Edmund Wilson.

Edmund, whom John had met at the Tates' in Connecticut the summer he returned from England, and had seen each year on vacation in Wellfleet, had stopped calling him "Berryman" and begun to seek him out for conversation when he heard that John was engaged in Shakespearean scholarship. Edmund liked to quiz specialists. It was as though he had a folder labeled "Shakespeare" into which, throughout the year, he filed all the puzzles he had come on in the course of his reading. When he saw John, he pulled out the file and said, "Tell me, uh, tell me, John, what do you make of . . ." and listened attentively to John's response. Since parties were an unsatisfactory setting for this kind of exchange, he began, in the period after he and Mary McCarthy were divorced and before he married Elena Thornton, to invite us in for an after-dinner drink.

Coming as we did from a shack in the woods, it was always a surprise when we rang the bell of Edmund's year-round house on the edge of town to find him in a white linen suit and to be shown into a front parlor that had furniture, like the horsehair sofa on which we sat, which looked as if it might have come from his mother's house in Red Bank, New Jersey. As Elena later said, Edmund's political views might be radical but there was nothing bohemian about the style in which he lived. "Scratch the surface," she said, "and you'll find that underneath it's solid Red Bank."

"Hello, hello." Puffpuff. "Come in," Edmund would bellow in a stentorian voice, sputtering each phrase at the beginning of a sentence, discharging the rest in rapid fire. "Let me, uh, let me, uh, let me give you a glass of whiskey." A bottle of Scotch, ice and glasses were on a tray by his chair. His voice, his bulk, his suits (white linen in summer, brown wool in winter), his capacity for food, drink and serious conversation made him seem a leftover from another era. One felt he should have been a contemporary of Henry James (at the latest) rather than Allen Tate. Or he could have been a Roman senator. Certainly it was easier to imagine his portliness clothed in a toga than in a bathing suit.

It was hard for me to see him as the ladies' man I heard he had been, and still was. With me, he was a little vague. He never got my name straight. It was "Ellen," "Helen," "Eleanor." (When John teased him about this Edmund gave him a little lecture on etymology: They were all the same as "Eileen.") At a later period, during which we saw each other more frequently, he surprised me by remarking that at parties during the Christmas season I had appeared in different shades of green. On another occasion, when I was wearing sandals, he complimented me on the "Romanesque arch" of my foot. " 'Romanesque arch,' eh?" John said, much amused. "The old boy notices more than one suspects."

"Tell me John, uh, uh, what uh, what are you reading?" Edmund would say as we settled down with our drinks in the parlor in Wellfleet. Edmund, like Randall, wasted no time on small talk. "Crane? Crane you say? So"—puffpuff—"am I. Extraordinary writer, Crane, don't you agree?"

Edmund Wilson in Wellfleet

SYLVIA SALMI, COURTESY OF HELEN MIRANDA WILSON

What, in particular, was he reading? John wanted to know.

"I'm uh, I'm working my way through his *oeuvre*." Edmund was always working his way through the *oeuvre* of some writer. There was nothing haphazard about how he proceeded. He decided on a writer, read his entire work, wrote a long review, expanded it into an article, collected the articles into a book: No waste. If one heard that he was reading Wodehouse, one knew he was not doing it just to put himself to sleep. An omnibus review was in the making.

"I'm, uh, I'm rather puzzled by Crane's poetry. What what what do you make of it?"

"Ha! I have him!" I could hear John saying to himself. In the Harvard days, he and Delmore had agreed that Edmund was an untrustworthy critic of poetry. This was an opportunity to make him hear Crane's verse. "Let me say a little of it for you, Edmund, so you can hear it."

> Do not weep, maiden, for war is kind.
> Because your lover threw wild hands toward the sky
> And the affrighted steed ran on alone,
> Do not weep.
> War Is kind.

He wanted to convince Edmund, as he wanted to convince readers of his book, that "War Is Kind" was "one of the major lyrics of the century in America."

John's ability to make a poem come alive in the voice made me suspect that he could make a shopping list sound like a lyric had he wanted to. As he recited poem after poem, Edmund caught his enthusiasm. "Yes, but, uh what about uh, what about the . . ." When Edmund heaved himself to his feet and trotted off to the kitchen for more ice, John, unwilling to lose his pupil, followed at his heels, "What about . . ."

"Crane's unpoetic poetry? His 'pills,' as he called them?"

Yes, John said to me, he would write the section on Crane's verse with Edmund in mind. In the chapter called "Crane's Art," John was at his didactic best, as I told him. (He was like the professor teaching "Lycidas" in "Wash Far Away.") He depicts Crane as a "frightened savage anxious to learn what his dreams mean," the "pill" poems having the character of dreams. Reading John's drafts I began to understand what it was I had been feeling as I read these mysterious and spooky poems.

"So. You like these pages, do you?" John said, his ironic tone failing to mask his pleasure. The importance of my encouragement about the Crane surprised me at first, because when John was writing verse, or even fiction, he was able to tolerate long periods of agonizing uncertainty about how the work would turn out with no need whatever for encouragement. He wanted me, and others, to be there to read what he had written when he was ready. Until then, he worked in solitude. The Crane, not his idea to begin with, was quite another matter. He was fighting so many battles trying to finish it that he needed all the reassurance he could get.

There was the battle against Thomas Beer. Beer was to Crane what Eliot was to John's writing of criticism, what Yeats was to his writing of verse. Beer was not only a writer whose biography John thought brilliant (if unreliable). Beer was also an older man. John, who had had it drilled into him from childhood that older men were to be respected, was inhibited about "answering back." Now that John was in therapy, he saw Beer (Eliot, Yeats) as father figures who had to be engaged in combat and overthrown if he was to find his own voice. "Well, at least I'm no longer overawed by Beer," he announced one day, taking stock of where he was, and trying to discover why he was still not moving forward quickly enough.

If Beer was not holding him back, what was? It was the difficulty of trying to understand Crane. Why had this son of a saintly Methodist minister and his zealous spouse become a champion of prostitutes? Why had he lived in a common-law relationship with a woman whose past was unsavory, a woman he saw as "the ashes of other men's love," of whom he wrote:

> Ay, thou art death
> Black and yet black,
> But I love thee,
> I love thee—
> Woe, welcome woe, to me.

Freud had the answer, John told me, trembling with excitement after reading the paper called "A Special Type of Choice of Object Made by Men."

The danger was that if Freud explained Crane's behavior, he also threatened to explain John's. For, more and more, John saw similarities between Crane's life and his own. Crane had lost his father early, had been raised by a strong-minded mother who had favored him in a way that undermined his adult relationships with other women. He had been an apostate whose strong conscience tortured him over his sexual behavior. He had felt a need, as Mark Van Doren had written, "to live, at least as an artist, in the midst of all but unbearable excitement." He, too, had been pulled toward suicide. When John wrote such sentences as "His force the boy got from his mother," he wondered if he was writing biography or autobiography.

Thinking aloud to Edmund about the chapter that would be called "The Colour of This Soul," John said he would give a good deal to know more about Mary Crane, Stephen's mother. Edmund electrified him by saying that his own mother had known her: The two women had met at Asbury Park. Mrs. Wilson went regularly to the Jersey shore to escape the summer heat in Red Bank, Mrs. Crane to be with the Methodists at Ocean Grove. A public speaker and journalist, Mrs. Crane talked about and wrote on religious and social subjects. Among the things Edmund remembered his mother having said about her was that she was "a remarkable woman."

This was the word John often used to describe *his* mother. She was remarkably intelligent, remarkably energetic and, on the occasion of her recent fifty-fifth birthday, at which she had appeared as a platinum blonde, remarkably youthful. If John admired the way she looked, what he learned in the early months of therapy had put him on guard against her, for he was beginning to be aware of the heavy price he had paid, and continued to pay, for their close relationship. (When he read that Crane said of his mother, "You could argue just as well with a wave," he asked me, "Who does *that* remind you of?")

If he wanted to get on with this book, he would have to guard against mixing up Crane and Berryman (the trap we suspected Richard had fallen into with Adams), especially as he plunged deeper and deeper into Crane's psyche. To feel compelled to rescue sexually discredited women who belonged to other men, to seek them out repeatedly and compulsively to gratify an unconscious desire for an unattainable satisfaction—the longed-for mother—was, in Freudian terms, Crane's case. This, together with an exploration of the dominant symbols in Crane's work, was the burden of "The Colour of This Soul."

Reading draft after draft of these pages, I objected that while they would be enormously interesting to psychoanalysts, the literary and academic audience for the Series would almost certainly be baffled by his speculations and perhaps find them ludicrous. He deleted a few of the sections that I marked "psycho-meshuga" (a bastard-Yiddish term we used in Princeton for a woman in town who was so humorlessly Freudian that she analyzed even her dog's bark); others he rewrote so that they were less dense. By the end of July 1949, when the final version was completed and he had not so much handed in the manuscript as had it wrested from his grasp, I continued to be concerned. Wouldn't reviewers who were put off by this chapter be blinded to the virtues of the rest of the book? John saw the risk. "It's a risk I have to take. The writer who concerns himself with what reviewers will say is lost."

For the most part reviewers dealt with "The Colour of This Soul" more kindly than I had predicted. While they were doubtful of the need to evoke "the unhappy ghost of Freud," as one of them put it, their criticism was muted. The general consensus on the book as a whole was that it was "distinguished," as I reported to John. The Kirkus review was too good not to show him: "A lack of humor, an affected style, a lack of perspective common to *Partisan Review* writers." *"What?* No humor?" John cried. "I'll show them. The next thing I publish will be called *Berryman's Joke Book."*

The severest critic was not Graham Greene, though in *The New Statesman* he was very severe about "the tortured prose that is unable to convey accuracy." It was the author himself. He had been able to relinquish the manuscript only by telling himself that he would rewrite it from beginning to end before the second edition ("Will there *be* a second edition?"). When Farrar, Straus came to reissue it twelve years later, however, he must have felt better satisfied. Apart from adding a new preface, he let the book stand as it was. By then he had had the gratification of knowing that he had started a Crane revival. And he knew too, by then, how deeply Crane had entered his own soul.

Crane's fiction, rather than his verse, had become a powerful influence on his poetry.

When we went to the Cape for a brief vacation in August, John could imagine no such future, nor any possible gain from his labors. After a day or two of euphoria at being out of his study and away from Princeton, he became depressed and irritable. The respite we had both looked forward to—he from the Crane, I from my thesis, which I had submitted before leaving—seemed out of reach. He was convinced that the book was a failure, dreaded the battles he would have with his editor (a woman in whom he saw many of his mother's traits) over the prepublication details, and was apprehensive about Sloane Associates' lawyers who, he suspected, would slash passages they thought might be libelous.

As he walked on the beach trying to exhaust himself so that he could sleep, he was certain he would never have the energy to write verse again. The Bradstreet poem? He'd lost it. Alcohol, sedatives, stimulants: The abuse his nervous system had taken was irreparable. He was finished, finished.

Nothing I said could convince him that he would recover, that he would write verse again. He had felt this way after the summer of joblessness in New York and had recovered. He would again.

No. This time was different. And, what was more, he had also forfeited whatever chance he had had, we had had, for personal happiness. After Lise he had told himself that he could once again become the kind of husband he had been—"only better." He saw now that he had undergone what Ruskin called "a grievous metamorphosis," and there was no possibility of return. While he felt no drive to rescue discredited women as Crane had, he compulsively sought, and easily found, flirtatious women who belonged to other men, and who in their infidelity to their husbands mimicked his mother's infidelity to his father. Understanding this (his current analysis of his motivation) helped him not at all in governing his actions. "Cigarettes, alcohol, women. Need need need"—if Henry had not yet become a literary personality, he had already entered our lives.

Of all this I knew what I could bear to know and to guess from John's broad hints and lamentations about his "lost innocence" and the "sundering" of our relationship, which the Cape, with its memories of earlier summers, brought home to him agonizingly. (The pose of braggart he adopted only after we separated and the "flicker of impulse lust" continued to be beyond his control.)

For the first time, the Macdonalds found John a trying guest. At an evening beach party, the kind at which in previous years he had told ghost stories to the children and joined lustily in the singing, he blew up over an argument he had with Dwight, broke away from the group and strode into the ocean fully clothed. The icy water shocked him back to his senses before he had gone very far, but he had alarmed all of us on the beach. He had not meant to frighten us, he said, contrite. He had known he was out of control and, wanting to get away, had gone into the surf without thinking what he was doing. Dwight, realizing what bad shape John was in, made a gesture of friendship to patch things up between them. The next day, however, there was another quarrel and another. There were so many of them that by the time we left for home the relationship between the two men had been damaged. Though they continued to be friends, they never recaptured their old ease with each other.

While in Wellfleet we heard a rumor that Cal had gone South with Elizabeth Hardwick to be married at the Jarrells'. During the previous months Cal's life had been more turbulent by far than John's. At a time when John was at his lowest ebb, he heard that Cal, who had spent the winter at Yaddo, was flying high. Verse flowed from his pen during the day, wit from his lips at night. So brilliant was his talk that Elizabeth Hardwick, Flannery O'Connor and a group of others in residence had fallen under his spell. With what seemed like energy to burn, he had interested himself in the management of Yaddo. Becoming convinced that Elizabeth Ames, the director, and her friend Agnes Smedley (author of *China's Red Army Marches* and various other volumes on China) were not merely fellow travelers but active Communists, he requested that the board of directors be convened so that he could present his case against Mrs. Ames and ask for her dismissal. Other past and present residents, unconvinced by Cal's assertions, rallied to her defense. When the decision was made in her favor, Cal and his group quit Saratoga Springs for New York.

Gertrude, who saw them soon afterward, said, "Cal has hypnotized them. They don't seem to realize he's crazy."

Was he? John wondered, trying to recollect Cal's telephone call from New York to Princeton. Certainly he had seemed wildly excited about having written over a thousand lines of a poem. (Who wouldn't be?) But hadn't he been even more wound up about "a holy crusade" he wanted John to join? Cal's speech had been so uncharacteristically rapid and slurred that John had thought he must have been drinking and therefore hadn't taken the crusade seriously.

The next news we had I brought home after spending a night at the Macdonalds'. Dwight, Mary McCarthy, Elizabeth Hardwick and Cal had gone together to a meeting of the Cultural and Scientific Conference for World Peace at the Waldorf, to ask questions of the speakers that they hoped would expose the group as the Communist-front organization they were convinced it was. On that occasion Dwight had found Cal impressive—shrewd, articulate and incisive. Later, however, when they'd all gone back to the Macdonalds' apartment, Cal's behavior had been disquieting. He had pressed a ten-dollar bill on Nicky, the Macdonalds' younger son, and, in a gesture meant to be affectionate, had whacked Dwight on the arm so energetically that it had been painful.

Some weeks later we learned that Cal had been committed to a mental hospital. We didn't have a full account of what had occurred between the time he and his group left Yaddo and he was taken to the hospital until Elizabeth (whom John resisted calling "Lizzie" because he felt the nickname didn't suit her), together with Mary and her husband, Bowden Broadwater, stopped in Princeton in mid-April, on their way home from a trip to Virginia. John, who was in one of his not-to-be-disturbed-under-any-circumstances moods as he pushed toward another Crane deadline, was so eager for news of Cal that he broke off work and cycled home from the library as soon as he heard who our visitors were.

Reviewing the Yaddo episode, Elizabeth said that what very much complicated matters was that the day of the board meeting there had been an abrupt and striking change in Cal's behavior. At the hearing he had conducted himself with uncharacteristic arrogance and, for the first time, what he said sounded grandiose. Later that evening, when they were sitting around discussing the events of the day, he announced that he had gone back to the Church. Elizabeth didn't take him seriously until the next morning when he went to Mass. By the time they were in New York, and Cal was staying in her apartment, there was little question but that he was manic. He talked incessantly, telephoned everyone he knew (which was why the line had always been busy when John tried to reach him to arrange a meeting), buttonholed strangers on the street, sent telegrams flying all over the country, declared a million times that he felt "marvelous," that he loved everyone, that he wanted everyone he knew to be happy and was determined to see that they would be—even if it meant interfering in their lives. No, he was not drinking, Elizabeth said, in answer to John's question. Not a drop. He was also not sleeping, not a wink.

Allen Tate's life needed straightening out, so Cal called him and summoned him to New York, "to hear the will of God."

"Cal really is crazy, then," said John, who had been unwilling to believe the gossip. "Did he think *he* was God?"

He didn't claim to be, though he was certain he knew what the will of God was. When Allen declined to come East, Cal decided to stop in Chicago to see him, en route to visit his old Kenyon College roommate and close friend Peter Taylor, who was in Indiana. He left saying that he had to "bring Allen to know his sins. All must be known, and then all forgiven." Not only must Allen be brought to know his sins; Caroline must know them, too. Allen's love affairs must be exposed and repented of.

"Oh no!" John groaned. "He told Caroline? He named names?" We all knew some of them.

Yes indeed, he named names. Caroline had not been grateful for this information, and Allen had been beside himself with rage. Rage turned into terror as Cal, thinking he was being frisky, grabbed Allen around the waist in a great bear hug. In the ensuing fracas, Cal opened the window and shouted into the street. A crowd collected, the police were called and, after some deliberation, it was decided that he should be escorted to the train for Indiana. In the meantime, the exhausted and thoroughly frightened Tates called Peter Taylor, warned him that Cal was in a dangerous state and advised him not to let Cal into his house.

The wonder was that he got to Indiana. Peter, who had thought Allen must be exaggerating, quickly saw that his old roommate was acting strangely. He took Cal to dinner at a club and left him there for the night. Cal grew restless, went looking for him and, by chance, knocked on the door of a policeman's house. Afraid he would be apprehended, Cal struck the policeman. Others were summoned and, there being no mental hospital where he could be kept until his mother arrived, he was put in the local jail. Mrs. Lowell flew to Indiana with

Dr. Merrill Moore. Together they took Cal to Baldpate Hospital outside Boston.

Throughout this account John, who knew what it was to have a breakdown and had been imagining himself point by point in Cal's shoes, was slow to see the humor in the many comic details woven into this tragic story. He remained solemn on hearing that Peter had been locked in the cell with Cal for hours and had been unable to convince the guard that he was quite sane and should be freed. But he burst out laughing at an episode that Mary reminded Elizabeth she had forgotten. Sometime during the chaotic period before the trip to the Middle West, Cal went off to a Benedictine monastery to make a retreat (one corner of his fevered brain warning him that he needed isolation and tranquillity?). Through another misunderstanding, of which there had been so many, he was put with a group of businessmen who were alcoholics. Since there was little in the homilies the monks addressed to this group that applied to him, Cal became restless and left. His time had not been wasted, he felt, because he had used the occasion to address a few homilies of his own to the monks—on the corruption of the Church.

Telephone wires burned, letters flew through the mails, cocktail parties buzzed with what had happened to Cal. Jean Stafford said, "You see?" Those who had opposed Cal at Yaddo said, "You see?" Others who were convinced that he had been right about Mrs. Ames and Agnes Smedley said Cal was crazy like a fox. Rumor had it that at Baldpate he was reading Eisenhower's memoirs, that he had tried to talk the commander (Cal's father now, not Eisenhower) into checking in at the hospital, that he had refused to have Dr. Moore as his psychiatrist, that he had been put in the violent ward, that he was free to wander the grounds, that he was in wet packs, that he was having shock therapy, that he and Elizabeth were in love. John had a letter from him which, while not completely coherent, was certainly not the communication of a dangerous man.

After Cal had been shocked back to sanity and released, he was like a man awakening from a gigantic binge. What had he done during the weeks before he was hospitalized? All he could remember (this John found heartbreaking) was that he had never in his life been happier than during those manic weeks. The rapture he had felt was replaced, now that he was supposedly well, by a "purgatorial feeling." He would have been even more horrified to hear what had happened at the Tates' and in Indiana, had he not already begun to be gnawed by an anxiety he expressed to me sometime later, following his second breakdown.

After the opera one evening during the Christmas season, Cal suggested that a group of us go to the Stork Club, which he'd heard so much about but had never been in. How depressed he was I hadn't realized during dinner and the intermissions. He had seemed merely subdued. But on the dance floor there was no missing it. His legs were like a robot's moving in slow motion, oblivious of the music. Over the noise of the band, he asked me the question which was tormenting him: Would it happen again? He knew, as he knew I knew, that, the nature of his illness being cyclical, there was every chance of a recurrence. What haunted him was not simply the idea of another period of mania, during which he would do God knew what, nor even the incarceration in an institution and the horrors of electroshock therapy. It was the fear that the next time, or the time after, he would not recover. Or, if he did, that he would be released with the part of his brain he used for writing poetry burned out by the high voltages of the shock machine. Would his illness finish him as a writer?

There was no way to reassure him that he wouldn't have another attack, but I was convinced that, with his constitution, immense vitality and ambition, there was little likelihood of his turning into a chronic case such as he had seen shuffling around the wards. And there was hope that before long drugs would be found to replace the shock treatment.

In 1954, a year after John and I had separated, I visited Cal in a Cincinnati hospital following his third breakdown (which had occurred during the semester he held the Elliston Chair of Poetry there). An orderly took me through a series of locked doors to his room. Cal was lying on a cot, facing the wall. His favorite writing posture, I thought at first. But no, it was not that. His body was curled in on itself, his knees pulled up to his chin. When I said my name, he jumped up with the boyish gawkiness that had struck me in Damariscotta, and greeted me as if he was relieved to see a friend rather than a doctor. Lithium, the drug with which he was later to be treated, had still not been developed. He was in postshock purgatory. If he didn't repeat the question he had asked me at the Stork Club, it was there in his eyes. It quickly became apparent to me that while he had supposedly been eager for my visit, he disliked being seen in his present state. Nor did he want to talk about the onset of his illness, which had been triggered by the death of his mother.

Wily Cal deflected the conversation from himself to me. Why had I left John? In an effort to deny to himself that he had been going into a manic period, Cal had left Elizabeth (whom he couldn't fool, as he could people in Cincinnati who barely knew him) and had convinced himself that he was in love with a young Italian. Sane again, he saw this maneuver for what it had been. He and Elizabeth were going to be reunited when he was discharged. Surely John and I would be reunited too, wouldn't we? It was no easier for me to talk about my separation from John than it was for Cal to talk about his mother's death. We settled on a superficial exchange about mutual friends in Cincinnati, and after a little of this I made an excuse to go.

Having heard the details of the onset of this breakdown, and the psychiatrists' gloomy prognostications, I left the hospital feeling pessimistic. But the psychiatrists, underestimating Cal's strengths, were wrong. He was to recover more quickly than anyone would have believed possible.

The big news Richard brought to his first lunch with John at the beginning of the fall semester of 1949 was that the Tates were returning to Princeton. It was Allen, in 1939, who had started the chain of poets teaching creative writing on campus, he who had invited Richard to join him. The two men had had a falling out before the Tates left Princeton, Allen claiming that Richard had usurped his job. Richard was going to make an effort to get on with Allen—community life required it—and he urged John to do the same.

John was not filled with joy at the news of the Tates' arrival because he had heard stories from all sides about the way Allen had behaved toward Cal in Chicago. On our way to one of the first parties of the season, to which Allen had also been invited, John said that despite Richard's advice he planned to be aloof with Allen, and urged me to follow suit. It wouldn't be easy, because Allen would undoubtedly turn on the charm. Under these circumstances I was not looking forward to meeting Allen, although I felt considerable curiosity about this man I had heard described as a superb poet and critic, a generous mentor, an urbane host on the one hand; on the other, as a politician, even an operator, who in recent years (a time when he had not been able to write poetry) had become divisive and jealous over the success of others. What to believe? As John had predicted, Allen sought me out at the party. On first meeting him I was struck, as was everyone, by the size and curve of his forehead, the great bombé brow that he later told me had, during his childhood, made his relatives wonder whether he had water on the brain and was not "all there." It was their doubts about his intellectual ability, he claimed, that had given him, by reaction, his intellectual ambition: He'd show them that what was behind that brow was a powerful brain. I remembered a story John had told me about a football player who had come to the Tates' Princeton house courting their very beautiful daughter, Nancy, who at sixteen was the belle of Princeton. Allen tried for some time to make conversation with this "oaf," who could talk of nothing but his muscles. Losing patience, Allen said, "See here, young man, what matters is not what you have here"—striking his upper arm—"but here"—striking his brow.

COURTESY OF ROBERT GIROUX

Allen Tate

Approaching fifty, Allen had the slim build and gait of a much younger man. He wore a mustache which he used as a weapon in literary criticism. When he commented unfavorably on a poet's most recent publication, he twitched it up to the side and sniffed through one nostril. John had told me that Allen was a superb reader of verse, and listening to him speak I could well believe it. He was as charming as John warned me he would be. If he found me frosty in my effort to resist being won over, he gave no sign. He was warm enough for both of us.

"Well, what do you think of him?" John asked on the way home. I was puzzled. It would take more than one evening for me to judge a man as complex as Allen.

A few days later Allen called asking John for help in drafting a letter to the *Saturday Review of Literature* about the Pound-Bollingen affair. As Allen well knew, John found it difficult to resist a call for help, especially one that had to do with a literary matter. He set off for the Balt, where they were to meet, determined not to discuss Cal. If Allen began a sentence with, "That boy . . ." which John was certain would end with " . . . is finished," he planned to cut Allen off. No sooner had he sat down than Allen said Cal's breakdown had been the result of the Pulitzer: It had turned his head. John countered that it would surely take more than the Prize to cause a breakdown. They hadn't met to talk about Lowell. What about Pound?

After the Fellows in American Letters of the Library of Congress had selected Pound as the winner of the recently established Bollingen Award for *The Pisan Cantos,* the *Saturday Review* invited Robert Hillyer, a poet and ex-professor at Harvard to write two articles "assessing" the Fellows' choice. Their appearance caused a furor in literary circles. Hillyer not only attacked the selection of Pound (which, because of Pound's pro-Fascist broadcasts for Rome Radio during the war, as well as for his notorious anti-Semitism, many intellectuals had disapproved of), but also used the occasion for a broad attack on the new criticism, on modern poetry and especially on T. S. Eliot, "the foreigner . . . who gave up his country in favor of one he liked better." His envy of Eliot's success was so patent that many people laughed at the articles. Others, enraged, wrote angrily to the *Saturday Review.* A proposal for a congressional investigation of the "plot" against democracy, which Hillyer had hinted was behind the choice of a man under arrest for treason, was dropped, but because of the scandal Congress decided that the Library should no longer administer the Award.

Allen, a Fellow in American Letters of the Library of Congress (as was Cal), a writer of modern poetry and a new critic, was directly in Hillyer's line of fire on three counts. He felt that a letter signed by as many intellectuals from as varied backgrounds as possible should be sent to the *Review*. John thought it an excellent idea. Together they decided what the letter should say, and drew up a list of people to send it to. John wrote the letter; together they sent it out. In return they received eighty-four signatures. When the *Review* stalled about printing it, Margaret Marshall wrote a two-column summary of the affair and printed the letter in *The Nation*.

For many, the final word was had by Dwight Macdonald in an editorial in *politics*. He wrote: "Whether *The Pisan Cantos* is the best poetry published by an American last year or not, I am incompetent to judge. Nor is this the point considered here, which is rather that by some miracle the Bollingen judges were able to consider Mr. Pound the poet apart from Mr. Pound the fascist, Mr. Pound the antisemite, Mr. Pound the traitor, Mr. Pound the funny-money crank, and all the other Mr. Pounds whose existence had properly nothing to do with the question of whether Mr. Pound the poet had or had not written the best American poetry of 1948."

If Allen's aim in asking John to cooperate with him over the letter was a device for re-establishing a relationship between them, as I suspected it was, he was eminently successful. By the time their meetings and telephonings back and forth were over, John, no better able to resist Allen's charms than anyone else, was once again in the fold. Nothing made this clearer than Allen's invitation to us to attend the party Caroline was giving for his fiftieth birthday, and John's acceptance.

The house the Tates had bought, tiny and old, hugged Nassau Street at what was then the edge of town. How they fitted so many people into their doll-size living room and gave them all food and drink was a mystery. There were such copious amounts of the latter that midway through the evening I noticed that the laurel wreath Caroline had plaited and planted on Allen's head had slipped so that it partly obscured his right eye, externalizing the slippage all of us were feeling, to varying degrees, by that time.

Having heard from many people that Caroline was formidable and

Caroline Gordon

sharp-tongued, I had been disarmed the first time I met her (the day she introduced us to the Lowells) by her attempts to find kinship with me. There was no kinship certainly where family was concerned. She was a Southerner, I a Northerner. But wasn't I a Catholic? She was a recent convert. I was also the wife of a poet. Poets' wives, like coal miners' wives, or the wives of other men engaged in dangerous occupations, feel a certain solidarity.

It was as poets' wives that we knew each other during the early years. Beginning with the party for Allen, we saw each other frequently if not intimately. We, or they, always had other guests. Allen would call and say, "Bunny [Edmund] Wilson is here. Come have a drink." The men did most of the talking, Allen and Edmund ribbing each other, exchanging mildly insulting remarks.

Allen to Edmund, who had protested that he couldn't stay for another drink; he'd already kept his mother's chauffeur waiting too long and must get back to Red Bank:

"Chauffeur?" Allen sniffed through one nostril. Looking out the door to see who was behind the wheel of the Cadillac, he said disdainfully, "That's not a chauffeur, Bunny. Why that's just an ordinary field negra."

Edmund to Allen, who, on another occasion, was driving us errati-
cally through traffic to Lahière's for dinner: "Thank you uh uh, thank
you Allen for uh for uh for an interesting and hazardous experiment
in uh what it's like to drive on the wrong side of the road, an
experiment hohoho which I uh I want never to repeat."

Or the two men discussed the pros and cons of being married to
novelists—Allen to Caroline, Edmund to Mary McCarthy, Cal to Jean
Stafford and Elizabeth Hardwick, and, as we'd recently heard, Delmore to Elizabeth Pollet—deciding hohoho that the hazards here were
considerable too: One ran the risk of seeing oneself portrayed in fiction
in a less-than-favorable light.

It was as former wives of poets that Caroline and I saw each other
during the second period of our relationship, in the mid-fifties. She was
living in another tiny and ancient house, "The Red House," not far
from where she and Allen had lived. After eighteen years of marriage
the Tates had divorced, remarried (not long before they returned to
Princeton) and had now divorced again. The second divorce tore
Caroline apart. In this black and bitter period, she would invite me
to dinner and pour out her anguish at Allen's having left her. That I
had gone through two agonizing years after separating from John, and
knew what she must be feeling, she refused to believe. Our situations
were different: John had not left me for another woman; I had left him.
Only because he drove me to it, I reminded her. Brushing aside what
seemed to her a quibble, she said that I had had the satisfaction of
knowing that John had suffered greatly; whereas, from all reports,
Allen was shamelessly happy. Above all, John had not remarried. Allen
had. Any word of comfort I offered Caroline was certain to be the
wrong word. There was little I could do but listen. She was inconsola-
ble.

In the late sixties, after I returned from several years abroad and was
living in New York, I often visited Caroline in Princeton. If she was
still suffering because of Allen (who had divorced his second wife and
remarried again), time had dissipated her bitterness. Reminiscing about
the old days, she talked about Allen in a way that showed how
important he had been in her development as a writer. The critic she
admired above all others was her private critic. What she wrote, he
read. His suggestions were invaluable. Throughout the violent swings
in their marital life, they had been held together by a common South-

ern heritage (there had been a small Confederate flag on a wall of the
Nassau Street house), and by a literary comradeship which gave their
relationship a depth and breadth that marriage alone would not have
done.

Caroline, like Allen, had been born in Kentucky. Like him, she had
had a classical education. (She felt a mixture of pity and scorn for
writers who had not studied Greek as well as Latin.) After they married
and were living in New York, they had so little money that Allen
performed the janitorial duties in the Village house where they lived
to pay the rent on their apartment, while she worked as Ford Madox
Ford's secretary.

It was on Allen's first Guggenheim in 1928, when they were living
in Paris, that she wrote her novel *Penhally.* In the Paris days Allen was
little help to her as a writer. He and Hart Crane and their poet friends
were so self-confident, so sure of their talent, so far ahead of where
she was in a literary career, that she felt crushed by them. To Ford,
for whom she was again working, she confided that she had a novel
half finished and was stuck. Ford read what she'd written and said,
"That's good. Now: Tell me what happens next." She told him what
she imagined would follow. "Fine. Write it." Each time she lost
confidence and got bogged down again, Ford prodded her with,
"What happens next? Fine. Write it." He babied it out of her, she said,
with gratitude that forty years had not diminished. What gave this
formula its magical power was Caroline's hero-worship of an older
and famous man who, being a novelist, was a powerful counterweight
to "all those poets."

It was only after they returned to the United States and were living
in Tennessee that Allen became her critic. He was endlessly encouraging while she was writing *Aleck Maury,* and gave her the kind of
detailed criticism that is so hard to come by. He said, for example, that
if she wanted to write fiction, and not merely a character sketch, she
would have to forget her father (the person on whom Aleck was based)
and imagine Aleck. "Once you've heard it, you say: Of course! How
many times since have I had to give the same advice to my students?"

Although Allen was four years her junior she talked about him as
if he were the elder by some years. He had authority in domestic as
well as literary matters, even over the behavior of her beloved cats.
In her passion for cats she had let them come into their bedroom, first

one, then another, until one morning Allen woke up, stood on the bed, and thundered, "Get those damn cats out of here." He was probably the only person capable of making Caroline docile. It was one of the things she loved about him.

If Allen did what he could to foster her career, there was little he could do to provide her with the success she deserved. *None Shall Look Back,* the novel for which they both had great hopes, was published the same year as *Gone with the Wind.* To have a novel on a Southern theme come out at the same time as that blockbuster was bad luck indeed. For Caroline it was a blow so severe that she never fully recovered. Nor did she ever permit anyone to mention Margaret Mitchell's name in her presence.

What would she have done without Max? she wondered. Maxwell Perkins, the legendary editor at Scribner's, assured her that though her novels never sold more than 3,000 copies, while he was alive she could always count on being published by him. Allen read her manuscript first, Max second. If Perkins offered her detailed criticism, she never mentioned it. What was important was that "Max was always there."

She missed them both sorely when, in her mid-seventies, she was trying to finish her novel, *Hera,* and was having a very bad time with it. "I swear I'll never write another one. I'm too old." When her doctor started to tell her that she had arthritis and should use an electric typewriter to relieve back fatigue, she snapped at him, "I'm not interested in the diagnosis. Just keep me alive until I hand in *Hera.*" After he limited her alcoholic intake to two ounces a day (part of his effort to keep her alive, although, if one could judge from her energy, he was going to have an easy time of it), she'd hold up her glass at a cocktail party each time the host came around with drinks and say demurely, "Just two ounces please."

Caroline had little patience with married feminist writers who "whined" about having domestic chores to do. Her practice had been to organize the house first thing in the morning, then go to the typewriter. (How much, I wondered, had Jean Stafford's way of running the Damariscotta house been learned, as had so much about writing fiction, from Caroline?) "When I think of the cooking I did at 'Benfolly!' [the Tates' house in Tennessee]. We never had less than ten at the table. That summer Cal camped on our lawn . . ."

At "Benfolly" charades had been one of Caroline's favorite games.

After the toasts and the cutting of the cake the night of Allen's birthday party in Princeton, she suggested that we play. The guests, in pairs, chose a word and acted it out before the group. Richard, who was hiding behind the bar, and hoping to avoid having to perform (games made him shy), pointed to Helen and John who were whispering and laughing, "Those two are up to something." When it was their turn, Helen arranged herself languorously on the couch: the clothed *maja*. John, with his napkin folded at his neck like a Roman collar, rushed into the room and threw himself by the side of the couch so that his head rested in Helen's lap. Helen's look of abandon and John's melodramatic gesture sent a ripple of shock around the room.

The silence was broken when someone guessed, "Passion, is that the word?" John made a gesture of encouragement: Hot. "Demimondaine?" "Affair?" "Infidelity?" "Actress?" "Theater?"

Cold. Cold. Cold. Trying to prompt those who were getting further from the mark, John kept pointing to his collar. "Give up? Give up?" he cried triumphantly, when no more suggestions were forthcoming and even the wordsmiths were stumped. "The word is 'parnel'— a priest's mistress." John had come across it while engaged in one of his favorite pastimes, browsing in the dictionary, and had been burning to use it.

The next day, when we called to thank the Tates for the evening, Caroline said they already had evidence, the best possible, that the party had been a success. It had stirred up gossip. Allen had just returned from the Balt where the talk had been of the *scandale* Helen and John had created. She, Caroline, was delighted with the way the game had gone. In the novel she was working on her characters played charades. She had needed a word that was unusual and provocative, and John had given it to her.

Caroline could have it, John said, but he also planned to use it. Though where? It was one of those "lovely" words that kick around in the brain with no place to go. Years later, in what must have been a moment of exasperation, he gave it, together with a guitar, to Henry Hankovitch in "Dream Song #31," although surely Henry, never having taken Holy Orders, could not have been accused of having a parnel—whatever his other sins.

IX
MISTRESS BRADSTREET

The game of poetical chairs—in which writers move from campus to campus, pausing for shorter or longer periods depending on the whim of the whistle-blower, then moving on to another chair—came into fashion in the early fifties. Despite John's impression that the publication of *Stephen Crane* had as little effect in establishing his reputation as *The Dispossessed,* between 1950 and 1952 he received invitations from the universities of Washington, Vermont, Wayne, Cincinnati and Princeton.

Dylan Thomas, who was at the beginning of his fatal career as the star performer in the game, made a stop in Seattle while John was there in the spring of 1950 replacing Ted Roethke, who had been hospitalized with a breakdown. (I was working at the Rutgers Psychological Clinic at the time, and remained in Princeton for the semester.) The two men met at a large English department party for the first time since the day in London when Dylan had tried to get John drunk so that he'd miss his meeting with Yeats. In the intervening thirteen years Dylan's consumption of alcohol had become notorious, and while John had not yet begun to have a drink before teaching, or a reading, or before writing, Dylan would no longer have been able to accuse him of being abstemious or "effete."

The two men, who had looked forward to talking about what Dylan called their "sullen art," had had time for no more than a few words before the guest of honor was swept away by a crowd of admirers. Writing me about the occasion from Seattle, John said that even if it meant taking a day off from my work, I must not miss hearing Thomas when he came to Princeton.

The gossip had been telegraphed to Princeton about the Welsh poet's highly successful efforts to shock faculty and students, especially female, and Richard, who was to act as his host, was uneasy about how the visit would go. After the first meeting he said he found Thomas refreshingly "manly," a nice change from the "pansy poets from England" who had recently been through town.

On the platform Thomas had the self-possession and stance of a Shakespearean actor. While his face had lost the cherubic quality one knew from the Augustus John portrait, and he had put on what looked like an unhealthy amount of weight, his bigness made him impressive and, yes, manly looking. His witty and somewhat insulting opening remarks about academics, the academics responded to with good humor, each believing it was not his nose but his colleague's that was being tweaked. As he began to read:

> Now as I was young and easy under the apple boughs
> About the lilting house and happy as the grass was green,

it was clear that what made him so sought-after as a performer was his deep, rolling, theatrical voice (with, surprisingly, a lisp, exposed by lines like, "Seaward the salmon, sucked sun slips"). He took risks with inflection that would have been embarrassingly melodramatic had he had less than perfect control. His recitation of "John Kinsella's Lament for Mrs. Mary Moore," and especially the refrain lines:

> *What shall I do for pretty girls*
> *Now my old bawd is dead?*

brought down the house.

Afterward, at his meeting with undergraduates from the creative writing program, he was a great success. When the group broke up, Richard took his guest to his room at the Nassau Tavern and left him at his door, thinking that after the long day he must be tired. Tired he was, but also lonely enough to respond to a telephone invitation (extended to him on a dare) to a party that was going on at the Institute housing project.

One heard endless stories about Dylan's outrageousness at American colleges. Less was heard about the equal outrageousness of Americans who were supposedly offering him hospitality. At the party one of the guests, who had been drinking heavily, lost little time in attacking the poet he had earlier gone to hear read. "Why do you write that kind of stuff? Why don't you write so that people can understand you?" Thomas, who certainly had answers ready, turned away, unwilling to be provoked.

John expressed admiration for this remarkable control which, as he wrote, must have been made possible by Dylan's relative sobriety. Had he also been drinking heavily there would have been a free-for-all. What *was* it about poets that stirred people up this way? John wondered. When he had been similarly provoked in Seattle, he had lost his temper so badly he had become convinced, once again, that he was "unfit for human society." John's three months at the University of Washington, which were drawing to a close, had not been a success. The money he earned had evaporated, he had suffered greatly from loneliness, had constantly made and broken resolutions to cut down on drinking and smoking, and was as "mad" to get back to Princeton as he had been to get away, although what we would live on . . .

Perhaps a Hodder Fellowship, Richard said. Richard returned from Maine in the fall of 1950 looking as if he'd seen a ghost, and didn't want to talk about it. As first we thought this somber and withdrawn mood was a reflection of his failure to have made progress on the Adams book while he was away. It was true, he admitted to John, that he hadn't written a word. And because he hadn't, he felt powerless to move forward on other projects.

But when October came and went and there was no lifting of his mood, nor any word about when he was expecting Helen, we wondered if he had greater concerns than literary ones on his mind. He was as unapproachable about Helen as a man recently widowed who makes it clear that any mention of the deceased by others would be an intrusion on his grief. "We've made a mistake to let this go on for so long," John said, early in November. "I'm going to have lunch with Richard and make him talk." After they'd had a martini, John said, "Listen, Richard, we miss Helen. Where *is* she?"

Now it was John who looked as if he had seen the ghost. As he came in the door of the apartment, he blurted out, "She's left him. After twenty years, she's left him." How bad the marriage had been we knew, everyone knew. All of us had made the mistake of thinking that because it had lasted so long, it would go on forever. Richard was so paralyzed by the pain he was suffering that he would never have talked about the separation, John said, had he not put the question to him point-blank. "Neither of us seems to have been able to give what the other needed," Richard had said, his face pinched and drawn. "And there's nothing that can be done about this, is there?"

The separations and divorces of friends always shook John. Delmore and Gertrude, Cal and Jean, now Richard and Helen. If their marriages broke up, could not. . . ? Delmore and Cal had remarried. So, too, had Jean. While John was in Seattle I had sent him a clipping from *Mademoiselle,* a photograph of Jean at a Caribbean resort. On her head was a straw hat, a shield against the "detested" sun, on the table in front of her were four daiquiris, a shield against her doubts. We had seen little of her during her whirlwind romance with Oliver Jensen. From telephone conversations, it was clear that she was basking in the attentions of a suitor, the kind of attention she had never received from Cal. "Can you imagine Cal sending flowers?" she asked. "Or bringing gifts of perfume and champagne? I'm being courted." So little had she wanted to hear the warning voice of her psychiatrist, who suggested that she was marrying without sufficient reflection, that she broke off treatment.

The shell of Richard's life remained intact after Helen left. He kept the apartment on Princeton Avenue and, after his talk with John, reinstituted his Saturdays at home. He had his life on campus, his cronies at the Balt, his lunches at Lahière's and almost as many invitations to dine out as he could have wished. Although he disliked eating alone, he was, unlike Delmore or Cal or John, competent to look after himself. He had done so during the years Helen had worked in the factory and during the months each year when she was in Maine. Bachelorhood was neither unfamiliar nor unattractive to him. But inside the shell there was a great ache. He had lost Helen, whom he greatly admired and loved in his convoluted way. He had also lost Maine, that real and imaginary state. The studio he had helped build and the garden he had planted belonged to Helen. He would never see them again.

When Helen came to town to collect her possessions, she said that if Richard was suffering, it was not from loss of her, but from wounded pride. She was going to live in the country outside town, devote herself to painting and stay as far away from the academic community as she could. It soon became apparent that the separation meant they would now torture each other from a distance, by mail. Despite Helen's seeming independence, it took four years and a grave illness to propel her into the final break. When, in 1954, I went to visit her in Princeton Hospital, where she was undergoing radium treatment for cancer, she told me with great bitterness that not once in the two weeks she had been there had Richard been in to see her. His terror of illnesses, of hospitals had kept him away:

> The live man visiting the sick
> within him finds his own death quick.

As I was preparing to leave her room, a young man I thought I recognized came in, bringing flowers and a book of reproductions of Impressionist paintings. He asked how she was feeling and in general displayed the kind of solicitousness she had wished for from Richard. He was twenty-one-years old, a poet and a student of Richard's, she told me when she came to say good-bye before moving to Boston. "People will say I'm crazy to go off with someone so young. What do I care what they say? What's more dangerous than his youth"— she gave her hollow laugh—"is that he's a poet. But he wants mothering and is grateful when I give it to him, whereas Richard begged for it and resented his need."

The Hodder Fellowship, which Richard had told John he was being considered for, came through in 1951. It gave him an income for a year and allowed him to choose a subject for a series of public lectures. Since his work on *Lear,* he had been turning over in his mind a general book on Shakespeare. In "Shakespeare at Thirty," his opening lecture (planned as the first chapter in the book), his aim was to scrape away the layers of paint and clay on the "complacent image of the Apollonian Shakespeare," to expose beneath them the thirty-year-old poet and playwright with emotions "active and intense."

Moving swiftly through the mass of biographical scholarship, his racy language jolted the general public out of their pious attitude toward the Bard, so that there was no napping in the lecture hall. (The sound of heavy breathing came from those who had got lost, hurrying to catch up.) The faculty, many of whom had questioned the credentials of a man without a Ph.D. to talk on so hallowed a subject, were won over by his erudition: This was no dreamy poet (in gray flannel suit and shirt with button-down collar); it was a serious scholar who knew his stuff.

On a campus, word travels fast. At the second lecture the audience had doubled and was star-studded. His subject was *Macbeth,* the play that John felt had suffered more than any other from having been "castrated" by prep-school masters to make it presentable to adolescents —"They take a masterpiece, shred it and then wonder why students hate it." He focused on the ambiguity of Macbeth's nature, and through a close examination of the language showed why, even after the king becomes "demonic," he retains our sympathy: We see in the baseness of his character, as well as in the goodness, our own double natures. John, who sometimes spoke as if his nature were all baseness, and was more and more troubled by what he saw as the demonic component in his make-up, had, unlike the King, not murdered anyone; yet he so often dreamed he had that he came to believe the dream was reality (I have committed a murder), the reality a dream (I am innocent).

The most provocative lecture in the series was on *Hamlet.* It was one thing to make use of psychoanalytic theory to interpret Crane, quite another to interpret Shakespeare. Every seat, except one reserved in the front row, was taken. John shifted his papers about on the lectern, looked at his watch, looked at me and, tightening his mouth with impatience, gestured that he could wait no longer. Making an effort to master his vexation, he began. Halfway through his introduction there was a commotion at the rear door. The private drama, the play within a play, was about to begin. All eyes turned—who would have the brass?—to see enter, in vivid dress, Mrs. Berryman. She

Jill Berryman

walked straight down to the first row and took the empty seat directly in front of her son. What he had been thinking with impatience before he began was, "My mother! She said she was coming down from New York to hear me. *Where is she?*" Here she was, scene-stealing. The only indication of John's anger as he continued was that his head went into his neck-in-traction position as he fixed his eyes on a point well above her head.

Did his mother, who was hypersensitive to whatever John said in periods when things were going badly between them, as they were now, feel that there was a message for her in the interpretation of the relationship between Hamlet and Gertrude as oedipal? Did she feel that through the selected readings (Act II, Scene iv), her son was talking to her about his own father's death and her hasty remarriage? If she did, she didn't refer to it when she came back to the apartment afterward. Her revenge, if it was that, was to talk of other things, as if there had been no lecture. She was suffering from jealousy which John had stirred up by talking to her with great warmth about Mrs. Mackie, the mother of a close friend of ours. One day, when John had been out for a walk, he had dropped in on Mrs. Mackie, and coming upon her seated before a fire, having tea and reading a novel, had found in her his vision of the ideal mother. He began to call on her regularly, taking her books and staying to talk with her about them. Mrs. Berryman had felt John's attentiveness to Mrs. Mackie so keenly the one time the two women met that we were no sooner out of the Mackie driveway than there was a blowup. (Over Ed Cone's mother, another of John's ideals, there had been an earlier outburst.)

Wrung out from the strain of the lecture, John was not looking for a quarrel with his mother now. These days there were no scenes that ended with John fainting, such as I had witnessed when I first knew him. In the intervening years mother and son had perfected more subtle techniques for wounding each other.

The Hodder made John's reputation as a lecturer. It also convinced him that he was good at it. Whether he liked lecturing was another matter. The gratification that came from instant success—admirers crowding around afterward to make flattering remarks (all but one's mother, of course), being stopped on campus for days thereafter—as contrasted with the doubts that followed a solitary day in his study, certainly had its appeal. The Hodder also taught him that there was a price to be paid for this way of earning a living and making one's name. The nerved-up feeling beforehand, the trembling intensity that those in the front row could observe, the drenched shirt at the end, the played-out feeling the next day, gave away that he was not a natural. If he did not become actively ill the way Dylan Thomas did (so much for the self-possessed façade!), neither did he perform with ease as, say, Mark did.

Of greater concern to me was John's craving for society afterward. He misinterpreted the clear signal his body sent him that it was exhausted as a need for more stimulation—for people, cigarettes, alcohol. It was this concern that dampened what would have been my unbounded enthusiasm for the Elliston Chair of Poetry, the most important honor to come John's way so far, which the University of Cincinnati offered him for the spring semester of 1952. Aside from seeing students in creative writing for criticism of their work, he would be required to give two public lectures a week. What made the offer especially tempting was that the stipend was large enough to allow me to take a leave of absence from the clinic at Rutgers before going into private practice in Princeton.

Our arrival in Cincinnati was inauspicious. After sitting up all night in an overcrowded train, we took a taxi with suitcases full of books, a typewriter, a brief case bursting with manuscripts, a few clothes and empty wallets to the address we'd been given.

While John went to the comptroller's office on campus to beg an advance on his salary, I dealt with the Misses Regal, two sisters from whom we were renting, and who lived on the floor above us.

The Regals were characters out of a Jean Stafford story, as I told John. The younger, to whom I always talked, was the puppet of the blind sister, bedridden in a darkened room, who projected her voice from behind a half-closed door. It was immediately clear that they looked upon John and me, their first tenants, as Huns who would loot and burn down their house. Would we promise not to smoke? Would we promise not to deface the furniture? Would we promise not to slam the door? Would we promise not to make noise after ten o'clock at night.

"Not smoke? Are they crazy?" my three-pack-a-day husband exclaimed when I reported this conversation. "The university seems to have found us rooms in a monastery. Tell the dear ladies that what poets *do* is smoke; only occasionally, very occasionally, do they write verse. As for this furniture we must promise not to gouge our initials into . . ." We wandered around the dark, high-ceilinged, almost empty rooms, wondering how we could possibly make ourselves comfortable. Camp beds in the bedroom, a massively ugly table in the dining room, spine-puncturing chairs in the living room, a roll-top desk in the study and, in the far corner behind a screen—"So soon?" John sighed—a wheelchair. The gloomy apartment, days of rain, a faculty get-together at which cider and doughnuts were served caused John to say, "We're in for it."

What we were in for, it turned out, were four of the happiest months we had had in a long time. John lectured on Shakespeare one day a week, on poets from Whitman to Lowell (who was to follow him in the Chair two years later) on another. He ran a poetry workshop, read endless manuscripts, talked to every club that invited him, was interviewed and photographed by the local papers. Between times, he discovered at the roll-top desk that the Bradstreet poem had not vanished after all. He might even get under way with it before it was time for the wheelchair. The mail brought the good news that he had been granted a Guggenheim to write verse and work on the Shakespeare book in the coming year. And Wayne University, where he had held his first teaching job, paid him the compliment of inviting him to inaugurate its poetry room. The old-fashioned black telephone, which had been so silent the first week, rang with invitations from Cincinnatians who found the incumbent of the Elliston Chair as diverting as he was instructive. For the first time in his life John was being lionized and he loved it.

Van Meter Ames, a philosopher, and Alister Cameron, a classicist at the university, invited John to join a club with the tongue-in-cheek name of "The Jolly Boys" at which the members presented papers to be published later in learned journals. The discussion following the papers, reminiscent of the Broch-Kahler evenings at Evelyn Place, made John blush to think that he had been apprehensive, on leaving Princeton, about going off to an intellectual desert. Ames and Cameron, he said, were the audience he strove to interest in preparing his own lectures, for he knew they would follow closely what he said, listening with critical attention. After half-hearing the praise from those who came up to him at the end of his talk on Yeats or Eliot or Pound, John was eager to know from these two men how it really had been.

Through the Bettmans (Cincinnatians to whom we'd had a letter of introduction from a Princeton friend), through the Ameses and Camerons, we were introduced to a cultivated group of lawyers,

Alister Cameron and John in Cincinnati, 1952

doctors, bankers and psychiatrists, with some of whom I was studying, through a courtesy extended the wife of the holder of the Elliston Chair, at the University of Cincinnati Medical School. With the coming of spring, the most beautiful we had seen since our first year in Princeton, and the longer days, there were more and more parties. We danced until we collapsed and, unwilling to separate from our new friends, sat up talking, often until dawn.

When Allen Tate came through to visit his older brother Ben, a wealthy businessman, he invited us to Ben's country club for lunch and took us aside to find out how we were bearing up in Cincinnati. We were doing better than bearing up. We were having a roaring good time. Allen twitched his mustache with a mixture of disbelief and disapproval. "You must be in with a fast set. I didn't know there was one here."

If they were fast, our new friends said, it was because they had caught "Berrymania" (even to the point of imitating John's way of pronouncing "poem"). What they were responding to was not only John's "electrifying vivacity." It was also the capacity he had for throwing himself wholeheartedly into relationships. With those he cared for he was disarmingly open, no less funny than witty, eager to listen (as well as to talk), compassionate and generous. In periods when his demons gave him respite, as they did much of the time in Cincinnati, these qualities were as present as they had been when I first met him. During the long-drawn-out crisis over the Crane book, my sister had said, "There's nothing so much the matter with John that a little recognition wouldn't cure." In Cincinnati I was so close to being convinced this was true that I wondered how only a few months earlier I had thought I had no choice but to leave him.

The academic year following our return to Princeton promised to be an unusually lively one. Elena and Edmund Wilson were taking a house in town for six months, Robert Fitzgerald was coming to lecture, and Delmore, at Richard's invitation, was to replace him in the creative writing program.

It had also been through Richard that, three years earlier, Delmore had come to give one of the series in the Princeton Seminars in Literary Criticism, later and better known as the Gauss Seminars. The Seminars offered distinguished critics the opportunity to present a work-in-progress to an intimate group of their peers, in the hope that the discussion following the presentation would enrich the final version of the book. The excellence of the critics selected and the exclusiveness of the audience early established the prestige of the Gauss and made it a much-sought-after honor.

The World Is a Wedding, Delmore's first book in eleven years, had appeared shortly before he first came to Princeton. It was a critical success and a financial failure. Nothing could match the success of *In Dreams,* nor his unrealistic hopes of making a financial killing, so it was not the book's critical acclaim but its lack of financial success that churned in Delmore's mind. The need for money, which he felt especially keenly now that he had remarried, made the Gauss, with its generous stipend, extremely attractive. That he had to appear between two famous European scholars—Ernst Robert Curtius and Erich Auerbach—and would be followed by critics like Hannah Arendt, Francis Fergusson, Kenneth Burke, Herbert Read and Edmund Wilson made him more than a little nervous.

At the party following the first seminar, Delmore introduced us to his wife, Elizabeth Pollet. He had said that she was a novelist (her first novel, *A Family Romance,* was about to be published by New Directions), and that she was beautiful. Beautiful she was. Tall and fair, with pale skin and pale blond hair, a cape over her shoulders, she might have been a figure from a Norse fairy tale.

What did Delmore's mother think of his marrying a gentile? I wondered. When her younger son had married one, Rose Schwartz had said he would be better off dead. Anticipating an hysterical attack, Delmore might well not have told her about Elizabeth. More important, what did *he* think of marrying a gentile? Surely to a man whose subject, in poetry and fiction, was the Jew in America, it could not be unimportant.

Delmore's work-in-progress was the book on Eliot he had been writing intermittently for years. At the post-seminar party, polite comments were made about his first paper, though Richard seemed far from enthusiastic. After the second, Richard looked dour. Delmore had either seriously underestimated the intellectual level of his audience, or had been too depressed to prepare properly. He had been working on Eliot for so long one would have thought little preparation was necessary. Why then were his arguments loose, his responses to questions abstract and imprecise?

The Eliot series was a failure not only because Delmore was inade-
quately prepared, but also, and perhaps more importantly, because his
attitude toward the subject of his long-time and passionate interest had
changed. In the Harvard days his admiration for Eliot had been enormous, and his fabulations and speculations about Eliot's sex life had
been asserted in a good-natured way. He, and we, had laughed at his
claim that the author of "The Waste Land" had become anti-Semitic
after he had been jilted by a woman who was Jewish. By the time of
his Gauss lectures, Delmore was seriously charging Eliot with anti-
Semitism, and hinting that those who questioned his evidence, Richard
and John among them, did so because they weren't Jewish. Jews who
took exception to what he said were "the wrong kind of Jew."
Sometimes he went so far as to echo Hillyer's insinuation that Eliot
had been implicated in a Fascist plot to give Pound the Bollingen, an
attitude that baffled John because at the time of the Hillyer attack
Delmore had signed the protest that John and Allen had organized.

One couldn't help wondering, seeing Delmore bristle with hostility
toward Ed Cone ("the wrong kind of Jew") and others, whether he
didn't feel a need to disprove the accusations he must have imagined
his mother shouting at him: *He* was the wrong kind of Jew; how else
could he have married a goy?

About Princeton Delmore felt much as he felt about marriage. In
theory he thought it would be good for him. In practice it made him
uneasy. He felt he needed the association with an institution to avoid
feeling isolated, and after years of trying to manage without a steady
income he longed for the security of a professor's salary. In practice
Princeton's beauty, order and genteel-gentile style made him feel like
a newly arrived immigrant. The New School and New York University, at both of which he'd taught before the Gauss, could be characterized (crudely) as Jewish, bohemian, disheveled, literary; while Princeton was Presbyterian, stuffy, orderly, scholarly. Greenwich Village
versus the Groves of Academe. He'd had the Village and wanted the
Groves. That his flirtation with Princeton had not gone well did not
put him off his zealous courtship. On the contrary! He began to plot
and scheme for a permanent appointment, and bought a farmhouse in
rural New Jersey which was (again theoretically) a reasonable com-
mute by car to the campus.

"Baptistown?" John said with incredulity, as he searched the map.
Richard had just told us that Delmore had become a landowner. "Here

it is. Delmore is crazy. Why has be buried himself in the sticks? If he'd moved to Roosevelt where Ben Shahn lives, or near those chicken farmers who read poetry, I could see it." From time to time a group of refugees from the Bronx who had settled near Roosevelt and become chicken farmers invited John to read to them. They called for him in a pick-up truck and drove him to the house of the one with the largest living room, where ten or twelve of them listened with rapt attention as he read and explicated poems. Afterward they gave him coffee, the $25 they'd collected by passing the hat, and drove him back to Princeton. "Now that's what I call a reading," he said, following the first one. "No theatricals, no girls, no booze. Pure poetry. To think that those men who had been up since dawn feeding chickens are eager to listen to poetry at night! It restores one's faith in the human race."

Baptistown was in the opposite direction from the literary chicken farmers. Richard returned from his first visit shaking his head. Delmore *was* crazy. He had bought a rural tenement. "Tobacco Road," Richard called it. Saul Bellow, whose poet Von Humboldt Fleisher in *Humboldt's Gift* brings the Delmore of this period throbbingly back to life, describes the property his protagonist has just bought:

> The neighbors raised poultry on this slummy land. Burdocks, thistles, dwarf oaks, cottonweed, chalky holes, and whitish puddles everywhere. It was all pauperized. The very bushes might have been on welfare.

That was Baptistown. Richard wondered how a man who was incapable of keeping an apartment in tolerable order was going to manage in a house that would be constantly in need of repairs, with six acres of farmland which he would never look at, much less tend.

Richard worried about the housekeeping, John and I about the isolation. If ever there was an urban man, it was Delmore. Without the city streets to walk, cafeterias and bars to talk in, movies to go to, newsstands at which to buy papers and magazines at any hour of the day or night, what would he do? The fantasy probably was that he and Elizabeth would be alone with their typewriters, with no interruptions and few temptations. The chances of the idyll turning out well for the Schwartzes in Baptistown were slimmer than they had been for the Lowells in Damariscotta Mills—even if Elizabeth and Delmore were both able to work. And Delmore had confided to John that it was years since he had been able to write a line of poetry.

The courtship of Princeton University took another lurch forward when Richard invited Delmore to replace him while he was on leave, traveling in the Middle East for the Rockefeller Foundation. The ambivalent swain brought with him as ally a man who had become a close friend during his Village years, the novelist Saul Bellow, who was to be his assistant.

Why Delmore no longer looked on John as an ally mystified me at first. The Pound controversy had put distance between them. If Delmore had never accused John of anti-Semitism (as he had Cal), he nevertheless felt that John (together with Richard, Allen and Cal) had been on the wrong side. At the Gauss Seminar discussions about Eliot, John had again been on the wrong side. Also, much as John fought academia—the very thing Delmore was courting so assiduously—he was, in Delmore's eyes, on the wrong side here, too. John was a scholar; he even looked donnish. Restless though he might be to get away (to Europe especially), he did not feel alien to the community in which he had lived for almost ten years. Had the two men been thrown together teaching, had Delmore lived nearby so they could see each other frequently and for private conversation, rather than at parties, they might (so I sometimes thought) have been able to bridge the gap caused by the feeling each had that the other had changed.

A measure of how much Delmore had changed I had on the day I saw him hurrying to catch the train at Princeton Junction—hair wild, clothes in disorder. The little running steps propelling him forward in jerky starts and stops were slower now that he had put on weight. The head was as noble as ever, and the shy smile of greeting as engaging, but the hangover he said he was suffering from (a quotidian affliction now) only partly accounted for the puffiness in his cheeks, his mottled complexion and, most disturbing of all, a haunted look in his darting, over-alert eyes that I had never seen before. Or rather, I suddenly remembered, I had seen it in a milder form and until this moment had forgotten it. Delmore had worn it the night of our first dinner together at the Jai Alai restaurant in the Village, before he asked to change places with me so he would have his back to the wall.

On the train we sat together. In deference to the hangover, would he prefer not to talk on the way to New York? Not talk? He was so jazzed-up from drugs that sitting in silence was out of the question. Insomnia, alcohol, drugs—the story of his life these days—brought us directly to the subject of his psychiatrist. From what Delmore told me, I suspected he was an even more intractable patient than John had proved to be. Did Delmore continue to hope for anything from analysis? If, in the beginning, he had done so, he now looked upon his therapist as an educated ear, a pharmacist and a referee. The ear listened to Delmore's explication of Freudian theory, the pharmacist fed him drugs, the referee adjudicated his marital disputes.

Elizabeth and he were not getting on well. They stared at their typewriters, unable to work. Elizabeth had had the success with *A Family Romance* that he had dreamed of for *The World Is a Wedding*. It had become a best seller. And he had been pleased for her. So why wasn't she able to get on with her second book? Was it his fault? Did he inhibit her in some way? he wondered sadly, guiltily. "Two blocked writers in one house. What could be worse?"

What struck me on the train ride, and what I realized must have made another barrier between John and Delmore, was that Delmore was no longer able to listen in the attentive way he had done in the past. He had ceased listening, except to his own obsessive thoughts. The next time I saw him was at a party Saul Bellow gave in Richard Blackmur's apartment (which he was subletting) shortly before Christmas. We arrived late, having been to an earlier party at a house in the West End where there had been a lighted tree, milk punch and carol singing. The music we heard as we approached 12 Princeton Avenue was the growl of a saxophone. We entered a dimly lit, smoke-filled room where people were standing around with no-nonsense whiskey and gin drinks in their hands.

Saul, whose dark good looks had made the heart of more than one Princeton matron beat more rapidly—it was generally agreed among them that Bellow was "a dish"—greeted us with an open-mouthed smile which made one smile in reflex. He seemed to be the only person present who was in a genial mood. What accounted for the thumb-pricking, edgy atmosphere? Helen Blackmur, a guest (with what feelings?) in the apartment she had not been in since she'd collected her belongings on leaving Richard, had cleared as much furniture as she could from the bedroom, put on records and was trying to interest those clustered near the bar in dancing. They preferred disputation. Ripostes whizzed back and forth like tracer bullets through the murky atmosphere. John, who had had more milk than whiskey to drink, and was sober but quickly catching the mood around him, suggested we help Helen out by dancing.

The bedroom was empty except for the Schwartzes. As we entered we saw Delmore approaching Elizabeth menacingly, Elizabeth backing off: a mock apache dance, I thought. They continued slowly around the room in this wary way. Suddenly Delmore made a grab at Elizabeth. John rushed to restrain him, I to restrain John. "Don't you see?" John shouted, throwing off my hand, "He's going to hurt her." As little able to believe Delmore capable of physical violence as John had been to believe it of Cal, I had not seen. John's shout alerted others. Elizabeth escaped. Delmore was subdued.

John was so distressed that he wanted to leave immediately. On the way home he said, "My God! Is *this* the way it is between them? What has happened to Delmore? And what will happen to Elizabeth?"

The next day we pieced together the sequence of events. Delmore, who had again been drinking heavily (and, though we didn't know it, also taking drugs) had seen Elizabeth accept a light from Ralph Ellison's cigarette. Yanking her by the arm to the back room, he accused her of flirting with Ralph. In a frenzy of jealousy, he had been bearing down on her as we began to dance.

Sometime after Richard returned from the Middle East there was another alarming episode involving the Schwartzes. They had left Princeton, after one of the few parties they came over for that winter, and were driving back to the farm. Although Delmore had drunk little and had seemed sober when they left, his handling of the wheel was so erratic that Elizabeth insisted he let her drive. When he refused, she got out of the car and began to walk along the road. He sped off, sobered up enough to worry about having left her alone, sped back and crashed into a telephone pole. The police picked him up and put him in jail. Sobering up another notch, he gave them Richard's name. Recounting the events of the night—the hours of driving around searching for Elizabeth (who had walked four miles to Helen's house), Delmore's shouting at the police, "I'm guilty, guilty. Punish me"— Richard commented grimly, "A scene out of Dostoevsky."

After Saul left for Christmas vacation, Ted Roethke took over the apartment for a week or so. During the time he was there, we heard rumors of lively goings on, but we didn't meet him until Christmas afternoon at the Wilsons'. We had seen something of Edmund the previous spring when he'd come down from New York to give his Gauss Seminar on the Civil War, later published as *Patriotic Gore.* He and John had had lunch, or Edmund had come to dinner or to a party we were giving. Before one cocktail party, he said he had a favor to ask: Would we invite the Arthur Koestlers, who were living near New Hope?

"Koestler's work interests you?" John asked.

"Koestler? Oh, he's all right. It's uh, it's rather Mrs. Koestler who is interesting," Edmund said with a pursed-lip smile.

After the other guests had left what Walter Clemons, a Princeton senior, and the only undergraduate present, called "the Berrymans' Brush-Up-Your-Hebrew party"—Edmund, Saul Bellow, Irving Howe and Arthur Koestler had become deeply and animatedly involved in a conversation about Hebrew studies and the Dead Sea Scrolls—Edmund confided that the pretty, fragile-looking Mrs. Koestler was Mamaine Paget, with whom he had been in love when he was in England in 1945. Since then, they had continued to correspond. (She was as fragile as she looked and died not long afterward of tuberculosis.)

Ted Roethke

In the fall of 1952, and throughout that winter, we saw a good deal of Elena and Edmund, visiting back and forth for drinks and dinner. Christmas afternoon we were the first to arrive at their house because Edmund had called, asking us to hurry over; he had finished his day's work and was impatient for conversation. When we arrived Elena was arranging flowers Ted had sent her: three dozen anemones of a superior variety, each blossom large and drenched with color, sent down from Max Schling in New York. "He must have been paid a generous advance on a book," Edmund said. "How else could he afford them?" John remembered having heard, when he replaced Ted at the University of Washington, that Roethke's parents had owned famous greenhouses. Family ties may have allowed him to run up sizable bills at Schling.

Ted entered the room like a prizefighter entering the ring. A big, heavy-set man, he had an unconvincing tough-guy manner that seemed to say: Just because I write poetry and am an expert on flowers is no reason to take me for a sissy. He greeted his hostess with Old World grace, barely acknowledged Edmund's presence, called me "Doll," and accepted the introduction to John as though he'd never heard of him. He shambled into the dining room where he helped himself to copious quantities of food from the buffet and shambled back with a bunch of white grapes, which he draped over the back of his hand. When the seat on the couch next to Edmund became free, he took it and sat in silence, his eyes fixed on Edmund's face. From time to time he plucked a grape and put it in his mouth. When Edmund had finished what he was saying, Ted leaned over, grabbed one of Edmund's jowls in his massive hand and said, "What's this? Blubber?"

What sort of man was this, who would court his hostess with an extravagant gift and insult his host, especially when his host happened to be a formidable critic he had requested a meeting with? One didn't speak to Edmund Wilson in this way—if one was in one's right mind.

Edmund, recovering more quickly than the rest of us, laughed like Old King Cole, and pointing to the grapes on the back of Ted's hand said, "Who, uh, do you think you are? A half-baked Bacchus?"

Not sorry for the arrival of other guests, Elena went to greet them. Ted, stung or dazed by Edmund's rejoinder, followed her to the entrance hall. She introduced Nancy Wood (Caroline and Allen's daughter) and her husband. "Dr. and Mrs. Wood, Mr. Roethke."

COURTESY OF ROBERT FITZGERALD

Robert Fitzgerald

Percy Wood extended his hand and was struck a blow so hard he landed on the floor. On hearing that Percy was a doctor, Ted had defended himself against being apprehended. In the state he was in, he could not believe that Percy was a friend of the Wilsons' who had come for a Christmas Day drink. He was a doctor who would commit him to a hospital. (Had Ted heard or guessed that Percy was a psychiatrist?) The friends who hustled Ted back to Princeton Avenue assured us that he was not dangerous. He had never been known to attack anyone before.

Ted was not in his right mind. Cal, in Salzburg, had gone clear out of his again. Delmore had changed so heartbreakingly one could no longer use the word "crazy" in the old innocent way when talking about him. Saul was sane. The "ease and light" Cal had found in John's company in Damariscotta John now found in Saul's. Until December the two men had met only in the company of other people, on campus, at the Seminars, with Delmore, at the house of mutual friends. Returning from a Sunday walk down by Lake Carnegie with Monroe Engel and Saul, John said to me, "I like Bellow more each time I see him. A lovely man. And a comedian. He threw a log he found at the edge of the lake into the water and, with a gesture of command, said, 'Go. Go be a hazard!' "

A few days later John came home with the typescript of Saul's new novel and said, "I'm going to take the weekend off to read this." Seated in his red leather chair, immobile for hours except to light a cigarette, make a note on a small white pad, run the corkscrew he liked to toy with through his fingers, or let out a high-pitched "eeeeeeeeeeeee," which meant he was laughing so hard he couldn't get his breath, he trained his intelligence on *The Adventures of Augie March,* giving it the kind of reading every writer dreams of having. After the first chapter, he said, "It's damn good." When he finished, "Bellow is *it.* I'm going to have lunch with him and tell him he's a bloody genius and so on."

At lunch, John delivered his long, detailed, carefully considered rave review. That *Augie* marked a turning point in its author's literary career was probably not news to the future Nobel Prize winner. Still, it could not have been disagreeable to have confirmation that he was "a bloody genius and so on" from a discerning critic not given to wild enthusiasms, unless there was something to be wildly enthusiastic about. The lunch marked the beginning of their friendship.

Wittingly, John had given Saul a boost. Unwittingly, Saul had given John a shove. Saul's talk at lunch of how he had felt impelled to break with the Flaubertian tradition (which had governed *Dangling Man* and *The Victim*) to write a free-wheeling, picaresque novel, gave John the push he needed to make the final break, prepared for during his sessions in therapy, with his hero-worshiping attitude toward father figures, Yeats above all, and the constraints that had imposed. That Saul had allowed his ambition to rip in a long novel also helped John to see what had been under his nose, but which, because of a failure of ambition, he had not grasped. His conception of the Bradstreet poem had grown so large it would have to be ten times the length of the longest poem he had so far written. He had had his two stanzas for years; he had had his folder of notes since Cincinnati. What he needed to get going on a work as ambitious as the one he had in mind was sufficient "gall." He also needed a shove or two from other directions.

In mid-January the poem erupted. The first two hundred lines were produced at white heat. John would come down from his studio for lunch or dinner and say, "Listen . . ." and read the stanzas he'd written between meals. If he was especially excited, he burst in between times. I was home all day, recovering from an operation, free to give him the kind of undivided attention he craved.

Mistress Bradstreet was vividly present in the apartment at all hours of the day and night (John's working schedule). Her life was so intertwined with ours it was sometimes difficult for him to distinguish between her and himself, between her and me. After years of childlessness:

> The winters close, Springs open, no child stirs
> Under my withering heart, O seasoned heart

she becomes pregnant. It had been to remove the one possible physical impediment to my conceiving that I had just undergone elective surgery, and returned from the hospital full of optimism (Oh, Randall, you were right), an optimism which, in the face of John's ambivalence, was highly unrealistic. While he couldn't bring himself to say he didn't want a child (only a monster could say that. Besides, in the same way he wanted other forbidden things, notably happiness, he did want one), he had gone so far as to leave Lorca's *Yerma* out for me with a note, *"Read!"* Warned off by the italics and imperative, I did not read it until later. (In this Spanish tragedy, a peasant woman, Yerma, longs for the child her husband, Juan, denies her by working the land on which they live so obsessively that he has neither time nor energy left for their marital life. Bound by a rigid code of honor which makes it impossible for her to be unfaithful to him, she finally becomes unbalanced and kills him.)

Later, I also learned the reason for John's abrupt break with therapy. Following our return from Cincinnati, his psychiatrist had decided that since they were making little progress in individual therapy on the "need need need" that was so disruptive of our marriage, he would try John in a group. This daring proposal (with its implication that his neuroses were no more exotic or worthy of special handling than those of a miscellaneous group of patients) John accepted warily. But after some weeks of standoffishness, he became deeply involved with the others, often going on with them to a coffee shop at the end of a particularly explosive session to comfort whichever one had that day been "given it" by the group. About the help they gave him, he said little. He seemed so much better, however (another reason for my false optimism), that when he came to visit me in the hospital fresh from the psychiatrist's office, trembling with rage, and saying he was fed up with the group, would never return to it and didn't want to discuss what had happened, I was bitterly disappointed.

What had made him storm out of the session, I learned later, was that the other members of the group, in the blunt way patients have with one another, had confronted him with his unwillingness to have a child and, oversimplifying the reasons for his unwillingness, had charged him with being afraid to have a rival for my attention.*

At the climax of the stanza, the child is born:

> Monster you are killing me Be sure
> I'll have you later Women do endure
> I can *can* no longer
> and it passes the wretched trap whelming and I am me
> drencht & powerful, I did it with my body!

---

*Discussing the genesis of "Homage" in the *Paris Review* interview, John gives another version of these events. He says that I went to the hospital for "a woman's operation, a kind of parody of childbirth. Both she and I were feeling very bitter about this since we very much wanted a child and had not had one." In another place he refers to my "tragic operation." A myomectomy for the removal of a fibroid (benign) growth in no way resembles childbirth, and does not prevent conception but, on the contrary, is performed to facilitate it. Far from being "bitter," I was absurdly optimistic on leaving the hospital.

Why these distortions? Were they necessary to assuage the terrible guilt John had felt and perhaps continued to feel? Were they part of a smoke screen to throw graduate students and his future biographer off the track—not unlike "a certain sly desire [poets have] to baffle the on-rushing critic"? Were they because, "poets are feigned to lie"? Or were they the result of a memory defect brought on by brain damage? (When Hayden Carruth's review of *Love & Fame* appeared in *The Nation,* John responded to it with a letter, a copy of which he sent me, in which he accused Carruth of not being able to "read correctly" a feeling he, John, had expressed in one of the poems, likening it to one "with which a lover memorializes the date and place of his first kiss." In a cheeky parenthesis, he added, "I kissed my first wife under the mistletoe in her aunt's apartment on West 9th Street on New Year's afternoon 1941, Mr. Carruth. How about you?" In my reply to John, I teased him about "kissing, telling and misremembering": The kiss had been exchanged in an apartment on Twelfth rather than Ninth Street. Much amused, John offered in explanation of his error: "Twenty-three years of alcohol hard on memory.")

John being John, what is most likely is that not just one of these explanations, but some of all of them, account for these unmarked "delusions" (the word he used to correct other inaccuracies for which he was responsible in the proofs the editor of the *Paris Review* sent him).

John handed me this passage and threw himself down on the floor
next to the couch where I was stretched out. "Well, I'm exhausted,"
he said. "I've been going through the couvade. The little monster
nearly killed *me.*"

Three stanzas later the child, Sam, has an exchange with his mother
on the subject of death. It was an exchange which—twelve years
earlier, on the death of the uncle who had given me away when John
and I married—my nephew, Billy, had had with my sister. After Marie
told Billy Uncle Charlie had died, he said, "Aunt Hilda too?"
Marie said, no, Aunt Hilda was still alive. Surprised and uncertain that
he had understood correctly, Billy said, "Then God takes us one
by one?" When I read it aloud from Marie's letter, John had
wept.

> . . . Sam, your uncle has had to
> go fróm us to live with God. 'Then Aunt went too?'
> Dear, she does wait still.
> Stricken: 'Oh. Then he takes   us one by one. My dear.'

The white heat of creation dropped to a lower temperature. John
came down from his studio empty-handed. He fretted and paced and
brooded. Was he stuck? Not exactly. The poem would have to be even
longer than he had thought in mid-January. He had decided to have
the poet enter into a dialogue with Anne Bradstreet. "The trouble is,"
he said (as though asking permission?) "the poet wants to seduce
her."

Sleepily, for it was either very early morning or very late at night,
I thought: He wants to seduce a "pox-blasted" puritan who is, besides,
dead? "Why not?" I said.

"Why not, indeed!" Up he went to tempt this highly moral, devout
married woman who, despite her vexations with the tedium of domestic life, never for a moment considered being unfaithful to her much
older, and much loved, husband—until the poet appears to her out of
the mist. Was it her moral stature (as contrasted with the easy availabil-
ity of the women he found around him), as much as her being a
link, though a weak one, in the great chain of poets from Homer to
his day—the poet he might have been had he been a woman and

lived in Colonial America (although surely with better taste in select-
ing earlier verse-makers to be influenced by, and less given to
writing "bald abstract didactic rime") that attracted him to Anne
Bradstreet as a subject? Or was it her moral stature? The ultimate
seduction!

Parts of the dialogue between the poet and Anne had a familiar ring.
How many times had John awakened in a fright, saying something not
far from:

> I trundle the bodies, on the iron bars,
> over that fire backward & forth, they burn;
> bits fall. I wonder if
> *I* killed them

And I, attempting to reassure him, had said, at greater length and
unpoetically:

> —Dreams! You are good.—

How many times had we taken opposite sides on the question: Does
God exist? Would Anne, with her greater knowledge of Scripture, be
more successful at convincing him, as he yearned to be convinced, than
I had been?

It looked for a while as if she would be. In a state of manic
excitement, he said he was having a religious experience, was on the
point of conversion. Remembering Cal, I was alarmed. John called the
Fitzgeralds in Connecticut and asked if he could stay with them
for a few days. He needed to talk to Robert, and he needed to get
away. It was like asking Sally and Robert if they would be willing
to put a lighted stick of dynamite in their room over the garage.
Being the kind of friends they were, they were willing. With their
kindness, a change of scene and long walks to tire him physically,
the flame moved along the wick more slowly. In the woods near
their house:

> —It was Spring's New England. Pussy willows wedge
> up in the wet. Milky crestings, fringed
> yellow, . . .

On his return there was no further talk of a conversion. Anne Bradstreet's children grow up. Her father dies. She is ill. In the nightmare period when she is dying, during which John behaved, alternately, as if he was dying, and as if he was killing her off, I ran into Elena and Edmund in Lahière's one evening. No need to fabricate an excuse for being in the restaurant alone, something in Edmund's manner told me at once. He could imagine the scene that had preceded my coming to the restaurant: the terrible quarrel, my flight from the apartment, my taking refuge in the only place in town open at that hour. In an earlier marriage he had acted one of the roles in a like drama.

Sympathy had been added to the respect Edmund felt for John during the recent months when the two men had seen each other frequently. Edmund had advised John on his career ("You want to live by free-lance writing without financial backing? Impossible. Give up the notion. It will only cause you trouble.") and talked with him about his writing. Once or twice after John had begun work on the poem Edmund had met him on the street and seen that he was on fire.

He knew what it must be like to live with that kind of excitement, Edmund said, indirectly and delicately expressing compassion for both John and me. When were we leaving for Europe? End of April. Some months abroad might make the difference, he went on, trying to encourage me (although later Elena told me that that night they had seen my desperation and had guessed, even before I knew it, how close I was to making my decision). This man, who often seemed so vague about people, and still didn't have my name straight, had a deeper insight into our marriage than our closest friends, for he saw in John the husband he had been in an earlier marriage, and saw in me that wife.

John was contrite when I got home. Where had I been? (Had I gone to New York? Had I left him for good?) The Wilsons had urged me to go with them to a movie after dinner. John had been out of his mind with worry at my staying away so long. "You may not believe this," he said, "but I have never before tried so hard to control hysteria. I am like the man who cried wolf. *Lear* and *Crane* were fake cries. This is the real one. I'll soon be finished. She's almost in the ground."

About the crisis he wrote Robert Fitzgerald at the end of March that, after the time in Connecticut, he "went through bad times again.

It took me 30 hours to get her first last lines done (that is, to let her die)—and before that, for several days I hated the world so intensely in my exhaustion that I decided to abandon the poem where you saw it [stanza 51] . . . and make her live forever in every sense. I got over that at last."

Finally he was willing to let her go:

> We commit our sister down
> One candle mourn by, which a lover gave,

Three years after we separated, when the poem appeared in book form (after another of those interminable waits so characteristic of each step of John's career), he inscribed the copy he sent me:

> w. relief & gratefulness
> (it really ought to be
> dedicated to you, but
> I decided to leave it all hers)
> & dearest love

For a moment I puzzled over the "hers." A woman he had fallen in love with? No, "she" and "her" meant only one person, his phantom mistress, Mistress Bradstreet.

Recognition from the writers John most admired came quickly. In mid-March, at the specially arranged Gauss Seminar at which he gave the first public reading of "Homage to Mistress Bradstreet," Delmore claimed the poem for *Partisan Review,* where it was published a year later. Edmund compared it to "The Waste Land," and asked for a repetition of the reading at home, so that they could discuss the poem in detail. (Recalling that occasion Elizabeth Bowen remembered John as having been "tortured and half-incoherent." Leon Edel, the other guest, was struck by John's "personal anguish," and the way Edmund "quietly and tenderly" led him from stanza to stanza. What neither realized was that John had expected that we would be alone with Edmund and Elena. He was not yet ready to read the poem in so intimate a setting with strangers in the room. Only his unwillingness to offend the Wilsons, whose sympathy toward him he had been feeling so strongly, pushed him into his "tortured" reading.)

In April Allen wrote that "Homage" was "a masterpiece." Conrad Aiken said it was "one of the finest poems ever written by an American." It was published, in a production as elegant as John could have wished for, by Farrar, Straus, with Bob Giroux as editor. The dream had become a reality. John was on his way to fame. And to the realization that

> The secret is not praise. It's just being accepted
> at something like the figure where you put your worth
>
> . . .
>
> Of course, praise is nice too,
> particularly when it comes to a stop.

X

AFTERWARD

. . . to those who are not artists the gratification that can be drawn from the springs of phantasy is very limited; their inexorable repressions prevent the enjoyment of all but the meagre day-dreams which can become conscious. A true artist has more at his disposal. First of all he understands how to elaborate his day-dreams, so that they lose that personal note which grates upon strange ears and become enjoyable to others; he knows too how to modify them sufficiently so that their origin in prohibited sources is not so easily detected. Further, he possesses the mysterious ability to mould his particular material until it expresses the ideas of his phantasy faithfully; and then he knows how to attach to this reflection of his phantasy-life so strong a stream of pleasure that, for a time at least, the repressions are out-balanced and dispelled by it. When he can do all this, he opens out to others the way back to the comfort and consolation of their own unconscious sources of pleasure, and so reaps their gratitude and admiration; then he has won through his phantasy—what before he could only win in phantasy: honour, power, and the love of women.

—Sigmund Freud

On the morning of January 8, 1972, I picked up the copy of *The New York Times* that was at the door, and took it together with the breakfast tray to the bedroom. Despite the outdoor temperature, a record low, the room was warm and bright, flooded with winter sunlight. It being Saturday, we could dawdle over coffee and read the paper in a leisurely way. We split it, Bob taking the first section, I the second. In my habitual way, I turned first to the obituary page. There might be an interesting biography of a theatrical figure one had supposed long dead. Or a notice that an elderly acquaintance had succumbed "after a long illness," reading which one would say: a blessing for the family.

That I knew the man in the photograph at the upper left-hand corner of the page I was able for an instant to deny, so different was the configuration of the face from the bony, ascetic one I had known so well. Yet I had seen the beard often enough in recent years on book jackets and in newspapers to feel the unaccountable sensation of oppression that had troubled me the previous day flare up again. It could not be . . . Someone would have telephoned . . . But, I remembered, I had been out all day, and in the evening had met Bob for dinner in a Village restaurant.

The unambiguous headline grabbed me by the throat:

JOHN BERRYMAN, POET, IS DEAD
WON THE PULITZER PRIZE IN 1965

The discreet wording allowed me to hang over the one new, unwanted fact for a moment before the alarm went off in my brain: *How* had he died? Terror gripping me, the old terror I had not felt for years, I said a prayer that the poet's prayer—"In sleep, of a heart attack, let Henry go"—had been answered. Had John had that "most marvelous piece of luck" he'd been waiting for impatiently, and had had a vivid premonition of six months earlier?

In August 1954, at the end of a year of separation, John wrote me on the Cape, asking me to meet him in Boston on my birthday. After dinner he walked me up and down Beacon Hill, past the Saint-Gaudens monument (which both Cal and he had written poems about), the State House, Pinckney Street, Revere, Louisburg Square, Mount Vernon Street. At 49 Grove Street we stopped.

"Are you aching with memories?" he said, in a hard-soft voice that warned me there was danger ahead. "Good. That's what it's been like for me all summer, teaching at Harvard again. That's why I brought you here." We dropped arms and faced each other. With a diffident smile, he said, "I want you to go out to Iowa with me in September. I'm no longer asking you to 'hold me up.' I'm no longer saying, 'As long as you do not reject me, I am not lost.' I'm also not claiming to be a changed man. But I have learned a thing or two during this ragged year on my own. I have a job. I've cut back on drinking. I think we have a chance. No, don't say anything now. I want you to consider carefully. When I finish at Harvard at the end of August, I'll come to New York to hear your answer."

On our return from Europe the previous summer, I had told John that I was leaving him. In *Recovery,* he gives as my reasons his "drinking and bad sex." Certainly, both had made life intolerable off and on during the second half of our marriage. But it was more his need to live in turbulence—if it wasn't drinking and women, it was the way he worked on *Lear, Crane* and *Bradstreet*—that finally forced me to make my decision.

In Paris, where John and I stayed at the Hôtel des Saints Pères for ten days on our arrival at the end of April 1953, there had been a scene that was a trope for our marriage. I wakened in the middle of the night in panic: Where was John? I had heard him come in hours before and crash into the armoire that jutted out from the wall before dropping into bed. Now his bed was empty. The French windows, which opened onto a narrow balcony, were ajar. In the glaucous moonlight, I could just make out his pajamaed figure, poised on the balustrade. Suppressing an impulse to cry out, I went as quickly as I could to his side and said his name. Without a word, he took the hand I held up to his, as he had done on his mother's terrace, and allowed me—eyes open or closed? I could not see—to lead him back to bed. When his breathing became deep and regular, I locked the window. The remainder of the night, I sat in a chair thinking.

John's life had become a high-wire act. He was flirting with his subtle foe in the certainty that there was an invisible net, held by me, which would catch him should he lose his footing. The job of net-holder had exhausted me. More important, I realized that by making myself available in this way I had been encouraging him to be more and more incautious, less vigilant against the current that was always threatening to suck him under. By morning I knew that I could not, should not, hold up the net much longer.

Early the next day we left Paris for Autun. John complained of a hangover. "Idiot that I am, I sat up in a café drinking brandy, brooding over the mistakes I've made in the management of my life during the fourteen years since I was last in Paris." As was so often the case, he remembered having drunk too much, but had forgotten what he'd done while drinking. As was also often the case, I was unable to forget. It seemed to me, as we wandered through central France and down to the Riviera, that John's phantom mistress (whom, having done with, he was now desperate to shake) rarely gave us a moment's peace. During his "three-day drunk at the fête of St. Tropez," he recited "Homage" nonstop to whomever would lend an ear. The final night of the fête, when the last of the revelers had gone to bed, he cornered the local bakers trapped at their ovens, and recited to them. Covered with flour from the dough they were kneading, perplexed by their strange visitor who pushed his eyeglasses up onto the bridge of his nose as he declaimed:

> How long with nothing in the ruinous heat,
> clams & acorns stomaching, distinction perishing,

they listened with wonder and awe, understanding only that the pas-sion behind the lines was trying to burn itself out so that the exhausted poet could, like the carefree revelers, get some sleep.

Although there had been many good periods during our months abroad, the change of scene brought no miracle to dissuade me from my conviction that I must leave John. What I lacked, what I spent the time in Europe trying to summon, was the courage to face the anguish I knew the break-up would cause both of us. When, on the evening we returned to New York, I told John my decision, he accepted "the worst words ever spoken to him" with "horror and assent."

The emotions I had expected to feel on separation, the predictable anger and bitterness at the failure of a marriage, were smothered under a blanket of grief. The new loss reactivated the pain of childhood losses. Feeling freshly orphaned, I mourned. When I wasn't staring into space, or weeping, I struggled with the host of physical ills I suffered from. Mid-year, after I had regained my health, I devoted all my energy to my profession. Work, as I had so often found in the past, was the only analgesic that took the edge off psychic distress for me. I worked time-and-a-half building up my practice as a psychotherapist. While I knew the year ahead would also be difficult, by August, when John and I met in Boston, I felt that the worst was over. Had I been wearing mourning garb, I would have been ready to change from black to gray.

John may have suffered equally during his "ragged year" and had undoubtedly "learned a thing or two" as he claimed. But his having "cut back" on drinking sounded provisional and insufficiently reassuring for me to be able to consider a reconciliation.

In September 1954 he accepted my decision not to go with him to Iowa less with horror than with resignation. As we embraced in parting, I could feel his dread of the semester ahead. Except for the company of his students and one or two friends from New York who were there, he felt like an exile in Iowa. He was discouraged about "Homage" which, after the initial excitement and appearance in *Partisan Review,* had got stalled so badly on the way to publication in book form that he wondered if it would ever come out. He had little money and heavy debts. Worst of all, he was not writing and was afraid, terribly afraid, he would never write verse again.

"She drained me dry," he said.

"Temporarily," I said. "You're still recovering."

Repeating the dialogue we'd had so often in the past, he said, "No. This time not even images come into my head. I'm finished."

We had agreed to write regularly, and to meet in New York during Christmas vacation.

Three weeks passed without a word from John. A nightmare I had, in which he was in grave trouble and screaming for help, caused me to send him a telegram, asking for reassurance that he was all right. The telegraph office in Iowa City reported back that he was unknown at the address I had given. Through a series of long-distance calls I traced him to Minneapolis.

"Your unconscious got the message, all right. I was at rock bottom.

Allen took me in. Don't worry about me now. The worst is over."
He had a letter in the typewriter which would tell me the details of
the "Iowa debacle."

The fall semester had begun badly, the letter reported. Life in Iowa
City had seemed even bleaker than it had the previous spring when,
grateful to have a job again, he had thrown himself into teaching. At
that time he had also had "a lucky break," a fractured leg, the result
of a tumble "cold sober" down a flight of stairs (so badly designed that
other tenants had fallen). The cast had given him an external and
palpable object to distract him from his inner turmoil. While in-
capacitated, he had entertained himself studying Hebrew. "Ha! Now
I'll be able to talk to Wilson, Bellow, Howe et. al."

In place of the fracture, the fall semester had begun with a furious
political quarrel in a campus bar. He'd drunk too much and, in a
bruising humor, had gone back to his apartment. Finding he'd forgotten his keys, he'd awakened his landlord. The two of them shouted at
each other, John's invective so shocking the strait-laced landlord's wife
that she had summoned the police. As little of interest was going on
that day in Iowa City, the local papers carried the story of John's
having been put in jail for disorderly conduct. News of his where-
abouts reached the university authorities, and on his release they summoned him before a committee and dismissed him. Enraged, frightened, humiliated, chastened, he had fought through these feelings to
one clear idea: He must call Allen Tate. Tate, at the University of
Minnesota, urged him to get on a plane for Minneapolis. When John
arrived, Allen met him, put him up, helped him find an apartment and
arranged, through Ralph Ross in the Humanities department, for him
to have a job the following semester.

I was not to worry about him now, John said. He had hit bottom
and was on his feet again. In the months he had free before he began
teaching, he planned to review his life. *And put it in order.*

On hearing that he'd gone to Minneapolis, my first thought was:
He's gone in search of his father. John Allyn Smith came from Minnesota. Throughout our last year together, John had brooded uneasily
about what it meant to him to approach thirty-nine, the age at which
his father had committed suicide. Three months after we separated,
John survived—"but just barely"—his thirty-ninth birthday. The sur-
vival had been fraught with anxiety not only about his age, but also

about his, so far, modest successes, each one of which could be interpreted as a sign that he was out-performing his "weak and ineffectual"
father, who had failed in marriage, in business, in everything but in
his determination to end his life.

Immediately following our separation John had gone to live in New
York. Unable to find a job, he had given up the room he'd taken and
moved in with his mother. They had spent evening after evening going
over the family history again, circling the truth, Mrs. Berryman cast
once more in the role of myth-maker, with no lack of talent for
inventing fresh variations and details. She retold the story of her life
with Allyn: their courtship, during which, in this version, he was made
to appear brutish rather than merely seductive, Allyn's swimming out
in the Gulf with John on his back, the "accident" with the gun at
daybreak. This period of mother and son living together, which had
its predictable explosions, marked the end of John's moving in her
orbit (although it by no means ended the intensity of their relationship).

Being in Minneapolis now put him closer to his father than he had
been since the final days in Florida. During the winter months of 1955,
while he waited for his teaching job to begin, he spent hours every
day in self-analysis ("Still unable to write. I told you I was finished."),
and came to believe that he had provoked the scandal in Iowa so that
he would be forced to leave. Allen, who had John's father's Christian
name, was living in his father's state. Allen took in the prodigal and
did for him what a benevolent father would have done. John had felt
a compulsion to go in search of his father's ghost, a search which,
though he wasn't consciously aware of it, would lead him to a new
poetic subject and *The Dream Songs*.

All this I learned from his letters, telephone calls and visits to New
York during the three years of our "intense separation," until, soon
after he sent me a copy of "Homage" in 1956, we were divorced and
he remarried.

In our letters we had also written each other news of mutual friends,
John to me about Allen, Saul and Randall, I to him about Richard,
Delmore, Cal and Elizabeth Hardwick. The news about Delmore was
mostly sad; about Randall, who had remarried, happy. Direct news of
John I had from Allen when he came to Princeton to see Nancy and
Percy Wood and his grandchildren. If Allen began a sentence with

"That boy . . ." I knew he was going to tell me John was being difficult again. Difficult or not, Allen admitted that John was teaching brilliantly and conscientiously, and was no longer quite so certain he was finished as a poet.

Following John's separation from his second wife in 1959, he and I corresponded episodically until 1960, when I married Robert Simpson. After I went to live in Paris, John wrote from time to time, sending his books as they appeared. I found these letters impossible to answer, partly because I was unable to read verse for some years. When I began again, I read either French poets or (perhaps because of my adolescent pull toward things Russian) Pasternak, Mandelstam and Akhmatova, in translation. It was only after we returned to the United States in 1966, and my husband suggested that we read American poets aloud, that I caught up on what John and the other writers I had known had been publishing. (To Bob, Berryman, as he called him, was a writer whose work he greatly admired, who, in a time so long past as to seem prehistoric, had been my first husband.) It wasn't until the year before John died that he and I began to correspond again.

Dylan Thomas was the first of this generation of poets to die. In November 1953, a few months after John and I had separated, he telephoned in the middle of the night, sobbing, to tell me the news. His lamentations, which seemed excessive to many who took part in the dramatic scenes enacted in the halls of St. Vincent's in New York (where Thomas had been hospitalized) were neither surprising nor incomprehensible to me. While John and Dylan had met infrequently after their week together in London, they had been intimate during that period in a way for which only the young have the time, energy and freedom. John was mourning his almost-twin (Dylan was born a day earlier) in a kinship that substituted poetry for blood, and was no less strong for the substitution. He also saw in Dylan an object lesson, for the Welsh poet (the cause of whose death was given as "insult to the brain") had done to himself what John was fearful he might do, if at a pace so much slower that it was less obvious: insult the organ in his body upon which the writing of poetry depends.

Although in *Recovery* John says of his character Alan Severance that after his wife told him she was leaving him, "He could never, comfortably, never comfortably drink again," Severance's creator had, all fall, been drinking heavily, if uncomfortably, as other late-night telephone calls had told me. How much alcohol, John wondered, downing martinis with more guilt than pleasure, did it take to "insult" the brain?

Caitlin Thomas says of her husband: "He had never been keen on life." Approaching forty, the causes of his despair were manifold: chaos in his (not-so) private life, anxiety over the ailments he would suffer as a result of the punishment he had given his body and, most important of all, the conviction that the muse would never again allow him to practice his sullen art. Paul Ferris reports in his biography that a year before Dylan's death, he wrote his publisher to explain why he wasn't making progress on a book he'd promised. "For a whole year I have been able to write nothing, nothing, nothing at all but one tangled, sentimental poem as preface to a collection of poems written years ago."

Between the gnawing anxiety that one may never again write poetry (the predictable symptom that follows a successful act of composition) and the certainty that one will not, there is a difference similar to the hypochondriac's obsession with cancer and his certain knowledge, from signs and symptoms he can read even before a doctor can, that the disease process has begun. Dylan had had his share of panics during barren periods when he was afraid he had run dry. Then came a moment of certainty. Thereafter, he could see no reason to continue living.

Ted Roethke was the next to go. While he and John had never become close, they had a mutual respect for each other's poetry and, during the summer of 1953, when we and the Roethkes were in Europe and our paths criss-crossed, they came to know each other better. By the time of our meeting in Rome, John was somewhat calmer than he had been in St. Tropez, or at least was less driven to declaim his stanzas to the world. Ted would not have been attracted to such monomania because he was having difficulties of his own. Though sweet-tempered and not at all combative as he had been in Princeton, he was high, if not manic, as we guessed the night he insisted that a group of us who had had dinner together go with him to a German restaurant to have another meal. Another meal—was he crazy? Well, yes, a little. But he was so eager for us to accept his invitation—lire notes tumbling out of his pockets as he insisted he would be the host—that we faked our way through the second dinner with fruit and more wine, while he consumed course after course of the dishes his mother had prepared during his childhood, as if he hadn't eaten in weeks. The suspiciousness he felt toward John (based, I think, on John's having replaced him at the University of Washington when he was in the hospital—i.e., John's having taken over his classes behind his back), gradually diminished as the two men met again in London later in the summer.

On his return to the United States Ted went back to Seattle, where, in ten years, he published twelve books of poetry, won the Pulitzer Prize (1954), had a series of manic episodes requiring hospitalization for psychotherapy and shock treatment, taught brilliantly and drank and womanized until 1963. A coronary occlusion killed him when he was fifty-five.

John, who was assuming the role of official mourner for the group, wrote in "A Strut for Roethke" of "the Garden Master" who would never "cadenza again of flowers," and said he envied Ted's escape from the grinding labor of "daily, trying to hit the head on the nail."

The next loss, that of Randall Jarrell, struck closer to John's heart. Despite the failure of the meeting staged by Cal, when Randall came to Princeton to give a Gauss lecture and teach creative writing in 1952, he and John became closer friends. Soon after Randall arrived, he and I met as we were getting off the train from New York, and walked together up from the station to the house he had sublet for the year. On the way I said how sorry I was to hear that he and his wife were divorcing (meaning I was sorry for the pain it must be causing him).

"You needn't be," he said, as if he were talking about another couple, one he neither liked nor approved of. "Our interests had changed." That this coldness was a façade I understood only when we stopped at his house to get a book he wanted me to give John, and I saw the way he was living. Although he'd been in residence for only two weeks the place was in shocking disorder. On every surface there were plates of half-finished meals (obviously eaten with little appetite), clothes strewn over the furniture, stray cats he'd taken in from the streets for company—"a whole house of undone rooms and dishes and God knows how many street cats" was the way he himself described it to Hannah Arendt. I thought of how Delmore's Ellery Street apartment had deteriorated, and realized that Randall was far more depressed than he appeared.

That semester, when he came to have dinner with us, we were struck by how seldom he said, "Ba-by *Doll!,*" or otherwise showed the enthusiasm that had been so characteristic on earlier meetings. He also seemed less formidable, milder in the expression of his opinions. Had we not been concerned about what this meant we would have enjoyed the change, for it made him easier to talk to, more companionable. John and he spent little time on any subject but the real one: poetry. Their conversations confirmed John's opinion, already formed by reading Randall's essays, that he had "a natural taste in poetry hardly inferior to Tate's."

Every once in a while during this period we had a reminder of the old, disdainful Jarrell manner, as the day he saw me carrying an elegant umbrella sheathed in green snakeskin (a hand-me-down from John's mother). He looked from it to me and back again, then said, *"Poor snake!"*—as if I had skinned it alive.

After John and I separated, it was through Cal or Jean Stafford that I heard about Randall. He had remarried, Cal said, was a devoted father to two stepdaughters, and enjoyed teaching at the Women's College in Greensboro, North Carolina. Jean reported that he'd grown a beard, had a jazzy wardrobe and an even jazzier car.

In Paris I heard about him occasionally via Richard's letters. They did not report, and I only learned later, that Randall had had a manic episode, was hospitalized for some months and treated with drugs. Discharged as recovered, and seemingly doing well, he went to another hospital to have therapy on one of his hands. While there, he went for a walk along a highway one evening, just as it was growing dark. The sports-car fan and reader of *Road and Track* was killed, as his adored Persian cat had been killed, by a car. There are those who are convinced he died an accidental death (as it was listed in the coroner's report). Cal, mourning his loss in one of the three poems about Randall in *History,* recalls their years of friendship going back to Kenyon College days. Of the walk on the highway, he says:

> Then the night of the caged squirrel on his wheel,
> lights, eyes, peering at you from the overpass;
> black-gloved, black-coated, you plod out stubbornly
> as if in lockstep to grasp your blank not-I
> at the foot of the tunnel . . . as if asleep, Child Randall,
> greeting the cars, and approving—your harsh luminosity.

How little I understood Randall is shown by my having thought that he was not like the other poets I knew. What threw me off—aside from his not drinking, womanizing or tearing himself apart with excesses of writing—was that he was unlike any other human being I have ever met: Randall was uniquely Randall. Yet his illness, if not his death, as well as his late, openly autobiographical poems, suggest that in psychological makeup he was not so different from the others in the group.

A mentor rather than a contemporary, and a pivot around whom these poets had moved, Richard Blackmur died in 1965, the same year as Randall. Although they had been out of touch for a long time, John must have grieved when he heard the news. For me, the loss was immense. Richard and I had remained close friends. During the years following my separation, he came to dinner regularly and, as was his habit, stayed and stayed until I put him out (no less surprised and wounded if the hour of his expulsion was 3:00 A.M. or midnight) with the reminder that I had to see patients in the morning. How could I be tired, Richard seemed to be wondering, when he was more awake than he'd been all day?

In the summer of 1956, when we were both in Europe, we often met in Paris and London. Walking on the Boulevard St. Germain with him on the way to the Brasserie Lipp for dinner, I recalled our first walk together down Nassau Street as we shopped for Thanksgiving dinner. His pace was even slower now. At moments when, because of Buerger's disease, he felt the circulation in his legs become so sluggish he couldn't take another step, he'd pause in front of a shop window, as if by design, and using the objects displayed—umbrellas, canes, buttons, jewelry, china, silver, lingerie—as a stimulus, associate freely from the lingerie to Joyce, to Molly Bloom, to his first love, Tessa, to women's sexuality, to their bottoms, to a particular Princeton bottom, until he felt the circulation return to his legs again and we could continue our slow progression to the restaurant. Once there, he drank while I ate. The richness of French cuisine was too much for him, he said. As far as I could see he subsisted on bread and wine.

In London he was happier with the food and, of course, the language. The man who read and translated French poetry and prose with ease but became tongue-tied when he had to speak the language, no longer had to force himself into spasms of French phrases when talking to a waiter, and could enjoy chance encounters on the streets. "In London one understands what the whores are saying, and knows that what one says to them in response is understood." This fact alone made England the superior country.

When I remarried, it was Richard who gave me away. He had met Bob years before I had, when Bob had been an assistant dean at Princeton before going to Egypt as a diplomat. Richard enjoyed talking international politics with him and especially liked to pump him about the Middle East.

At the wedding ceremony Richard was grave and dignified, delighted to play an avuncular role. He promised to visit us in Paris, where Bob's job was taking us, but his deteriorating health made travel uncomfortable for him.

When we returned home on a visit in 1964, we spent an afternoon with Richard at the house he had built on McCosh Drive. At last he had a garden again, and also a greenhouse. We talked as he potted in a desultory way, his energy so low I became concerned that he was gravely ill. My questions about his health he turned away with a "Hmmmmm," sketching with his middle finger the outline of his liver on his tweed jacket. As I hugged him in farewell, and he and Bob exchanged a long handshake, we knew we would never see him again. He died not long thereafter, at home and alone.

Richard had been my prime source of information about Delmore. After Elizabeth left him, in 1955, he stayed on alone at Baptistown, the farm falling into decay as Richard had predicted it would. There was a rocky reconciliation of the marriage, but in 1957 Delmore's paranoia, which had been increasingly difficult to control, exploded in an episode in which he accused Elizabeth of infidelity with Nelson Rockefeller (an accusation which, from another husband in earlier years, Delmore would have found richly comic), threatened to kill another supposed rival and was hospitalized in Bellevue. When Saul Bellow organized a collection of funds so that Delmore could be transferred to Payne Whitney, he turned against Saul, Dwight Macdonald and the others who had been most solicitous on his behalf, accusing them of swindling him.

The cycle of hospitalizations, moves from one rundown flat or hotel to another, confinements in jail, talking jags at the White Horse Tavern (where, when he was only mildly manic, he could still be a brilliant monologuist)—interspersed with brief periods during which he surfaced in the literary world for a public occasion—continued for years.

In a 1963 letter John sent to Paris, attempting to reestablish contact with me after he had remarried for the third time, he brought me up-to-date on Delmore's tormented life. At the National Poetry Festival in Washington, John and Richard Wilbur had had to get Delmore out of jail in the middle of the night. He'd been locked up for having torn his hotel room apart—he'd "hurt" his room, John quoted Wilbur as having said—by yanking the phone out of the wall in a crazy rage which, when he then tried to place a long-distance call and failed, drove him into an even crazier rage of frustration and incomprehension. John, who had been abroad during the Bellevue-Payne Whitney episode, had a taste of what it must have been like for Saul at that time.

In July of 1966, en route home through Italy, Bob and I were sitting in the Campo in Siena when he handed me the copy of the Rome *Daily American* he had been reading, saying, "Here's news that will sadden you." It was Delmore's brief obituary: On July 11 he had died of a heart attack, aged fifty-two. The tragic details I didn't learn until I saw Nancy Macdonald in New York. Delmore, a recluse, who had once been "flagrant" with "young male beauty" and so gifted that it was thought he would be the star of his generation, had fallen dead in a hallway outside his squalid room in a fleabag hotel in Times Square. The heart attack that took him was neither easy nor quick. He had been "tearing his sorry clothes" for over an hour before the noises of struggle attracted attention. An ambulance took him to Roosevelt Hospital (where, when his time came, Cal would also be taken) to be pronounced dead. At the morgue, because "there were no readers of modern poetry" around, as Saul wrote of his character Humboldt, Delmore's body lay unclaimed for two days.

My tears were not for the death at the Columbia Hotel. They were for the ten years of living hell—of paranoid rages, terrifying anxiety and, in more stable periods, aching insight, loneliness and despair over his lost promise—that Delmore had suffered before the heart attack. As Auden said at Louis MacNeice's memorial service: "In this age, to die at fifty-five is, statistically speaking, to die early, but worse things can befall a poet than an early death. At least Louis MacNeice was spared that experience which some poets have had to endure, and for many years: the experience of being condemned to go on living with the knowledge that the Muse has abandoned them."

Delmore had been spared nothing. The wonder was how this man who, as Dwight wrote, had "a positive genius for self-destruction" had been able to wait so patiently for the death of his body to catch up with the death of his spirit.

John grieved and grieved for Delmore, and was haunted by the way in which his old friend had died. If there was no one to claim Delmore's body, and only a handful of people to follow it to the cemetery, there are the *Dream Songs* to mourn his death—"Ten Songs, one solid block of agony,"—in which John cried out his anguish. The years of estrangement faded. The scenes of their youth became vivid again. It was the Delmore of the Cambridge days whom John tried to put in the place of the anonymous man who had been taken to the morgue. It was the fellow poet who had been his chief support during his own years of failure and obscurity. The one solace John offered himself was the belief that as long as poetry was read, Delmore would not be forgotten.

After the grief became more manageable, John took stock:

I'm cross with god who has wrecked this generation
First he seized Ted, then Richard, Randall, and now Delmore.

He was so cross he named Richard, who was not of their generation, and forgot Dylan, who was. Who was left? Only Cal.

Throughout the years I continued to see Cal intermittently after he and Elizabeth returned from living abroad. We met at Bob Giroux's opera evenings and at the Marlborough Street house Elizabeth and he bought not far from where he had grown up. The first time I went for the weekend Cal took my suitcase and loped up the stairs to the guest room as he had done in Damariscotta. No shirttail hanging out now. He wore a proper suit and could have passed for a proper Bostonian. His hair had turned gray and the contact lenses (which, according to Jean, he had left in place for weeks during his first breakdown and had been told he must give up wearing), had long since been replaced by horn-rimmed glasses. Whereas in Maine he had looked younger than his years because of the "terrifying innocence" in his face, he now looked older because of the marks illness had etched around his eyes and mouth.

At the dinner party Elizabeth gave my first evening there, Cal made drinks, carved the roast, lit the fire in the study and in every way was attentive to his guests. If the manic poet was hiding behind the mask of conventional host, it didn't show. He was well—not writing, but teaching at Boston University. The desire to say precisely what he wanted to say to his students had reinforced the scowling and hesitating that had struck me at our first meeting in Princeton. His mannerisms, which the aspiring poets in his classes imitated, were becoming more pronounced, more Lowellian.

The morning following the dinner party, he was easy and funny at breakfast—more like the man I had known earlier—joking about "No-Cal" beverages he was drinking in place of alcohol, making wicked comments on the guests and life in Boston.

Jean could be counted on to give a seismographic reading of Cal's state, especially just before, during and after a breakdown. She always had the bad news first. Had I heard that Cal was drinking "No-Cal"? Jean grimaced with disapproval over this bit of bad news. And had I heard that he had a daughter? Cal a father: What could be more improbable? And had I heard that he was back in the bin again? Crazy as a loon.

Jean wasn't crazy, but she was drinking heavily, as I learned the weekend she came to stay with me in 1957. Her second marriage had failed and she'd had another breakdown. Sometime after her recovery she had left Westport, Connecticut, where she had been living, and had taken an apartment in New York. During the Princeton weekend she turned night into day. After the guests I'd invited to dinner to meet her had left, she poured herself a nightcap and curled up in a chair to talk. Nightcap followed nightcap until 6:00 A.M., when she was finally willing to go to bed. She slept, with the help of sedatives, until cocktail time. No, she wasn't hungry, she said when she got up. If she could just have a little drink . . .

Occasionally we met at her Upper East Side apartment in the city before going out to dinner. One more drink and we'd go she'd promise, when I complained of hunger and noted that it was getting late. On one occasion she displayed an impatience to get to the restaurant that intrigued me. Well, it wasn't exactly a restaurant, she said, as we headed for Third Avenue. It was a bar and grill haunted by *New Yorker* writers. That evening Costello's was almost empty, so she was free to call to the bartender from the booth we were in. "Any news from Joe?" The only thing more agreeable than talking to one person about A. J. Liebling was talking to two people about him.

Halfway through the evening I pointed out to her that we were behaving like high school girls sitting in an ice-cream parlor, talking about boys over our sodas. We had both recently fallen in love, she with Joe, I with Bob. Like high school girls we gave each other useless advice. She had met Bob and thought him too handsome to be trustworthy, and too old, at thirty-six, to give up being a bachelor and make a good husband. Experience had taught her that good-looking men made poor husbands. (Happily, she was wrong on both counts.)

Not the least of Joe's attractions for her was that he was not good-looking. He was "positively ugly," she said with girlish delight. And he spoiled her marvelously—took her to fancy restaurants in London, fed her all the drinks she could down without a murmur of disapproval (so different from you-know-who) and was a fan of her writing. I could see, could I not, why she was impatient to remarry?

I could, but I urged her not to hurry him. With two wives to support, one of whom he was still married to, it would take time, and perhaps courage, to enter into a third union. It did take time—three years—during which she lived on his letters if Joe was away on an assignment, and went to Costello's, where, under cover of *New Yorker* chitchat, she had an excuse to talk to the bartender about him.

After she became Mrs. Liebling, Jean continued to have the dope on Cal, and often on John as well. In the letter John had written in which he told about springing Delmore from jail, he said, "Cal is fine. We took turns in the same mental hospital in Boston last fall." This was reported as jauntily as if the two poets had spelled each other reading at the Y. So, I thought, no cause for concern. When I next met Jean at a Giroux opera evening in 1967 (after Joe had died), she was full of bad news about our former husbands. Cal was off his rocker. And John was drinking too much she said, in the censorious way heavy drinkers report on the heavy drinking of others. He was a wreck.

What I wanted to hear was how well John was doing. Bob Giroux, who continued to be his editor from the publication of *Homage to Mistress Bradstreet* until his death, was the one person I could count on for a balanced picture: John was married and as happy as he allowed himself to be. He had a daughter he doted on, and had accepted, now with gratitude, a professorship that gave him a good salary and security. The recognition and prizes so long denied him were finally coming his way. His books were even making money!

Nevertheless, the collective accounts, as well as the poetry, made me suspect that he didn't have many remaining years. Breaking my long silence, I wrote him in 1970. I had been looking for a favor to ask him, I said. Now I had the kind of favor that he was well equipped, no one better, to grant. I confessed to him what I had told no one but my husband: that in Paris I had begun writing fiction and was working on a group of stories with a Paris setting. Would he criticize them for me? He answered promptly:

> About your stories: of course. Send me as many as you like, as soon as you want. Maybe I can really help you—I am a damned good judge of stories at all levels of execution. Better judge than story-teller.

In the correspondence that followed, John became critic and teacher again, making comments on the stories, recommending what I should read. He wrote about what he was writing, and sent the "Addresses to the Lord" as he finished them. He described his situation at St. Mary's, an alcoholic treatment center, again jauntily, and added:

> If we had known I was an alcoholic—or maybe you did, but you can't have known anything abt the disease or you wdn't have hoped analysis could help—maybe AA cd have saved me. However, I don't repine.

No, I hadn't known he was an alcoholic. He had been diagnosed as being a "problem drinker." And I had been convinced that drinking was window dressing—very fancy, very messy, very noisy, very convincing window dressing, camouflage to permit him to hide from the real threat: his subtle foe.

He asked if we could meet when he came to New York. I agreed, not realizing that he planned to come East in a few weeks. At Christmastime he called from the Chelsea Hotel. We agreed to lunch at

Lüchow's. On the eve of our meeting he called again, his voice thick this time, his tone edgy, to remind me, he said, that it was at the Chelsea I'd spoken "the worst words"—that is, that I was going to leave him. I had agreed to meet him because he said he wasn't drinking. Since he obviously was, I called the hotel in the morning to beg off. The operator said he had left instructions not to ring the room. With great reluctance, I went to the restaurant. He was not there.

A month later, in January 1971, hospitalized again, this time for his now-or-never cure, he wrote apologizing for standing me up, as he put it: He had been "scared" to meet me. Throughout "twelve dreadful days at the damned old Chelsea," he had been in very bad shape, calling people in the middle of the night, and in general making so much trouble that he had "alienated & alienated" all his New York friends. He signed the letter "Love & Shame" (a reference to his undisguisedly autobiographical book of poems with the ironic title, *Love & Fame,* which was criticized severely by many of his friends, particularly Allen and Edmund, and was savaged by some reviewers).

A February letter was full of optimistic plans for public readings and travel to Europe following his recovery; he was never going to have another drop. As for his work, "I am writing lyrics like a maniac, 2 or 3 a week, but *very calm,* oddly." He had also thrown himself into an exercise program:

> 4 barbells, 10 each, hopping (worst of all) and running in place until I drop. Recommend it, dear. Twice a day all this. I plan to die healthy.

It was in this seemingly innocuous way that the subject of death entered our correspondence, as I discovered when, trying to understand his fatal leap, I read and reread these letters.

In response to a comment I made on an article by A. Alvarez in *Partisan Review* (which later became a chapter in his book *The Savage God*), John wrote:

> I don't know why Alvarez is on this death-kick; we correspond spasmodically, but he hasn't told me, and I haven't seen the PR suicide piece, only had it described to me—app'y he cited me as well as Henry.

And he goes on to ask if I've read Jack Douglas's "anti-Durkheim powerhouse," *Social Meanings of Suicide.* (I had not, and although I put it on my reading list, didn't think it of pressing interest until six months later.)

From February to the end of July, silence. Then an extraordinary 2000-word letter (the number of words is important as a mood indicator). It began with more hitting-the-head-on-the-nail criticism of my stories and a suggestion that I read Unamuno's "hair-raising, 'St. Emanuel the Good Martyr' which I believe made me cry with pity." (This title, too, I noted, but did not read at the time. When I did, I also wept.)

One of the stories I had sent him was about a crisis a woman suffers when she confronts her own mortality for the first time. Referring to it, he said:

> That realization happened to me at Richard's & Helen's once in Maine, after the rest of you had gone to bed; there's a Dream Song about it, maybe in Vol. II.

As if I could have forgotten that occasion, or his reaction the following day! He continued:

> Premonition of *Death*—*soon* among the Douglas firs—serried, noble beyond Beauty, attentive—above ten thousand feet on Pike's Peak two weeks ago. Not unhappy about it, though ceteris paribus I wd rather finish some of the fourteen books I recently found I had in hand . . .

At the moment, he said, hurrying on, he was keenest on a novel to be called *Recovery,* and *Shakespeare's Reality* (a fifth revision of the Hodder lectures). He was going off to Berkeley to work on the novel:

> I want 250 pp by Labor day . . . Of course I am determined to produce the most powerful and shapely work of narrative art since Don Quixote—what else?—but even more, I am anxious to get a *readable novel* . . . "Simple, declarative sentences, John" Delmore once said to me when I hadn't written to him for a long time. Only literary advice I ever got, of a general sort, worth having.

After describing the subject of the novel, he added:

> My health is better, but subject to convulsive rages (and ungovernable tenderness—I don't know which is worse) . . . I'm sleeping better, strong with those "killing" exercises as you call them, very relaxed *except* when moved.

The pain caused by the attacks on *Love & Fame* had been mitigated, he said, by Cal's having written him that the "Addresses" in Part IV of that book, along with Book IV of *The Dream Songs* "is the crown of my work." John hoped that his new nine-part poem " 'Opus Dei' would put 'Addresses' in the shade."

The letter ends on a comic note. Responding to *Who's Who,* which had asked him to list his recreations, he had told the editor that they were "chess, dream-analysis, art-history, star-gazing, prayer & self-flagellation." He was delighted when the proof came back unaltered, and wished he'd added "Benevolent Tyranny."

This progress report on his life left me with a disquieting feeling, not because of the premonition (which I read for style—"serried, noble beyond Beauty, attentive"—rather than content), but because of the way he talked about the novel. His excitement had the hectic quality I remembered from the days when he used to jack up his mood by throwing himself into playwriting. Was he substituting for playwriting, which he had finally admitted with chagrin was not his medium, the writing of fiction?

In September he wrote briefly that he'd finished Part IV of the novel:

> first half of first 2/3. Need Saul to read, and Giroux—so I may be in New York over the week-end or early next week. Tried you on phone just now. The '831' circuit was out. Will again.

If he called again, the circuit was still out. At the end of October, the tone of the letter was strikingly different from what it had been earlier:

> Infinite trouble (no drinking, but *alcoholic* surviving . . . including *money*).

Did I have the insurance policy we'd taken out on him in 1953? If so, would I send it? A year or so after we separated, he mentioned the policy in a letter discussing what I should do in case of his death. He didn't much care where he was buried, but would like "if possible to be buried in consecrated ground." The "if possible" I read as a covert prayer that he would not do the one thing which would have made it impossible to have such a burial. (Until recently, when theologians began to pay increasing attention to the psychological state a person was in before taking his life, suicide was considered a grave sin, and the Church, therefore, denied the suicide burial in consecrated ground.)

The October 1971 letter continued:

I'll be 57 tomorrow. It suddenly seems grotesquely old, w. such dreadful responsibilities & so little weight (I was down to 140, and have lost 3 more pounds) or energy.

How did my "careers flourish?" he asked, acknowledging for the first time that he had not, after all, ruined my life (a chronic worry and source of guilt), for if he had I would not have remarried, nor would I be engaged in my practice and in writing.

A little over two months later, John did what he had been rehearsing at least as far back as the night of our engagement party: He jumped from a railing, this time of a bridge, with no net and the frozen Mississippi River below.

Though only his mother believed it was an accident, he was buried in consecrated ground, the Church recognizing that he had been in a severe depression before the suicide. (I had been able to deny what should have been obvious from his birthday letter by telling myself that he had been going through a typical birthday crisis—he'd had them annually while we were married—which was no more serious than the others. Even the weight loss didn't alarm me; when I knew him, 140 pounds had not been uncharacteristic during periods when he was working obsessively.)

Rereading his letters after his death, I saw that between September 16 (the date of the one in which he said he wanted Saul Bellow and Bob Giroux to read his manuscript) and October 24 (the one in which he asked me about his insurance policy), euphoria about the novel had been replaced by depression as he realized how extensive the revisions would have to be. They would require considerable energy—energy he no longer had at his disposal. This man, who, as Saul said, drew his writing "out of his vital organs, out of his very skin," had nothing left to draw on.

The day following his suicide I entered a hospital for knee surgery that had been scheduled six weeks earlier and could not be postponed. During the months of forced inactivity following the operation, I had hours on end to grieve. Like so many admirers of his writing, I went back to the poems. How impatient he had been for death the late Dream Songs make clear. He had finished his major work and believed, I suspect, that this time he would not write poetry again. It was the moment his subtle foe had been waiting for. The tugging and dragging began in earnest and did not let up until the victim, worn out in spirit, but agile from his exercises, made the leap. The body of the man who had for so much of his life been dogged by money worries was identified by a blank check that carried his name.

Many—I, too, at moments—blamed the suicide on John's having been a poet. The litany of suicides among poets is long. After a while I began to feel that I'd missed the obvious. It was the poetry that had kept him alive. His father had committed suicide at forty. With as much reason, and with a similar psychic makeup, John had been tempted more than once to follow his father's example. That he lived seventeen years longer than John Allyn Smith, that he died a "veteran of life," was thanks to his gift. It had not been the hand coaxing him down from the railing that had brought him back each time, he now believed, but the certainty that there were all those poems still to be written. Only when there were no more did he feel, as his father must have felt on the morning he pulled the trigger, that "It seems to be DARK all the time."

The official mourner for the group would not go unmourned in verse. Cal took on the role.

In the late fifties, and more infrequently in the sixties, whenever Cal and I met, no matter what our subject of conversation was, sooner or later he had turned the talk to John. After a rehearsal of *The Old Glory* (which was being produced by Jean Webster), Cal described their most recent meeting: "One knows, these days, that one is not going to an ordinary poetry reading when one goes to hear John. But who could imagine that he would read haiku. *In Japanese!*"

In Paris, at Mary McCarthy and Jim West's apartment, I watched Cal formulate, with thoughtful frown, hesitation, and much sketching in the air with his right hand, his answer to a question an avid fan and newspaper reporter had put to him, "Tell me, Mr. Lowell, are you still writing in your bitter vein?" Afterward, catching my eye and laughing, he said, "What do you think John would have said to that one?"

In December, 1971, after Cal and Elizabeth had separated and he was living in England, he telephoned to say that he was in New York. Could he come by to see me? He stayed for hours, talked about Harriet (his daughter) who was "fine." So was Elizabeth. It was he, the one who was asking for the divorce and planned to remarry as soon as it was final, who was suffering. "Being in New York again makes me feel as if the skin on my back is being raked"—a feeling one could read in his face. He left me wondering exactly why he had come. It had not been to gossip about Allen, though he did that. Had it been to tell me what bad shape John was in on this, John's "alienating" visit to New York? The meeting was inconclusive, troubling.

Our last conversation, in 1976, was over the telephone. In London on my way to Istanbul, I called to ask Cal's help with a question a biographer had put to me. Biographers were much on his mind. Did I know the man who was doing John? Delmore? Allen? Would they, who were "hideously young," get it all wrong? When the time came (one felt he thought that time was not far off), who would do him? After we said good-bye and I was about to hang up, he held me on the line. "Was that a real journal you quoted in *The Maze?*" (My novel had been published a few months earlier.) The journal was fictional. "Were those actual letters and notes of John's you quoted?" Fictional. "Did John keep his eyeglasses in his shoe at night, the way Benjamin Bold does?" John did. So, Cal said, did he, with evident satisfaction, as if putting a peg in place.

After John's death, Cal wrote about him in the *New York Review of Books.* He recalled their first meeting in Princeton, the good days in Damariscotta, their weekend together in Washington, an opera evening with Bob Giroux and the years after John became famous when he was "less good company and more a happening." The piece read as if it had been written out of duty rather than affection.

Not so the poem he wrote for John after reading the last *Dream Song*. (Was it not the next to the last Cal meant? The poem beginning, "I didn't. And I didn't.") By the time Cal wrote it, four or five years after John's death, he had come to feel that their kinship was closer than he had realized, especially during the last years, when they had seemed so different:

> Yet really we had the same life,
> the generic one
> our generation offered

They had been students, teachers, veterans of the Cold War; had gone to Europe, daydreamed of a drink at six. And, though Cal doesn't say so, they had had their breakdowns and incarcerations, talked to their psychiatrists about their seductive mothers and ineffectual fathers, won the prizes, been in *Life,* put their eyeglasses in a shoe at night so they could find them in the morning. The poem ends:

> To my surprise, John
> I pray *to* not for you,
> think of you not myself,
> smile and fall asleep.

John, in "the chambers of the end" must have shifted the italics and said with incredulity, "Pray to *me?*"

Cal, who wished for "a natural death / no teeth on the ground," had his wish granted. He died in a taxi on the way from the airport to Elizabeth's apartment, as he was returning from England in September 1977. At his funeral mass at the Church of the Advent in Boston, I thought of Ted Roethke's poem:

> In heaven, too,
> You'd be institutionalized.
> But that's all right,—
> If they let you eat and swear
> with the likes of Blake,
> and Christopher Smart,
> And that sweet man, John Clare.

Dylan Thomas, Randall, Cal, Delmore and John might have selected different companions from those Ted chose, but their view of
heaven was the same. As Keats imagined himself sitting beside Shakespeare in a tavern in the next world, so they saw themselves separated
from the rest of us, "institutionalized," surrounded by poets. Cal and
Randall would be able to ask Yeats what his three greatest lines were.
Robert Frost would at last "have it out with Horace," while John
nailed the author of *Lear* to solve a crux that had baffled him for two
decades.

They would recite one another's poems and talk for hours on end,
free at last of worldly concerns about where the next advance, the next
drink, the next girl or even the next inspiration would come from—
free at last to be obsessed with poetry.

REFERENCES

Letters, especially those I wrote two or three times a week to my sister, Marie Hall, were an invaluable aid in recalling the years 1941 to 1956. Unless otherwise noted, quotations are taken from them. Articles, reviews, short stories, novels and especially the poems of these writers frequently nudged into consciousness and sharpened details that would otherwise have remained pale and unfocused.

I. JOHN AND DELMORE

PAGE

3   "the first . . . Pound": Letter from Allen Tate to Delmore Schwartz which John Berryman used to quote. See also James Atlas, *Delmore Schwartz, The Life of an American Poet* (New York: Farrar, Straus and Giroux, 1977).

5   "low . . . room": John Berryman, "The Imaginary Jew," reprinted in *The Freedom of the Poet* (New York: Farrar, Straus and Giroux, 1976).

5   " 'a vocation' . . . being": Delmore Schwartz in conversation with John Berryman. Later developed in Delmore Schwartz's article, "The Vocation of the Poet in the Modern World," *Poetry 78* (July 1951).

10   "rowed . . . political": John Berryman, "The Imaginary Jew."

10   "yellow . . . hopes": John Berryman, *The Dream Songs,* #88 (New York: Farrar, Straus and Giroux, 1969).

15   "Do they . . . shame?": "Do the Others Speak of Me Mockingly, Maliciously?" from *Summer Knowledge* (New York: Doubleday & Co., 1959).

17   "For . . . be": B. H. Haggin, *Music on Records* (New York: Alfred A. Knopf, 1941).

19   "Come . . . Hungarian": "The Would-be Hungarian," *Summer Knowledge.*

II. BOSTON AND CAMBRIDGE

PAGE

25   "heavy bear": "The Heavy Bear," from *In Dreams Begin Responsibilities* (Norfolk, Va.: New Directions, 1938).

PAGE

31   "comes . . . bride": John Berryman, "For His Marriage" (privately printed).

31   "All . . . lives": Delmore Schwartz, unpublished poem.

32   "We . . . fear": "A Point of Age," from *The Dispossessed* (New York: William Sloane Associates, 1948).

39   "meeting . . . were": *The Dream Songs*, #152.

39   "satanic": "Monkhood," from *Love & Fame* (New York: Farrar, Straus and Giroux, 1970).

45   "We . . . madness": Delmore Schwartz, unpublished poem.

45   "the principle . . . 'Decade' ": James Atlas, *Delmore Schwartz*.

46   "You . . . O": *The Dream Songs*, #152.

III. JOBLESS IN NEW YORK

PAGE

65   "A bullet . . . knee": *The Dream Songs*, #76.

65   The "departure": *ibid.*, #1.

70   "unspeakably . . . MOTHER": John Berryman, *Recovery* (New York: Farrar, Straus and Giroux, 1973).

IV. PRINCETON AND THE BLACKMURS

PAGE

73   'The art . . . reality': John Berryman, "Olympus," from *Love & Fame*.

73   "new Law-giver": *ibid.*

78   "This marriage . . . eyes": "A Labyrinth of Being," reprinted in *Poems of R. P. Blackmur* (Princeton: Princeton University Press, 1977).

83   "Who . . . sheet": "The Second World," *ibid.*

88   *"The Editorial Problem in Shakespeare":* The Nation, August 21 1943, p. 218.

94   "The Lovers": John Berryman, *Kenyon Review*, Winter, 1945, Vo. 7. Reprinted in *The Freedom of the Poet*.

V. LEAR AND RANDALL

PAGE

101   "I accost . . . man": John Berryman, "The Mysteries," from *Short Poems* (New York: Farrar, Straus and Giroux, 1967).

109   "When . . . me": Randall Jarrell, "A Night with Lions," from *The Lost World* (New York: The Macmillan Company, 1965).

PAGE

110   "hard . . . lipstick": Randall Jarrell, "Bad Poets," from *Poetry and the Age* (New York: Alfred A. Knopf, 1953).

110   "like . . . anything": Randall Jarrell, "Changes of Attitudes and Rhetoric in Auden's Poetry," from *The Third Book of Criticism* (New York: Farrar, Straus and Giroux, 1969).

VI. DAMARISCOTTA MILLS: JEAN AND CAL

PAGE

116   "An Influx of Poets": Jean Stafford, *The New Yorker,* November 6, 1978.

116   "Oh, . . . face": Robert Lowell, "History," *Collected Poems* (New York: Farrar, Straus & Giroux, revised ed., 1977).

119   "We . . . house": Robert Lowell, "To Delmore Schwartz," from *Life Studies* (New York: Farrar, Straus and Giroux, 1959).

124   "Unseen and all-seeing": Robert Lowell, "My Last Afternoon with Uncle Devereux Winslow," from *Life Studies.*

125   "I knocked . . . cover": Robert Lowell, "Daddy," from *History* (New York: Farrar, Straus and Giroux, 1973).

127   the "tortured joy": Allen Tate in conversation.

127   "the chambers of the end": John Berryman, *The Dream Songs,* #90.

128   "Scorn . . . drunk": John Berryman, "In Memoriam (1914–1953)," from *Delusions, Etc.* (New York: Farrar, Straus and Giroux, 1972).

130   "Unwearied . . . still": W. B. Yeats, "The Wild Swans at Coole," from *The Collected Poems of W. B. Yeats* (New York: The Macmillan Company, 1956).

132   "Yes, . . . Lowell?": Randall Jarrell, in a review of "The Mills of the Kavanaughs," from *Poetry and the Age.*

137   "Here . . . blue": R. P. Blackmur, "From Jordan's Delight," from *The Poems of R. P. Blackmur.*

140   "it . . . island": John Berryman, "Henry's Understanding," from *Delusions, Etc.*

140   "he . . . fall": John Berryman, *The Dream Songs,* #144.

144   "The Philosophy Lesson,": Jean Stafford, *The New Yorker,* November 16, 1968.

144   "manic statement": Robert Lowell, "Memories of West Street and Lepke," from *Life Studies.*

145   "The . . . rack": Robert Lowell, *ibid.*

146   "the good days . . . syntax": Robert Lowell, "For John Berry-

PAGE

146   man," from *Day by Day* (New York: Farrar, Straus and Giroux, 1977).

VII. ANALYSANDS ALL

PAGE

149   "We . . . caution": Robert Lowell, "For John Berryman," from *New York Review of Books,* April 6, 1972

149   "Does . . . rivalry": John Berryman, *The Dream Songs,* #259.

153   "ease and light": Robert Lowell, "For John Berryman," from *New York Review of Books,* April 6 1972.

157   "Once . . . sang": John Berryman, *The Dream Songs,* #1.

159   "Analysands . . . despair": John Berryman, "The Lightning," from *The Dispossessed.*

166   "I made . . . mine": Robert Lowell, *New York Review of Books,* April 6, 1972.

170   "The poet . . . cigarette": John Berryman, from *Berryman's Sonnets,* #5 (New York: Farrar, Straus and Giroux, 1967).

VIII. "THE COLOUR OF THIS SOUL"

PAGE

177   "The drill . . . bite": John Berryman, *The Dream Songs,* #185.

177   "plights & gripes": *ibid.,* #14.

179   "an imaginary . . . middle age"; *ibid,* Note, p. vi.

184   "one . . . America": John Berryman, *Stephen Crane* (New York: William Sloane Associates, 1950; reprinted by Octagon Books, 1975).

189   "flicker of impulse lust": John Berryman, "Addresses to the Lord, #3," from *Love & Fame.*

IX. MISTRESS BRADSTREET

PAGE

204   "Now as I . . . green": Dylan Thomas, "Fern Hill," from *Collected Poems* (New York: New Directions, 1953).

204   *"What shall I do . . . dead"*: W. B. Yeats, "John Kinsella's Lament for Mrs. Mary Moore," from *The Collected Poems of W. B. Yeats.*

207   "The live man . . . quick": R. P. Blackmur, "An Elegy for Five," from *The Poems of R. P. Blackmur.*

PAGE

213   "electrifying vivacity": Walter Clemons, in review of *Recovery,*
           Newsweek, May 28, 1973.

216   "The neighbors . . . welfare": Saul Bellow, *Humboldt's Gift* (New
           York: The Viking Press, 1973).

224   "gall": John Berryman, acceptance speech, National Book
           Award, 1970.

224   "The winters . . . heart": John Berryman, *Homage to Mistress
           Bradstreet* (New York: Farrar, Straus and Giroux, 1956).

225   "a certain . . . critic": John Berryman, "The Sorrows of Captain
           Carpenter," from *The Freedom of the Poet.*

225   "poets . . . lie": John Berryman, *Berryman's Sonnets,* #43.

225   "I kissed . . . you": John Berryman's response to Hayden Carruth's
           review of *Love & Fame, The Nation,* November 30, 1970.

225–27   All poetry quotes in these pages are from *Homage to Mistress
           Bradstreet.*

228–29   "went . . . last": John Berryman in a letter to Robert Fitzgerald.

229   "tortured and half-incoherent": Victoria Glendinning, *Elizabeth
           Bowen* (New York: Alfred A. Knopf, 1978).

229   "personal . . . tenderly": from the Foreword by Leon Edel, in
           Edmund Wilson's *The Twenties* (New York: Farrar, Straus and
           Giroux, 1975).

230   "The secret . . . stop": John Berryman, *The Dream Songs,* #340.

X. AFTERWARD

PAGE

231   "To those . . . women": Sigmund Freud, from the general intro-
           duction to *Psychoanalysis* (New York: Garden City Publishing
           Co., 1943).

232   "In sleep . . . go": John Berryman, *The Dream Songs,* #18.

233   "drinking and bad sex": John Berryman, *Recovery.*

234   "three-day . . . Tropez": John Berryman, *The Dream Songs,*
           #343.

234   "How long . . . perishing": *Homage to Mistress Bradstreet.*

234   "the worst . . . assent": *Recovery.*

239   "He had . . . life": Caitlin Thomas, *Leftover Life to Kill* (Boston:
           Little, Brown, 1957).

239   "For a while . . . ago": Paul Ferris, *Dylan Thomas* (New York:
           The Dial Press, 1977).

PAGE

240   "A Strut for Roethke": John Berryman, *The Dream Songs,* #18.

240   "a whole . . . cats": Hannah Arendt, *Randall Jarrell, 1914–1965*
           (New York: Farrar, Straus and Giroux, 1967).

241   "a natural . . . Tate's": John Berryman, in a review of *Poetry and
           the Age* by Randall Jarrell, *New Republic,* November 2, 1953,
           reprinted in *Randall Jarrell, 1914–1965* (New York: Farrar, Straus
           and Giroux, 1967).

241   "Then the night . . . luminosity": "Randall Jarrell 2," Robert
           Lowell, from *History.*

244   "flagrant . . . beauty": John Berryman, *The Dream Songs,* #154.

244   "tearing . . . clothes": *ibid.,* #156.

244   "there . . . poetry": Saul Bellow, *Humboldt's Gift.*

244–45   "In this age . . . abandoned them": W. H. Auden, "Louis Mac-
           Neice, 1907–63" in *The Listener,* October 24, 1963.

245   "a positive genius for self-destruction": Dwight Macdonald,
           Foreword, "Delmore Schwartz, 1913–1966," in *Selected Essays of
           Delmore Schwartz,* edited by Donald A. Dike and David H.
           Zucker (Chicago: University of Chicago Press, 1970).

245   "Ten Songs . . . agony": John Berryman, *The Dream Songs,*
           #157.

245   "I'm cross . . . Delmore": *ibid.,* #153.

253   "out of . . . skin": Foreword by Saul Bellow, in *Recovery.*

253   "It seems . . . the time": John Berryman, "Despair," from *Love
           & Fame.*

254   "less good . . . happening": Robert Lowell, *New York Review of
           Books,* April 6, 1972.

255   "Yet really . . . offered": Robert Lowell, "For John Berryman"
           from *Day by Day* (Farrar, Straus and Giroux, 1977).

255   "To . . . asleep": *ibid.*

271   "In heaven, . . . Clare": Theodore Roethke, "Heard in a Violent
           Ward," from *Collected Poems* (New York: Doubleday & Co.,
           1966).

ACKNOWLEDGMENTS

I would like to express my gratitude to the following participants in the events described in this book who read the manuscript, or portions of it, to look for errors of chronology or fact, and who also reminded me of details I had forgotten or had not recorded in my letters: E. T. Cone, Sally Fitzgerald, Robert Fitzgerald, Marie Hall, Alice Loewy Kahler, Nancy Macdonald, Charles Phillips Reilly, Peter Taylor and, especially, Robert Giroux, who was so closely associated with these poets, their wives and this era.

Others to whom I am grateful for criticisms and suggestions are Jack Barbera, John Brooks, Joseph Caldwell, Michael de Capua, William McBrien and Grace Schulman. At Random House, I owe special thanks to my editor, Jonathan Galassi, and the copy editor, Jean McNutt.

My thanks also go to Kate Donahue for granting permission to quote from John Berryman's letters to me; and to the MacDowell Colony, the Ossabaw Foundation and the American Academy in Rome for their hospitality during the month I stayed at each of them during the past two years.

INDEX

Italicized page numbers indicate photographs.